The
GOLDEN
RETRIEVER

Jeffrey Pepper

Front cover: Am. Can. Ch. Russo's Pepperhill Poppy owned by the author and his wife. Photo: John L. Ashby. **Back cover:** Dual Ch. Tigathoes Funky Farquar owned by Dorothy Ramsay and Elinor Tribon, bred by Mrs. George Flinn, Jr. and Mrs. Robert R. Sadler.

Title page: Am. Can. Ch. Pepperhill's Basically Bear is shown winning a group placement. Breeder/owner-handled by the author. Photo: William Gilbert.

In memory of my father, Arthur A. Pepper. Without his loving support none of this would be possible.

ISBN 0-87666-668-3

Distributed in the UNITED STATES by T.F.H. Publications, Inc., 211 West Sylvania Avenue, Neptune City, NJ 07753; in CANADA by H & L Pet Supplies Inc., 27 Kingston Crescent, Kitchener, Ontario N2B 2T6; Rolf C. Hagen Ltd., 3225 Sartelon Street, Montreal 382 Quebec; in ENGLAND by T.F.H. Publications Limited, 4 Kier Park, Ascot, Berkshire SL5 7DS; in AUSTRALIA AND THE SOUTH PACIFIC by T.F.H. (Australia) Pty. Ltd., Box 149, Brookvale 2100 N.S.W., Australia; in NEW ZEALAND by Ross Haines & Son, Ltd., 18 Monmouth Street, Grey Lynn, Auckland 2 New Zealand; in SINGAPORE AND MALAYSIA by MPH Distributors Pte., 71-77 Stamford Road, Singapore 0617; in the PHILIPPINES by Bio-Research, 5 Lippay Street, San Lorenzo Village, Makati, Rizal; in SOUTH AFRICA by Multipet Pty. Ltd., 30 Turners Avenue, Durban 4001. Published by T.F.H. Publications Inc., Ltd., the British Crown Colony of Hong Kong.

Contents

About the Author

Since early childhood, Jeffrey Pepper has been involved with dogs. His first pet was an American Cocker Spaniel, followed some years later by a Standard Poodle. Shortly before marriage, he purchased his first Golden Retriever as a pet. Becoming interested in Obedience work, the dog was entered in several A.K.C. Obedience Trials and earned his C.D. degree. This was followed by conformation showing, the dog ultimately becoming Ch. Sir Richard of Fleetwood, C.D.

A show bitch was then acquired who became a foundation bitch at Pepper's Pepperhill Kennels subsequently named to The Golden Retriever Club of America Hall of Fame. Another bitch, Am. and Can. Ch. Russo's Pepperhill Poppy, a National Specialty Best of Breed Winner and member of the G.R.C.A. Show Dog Hall of Fame, was the first bitch in many years to achieve this honor. A second bitch bred by the Peppers is Am. and Can. Ch. Pepperhill East Point Airily, currently the top-winning Golden Retriever on the East Coast, owned by Dan Flavin and Helene Geary. Another homebred dog is American and Canadian Pepperhill's Basically Bear, two-time winner of the Stud Dog Class at G.R.C.A. National Specialties and a member of the G.R.C.A. Stud Dog Hall of Fame. Other dogs of their breeding have been Specialty Best of Breed winners.

With only a limited breeding program, numerous champions and obedience title holders have been bred at Pepperhill Kennels over the years, including a number that have won major points at Specialties and several that are Group winners.

Mr. Pepper has been active in dog clubs over the years. He served several terms as First Vice President of the Rockland County (N.Y.) Kennel Club and has served as President, Vice President and Treasurer of the Hudson Valley Golden Retriever Club, where he and his wife are charter members. Mr. Pepper is currently an officer of the club.

At the present time, Mr. Pepper is a featured columnist for the *Golden Retriever Quarterly*, and is Conformation Editor for the *Golden Retriever News*. *The Golden Retriever* is his first book. A Social Worker by profession, Mr. Pepper holds a Masters in Social Work degree from Adelphi University.

The Pepper family and their Goldens live in Putnam Valley, New York, along with two English Springer Spaniels, two Whippets and several cats.

Acknowledgments

Writing this book has been truly a labor of love. But it was a task that could not have been accomplished without the help of many people. My grateful thanks go to each and every one of them.

Anna Katherine Nicholas, the author of many books about dogs, including the recently published *The Book of the Golden Retriever*, first approached me about writing this book. Her suggestions and encouragement combined with her expertise have been invaluable. Without it, I doubt this book would ever have been written.

Many Golden fanciers have contributed time and materials toward my efforts in producing a new book on the breed. Their suggestions as the manuscript developed were most valuable. To the many breeders who generously loaned me precious photographs of their dogs so that they could be included in this volume goes a special note of appreciation.

Elliot More has written an excellent chapter on grooming Goldens. He has had a number of years of experience as a professional handler and has shown many Goldens to their titles and beyond. Before starting out on his own, Elliot worked with several of the best known professionals in the country, including Bill Trainor and Bob and Jane Forsyth. Elliot's skill as a handler and his rapport with a dog is something I have seen personally as he handled our "Poppy" to many of her most important wins.

Nancy Kelly Belsaas, with her husband Dean, provided all the material on juniors and Goldens and wrote the chapter on the subject. As a former champion junior handler herself, Nancy was able to provide a special insight into the subject. Sandy Akers has taken her years of experience with Goldens in the Field and compiled the wonderful chapter on Field Goldens. Judy Taylor graciously took on the responsibility of writing about the Golden in Canada, aided by Shirley Goodman's unique history of the Golden Retriever Club of Canada. Judy and her twin sister Jennifer McAuley have been involved with Goldens in Canada for many years and their Skylon and Chrys-Haefen kennels have produced some of the top-winning Canadian Goldens.

My grateful thanks also go to Sandy McDowell, who wrote the chapter on English dog shows and used to great advantage the experience she gained on a number of trips to visit English Golden Kennels. Special thanks are also due to Susan Fisher, the editor of the G.R.C.A. *Yearbook*, who took the time to get the newest available information on Hall of Fame dogs to me, even while she was working on publishing the 1982 edition of the book.

The truly unique chapter on eye problems in the Golden Retriever was written by Dr. David Covitz, one of the relatively few A.C.V.O. certified veterinary ophthalmologists in the country. Dr. Covitz agreed to write this chapter despite an extremely busy schedule. Over the years, he has seen thousands of Goldens both in his offices and at eye clinics.

Finally, my special thanks go to my wife Barbara who did so much of the proofreading of the manuscript, helped in the revisions of each chapter until they said what I wanted to say, and who provided so much indispensable criticism as the book grew from an idea to completion. Without her help and patience, the project would never have been completed.

An extra special "thank you" must go to the two dogs who really started it all, Ricky (Champion Sir Richard of Fleetwood, C.D.) and our foundation dam DeDe (Champion Cummings Dame Pepperhill). DeDe left us two years ago, Ricky supervised the typing of this manuscript as he lay at my feet. He died on May 8, 1983 at the age of fourteen and a half years.

Introduction

Ask the following questions of any person who knows about dogs. "What breed has the perfect temperament as a family pet?" "What breed is easily trained?" "What breed is clearly superior with children?" The answer you will undoubtedly receive most often is the Golden Retriever.

Once a relatively rare and unknown breed, today the Golden is one of the most popular purebred dogs in America. Goldens are seen almost everywhere: in the city and in the countryside, on numerous television commercials and in many print advertisements. Golden owners can be found living in royal palaces, in the White House, in city apartments, in suburban homes, and in rural areas. This beautiful yet easy-to-care-for breed can be seen strutting in the Best in Show ring, working at obedience trials and field events, hunting birds, or searching out narcotics or explosives. He is at home leading a blind person or playing with a lonely child. Truly, the Golden Retriever is an all-around dog.

Goldens are easy dogs to own. They require a minimum of grooming in comparison to many breeds; they suffer from relatively few genetic problems; they are easily trained, wanting little more from life than to please their masters; they have a deep, natural love for people, especially children. Although a relatively large breed, the Golden is renowned for his gentleness and he gets along well with other dogs, as well as with other family pets such as cats. A naturally clean dog, the Golden is relatively easy to housebreak, especially with the proper use of a crate. Obedience training is another easily accomplished task, particularly after the dog has been taught how to learn.

It is as a family pet that the Golden Retriever has made its greatest impact. Many authorities specifically recommend the Golden as the ideal family dog. The typical Golden has an innate love for children and is at his very best when he has a youngster to love. (A young puppy, however, may need some help in controlling his natural exuberance when dealing with the very young child. The older Golden usually seems to know instinctively when to be gentle with a toddler.) There is, however, one drawback to this gentleness. Because he is so people-oriented, many Goldens make perfectly awful watchdogs. Although he may bark when a stranger comes to the door, the Golden's tail will be wagging furiously at the same time. If the person outside is out to rob you of your valuables, your Golden is unlikely to try and stop the intruder. In fact, if he could talk, he'd probably say, "Hi! Will you play with me? The silver is over there."

Unfortunately, the increasing popularity of the Golden Retriever is already leading to some of the practices associated with careless breeding for profit. Because there is a ready market for Goldens, commercial breeding has become common. Since those interested only in profit give no thought to the welfare of the breed in general or to the quality of the individual puppies they produce, the unavoidable result is poor quality, unhealthy Goldens.

Throughout this book you will find suggestions on choosing, training and breeding your Golden. You will learn the methods successful breeders have used. There are many photographs of famous Goldens, both past and present, a number of whom may appear in the pedigree of your own dog.

Before making your final decision about purchasing a Golden, read this book carefully. Whether your new dog is to be a beloved family pet or you have hopes of competing with him in the show ring, obedience trial or field trial, the time you spend in study now will result in your ability to wisely choose and raise your puppy to reach his fullest potential as a member of your family and as a credit to the breed. There is no better dog than a Golden Retriever. Help keep him that way.

Opposite page: F.C., A.F.C., Can. Dual Ch. Rockhaven Raynard of Fo-Go-Ta. A member of the G.R.C.A. Field Dog Hall of Fame owned by Mrs. George H. Flinn, Jr. of Tigathoe Kennels, Greenwich, Connecticut.

One of the early home-bred champions from Golden Pines Kennels, this is Ch. Golden Pine's Brown Bear (Ch. Little Joe of Tigathoe*** ex Ch. Wessala Pride of Golden Pine). Handled here by Bob Watergate. This dog was one of four from his litter to complete his championship, all four finishing within two months of each other in 1957. One littermate was Ch. Golden Pine's Bambi's Lady, a repeat breeding produced Ch. Golden Pine's Easy Ace, a name you may find in your own show dog's pedigree. Brown Bear, a Show Dog Hall of Fame member was owned by Golden Pine Kennels. Photo: Norton of Kent.

10

Chapter 1

A Brief History of the Golden Retriever

THE ORIGINS OF THE BREED AND ITS EARLY HISTORY

The development of the Golden Retriever was no accident of nature. Rather, it is the result of many years of careful, well planned breeding carried out by a man dedicated to his task. This man was Sir Dudley Marjoriebanks (later, the first Lord Tweedmouth). During the nineteenth century, there was a constant search among the gentry for the perfect hunting dog. Many men attempted to reach this goal by acquiring good hunting dogs and then breeding them. Outcrosses to other breeds were commonly done in order to try to improve the working abilities of the dogs. Sometimes the results of these breedings improved the dogs; other times they did not, but the search continued nevertheless. Sir Dudley was one of the men involved in this search.

As with so many other purebred dogs, the Golden Retriever traces his ancestors back to England. The original story of the ancestors of the Golden Retriever has been disproved, but is repeated here since it is such a colorful tale. According to legend, the Golden began when Lord Tweedmouth allegedly purchased a troupe of Russian circus dogs. The story goes on to say that Lord Tweedmouth was attracted to these Russian Trackers (who supposedly weighed in excess of 100 pounds) because of their cleverness, intelligence, and pale yellow color. They had heavy, rough coats and stood about 30 inches at the shoulder. Lord Tweedmouth attempted to purchase a pair of these dogs and, when refused, bought instead the entire troupe of eight. From the circus, held in Brighton in the southern part of England, he took the dogs home to his estate, called "Guisachan," in Scotland where he used them to hunt deer. Later, in order to reduce the size of these dogs and to improve their scenting ability, he was said to have crossed them with a sandy-colored Bloodhound. According to the legend, the Golden Retriever is descended from this cross-breeding.

This tale was accepted as the truth by canine authorities for quite some time, though it was occasionally questioned by some serious Golden breeders. The 1950 edition of the *Yearbook*, published by G.R.C.A. still gives this story as the history of the breed. In fact, there is an article in the *Yearbook* in which some breeders expressed concern about the size of Goldens at the time and pointed out that the breed had been bred down from a much larger dog and therefore caution should be exercised not to breed back to the "original" large size.

Beginning in about 1952, when the original Stud Book of Lord Tweedmouth first became available for study, the true story of the ancestors of today's Golden Retrievers became known. This Stud Book, written in Lord Tweedmouth's own hand, became available through his descendants. The book contained a detailed record of the breeding operations at Guisachan from 1835 to 1890. Nowhere is there any mention of the purchase of any Russian circus dogs, something that would be expected of a careful record keeper—especially considering that eight dogs were involved and that they were allegedly transported a great distance from the south of England all the way to Scotland (not a short trip in those days).

The Stud Book does record, however, the purchase in 1865 of a yellow retriever named "Nous" from a cobbler in Brighton. The dog had been given to the cobbler in payment of a debt and was the only yellow in an unregistered litter of black Wavy-Coated Retrievers. This dog, according to the records, was taken back to Guisachan where he was used for hunting. Later, a Tweed Water Spaniel named "Belle" was purchased. This bitch was bred to Nous and the resulting litter produced four bitches who were named "Ada," "Primrose," "Crocus," and "Cowslip." All, expecially the latter, were to become most important to Lord Tweedmouth's thoughtful plan to develop a sound hunting Yellow Retriever. For over twenty years, Lord Tweedmouth carefully linebred back to Cowslip, an unusual plan in those days. At first, Cowslip was bred to another Tweed Water Spaniel that had been purchased. A bitch puppy was retained from this litter and was later bred to a descendant of Ada. In order to keep the line strong and improve its hunting abilities, over the years careful outcrosses were made to two black Wavy-Coats. An Irish Setter was brought in, perhaps to improve upland hunting ability and insure color, and later a sandy-colored Bloodhound was used to improve tracking ability. The coat texture of these dogs was reported to vary, as did the color, which ranged from fox red to cream.

Occasionally, puppies from Lord Tweedmouth's kennel were given as gifts to other people, friends and relatives, who were interested in the breed. Some of these people went on to breed the dogs and develop their own lines. It is not known whether any of these dogs were eventually bred back to the original line of Lord Tweedmouth, but it might not be incorrect to assume that at least some of them were. There are no written records of this, however.

The Wavy-Coated Retrievers used in the development of Goldens are the ancestors of today's Flat-Coated Retrievers. Then, as now, they were usually black. The breed had been developed in England from crosses of the St. John's Newfoundland and some Setters. The St. John's dog apparently was a native of North America that first appeared in England in the early 1800s aboard fishing vessels coming from America. They had an influence on all retriever breeds and were, according to the canine writers of the day, about the size of a Setter. This dog should not be confused with the dog we call a Newfoundland today. It is not the same breed.

The question of why black puppies do not appear in Golden Retriever litters is often raised. There is a complicated answer to this question having to do with coat color inheritance and genetics that is best left to books on the subject. For our purposes here, we must just accept that it doesn't happen.

The origins of the Tweed Water Spaniel, a breed now extinct, are long lost, but it is known that early water dogs were crossed with Land or Field Spaniels to develop Water Spaniels. Along the coast of Great Britain, Water Spaniels were an important part of family life, often relied upon to bring food to the table through their great retrieving ability. Canine writers at that time reported these dogs to be intelligent, good swimmers, and possessing a great desire to work—much the same qualities found in today's Goldens. The Tweed Water Spaniels were a rare Water Spaniel breed developed in the Tweed River area. They are described in contemporary dog books as resembling a small "liver"-colored retriever. (At that time "liver" meant almost any shade from brown to yellow.)

The Golden Retriever, then, as documented by the carefully kept kennel records of Lord Tweedmouth, is the result of years of careful linebreeding for type, color, and ability, carried out for many years at Guisachan. The resulting Ilchester line of Goldens is the original one, and these dogs are the ancestors of all Goldens today. There is no record anywhere of any Russian circus dogs being used at any time in the establishment of the breed. The legend of the circus dogs is, in actuality, just a colorful story. It has no apparent basis in fact. Our Golden Retrievers are the direct result of Lord Tweedmouth's vision and planning.

It wasn't until 1903 that the Kennel Club of England accepted the first Goldens for registration. They were, at that time, called "Flat-Coats—Golden." By 1904 the first Golden placement at a Field Trial was recorded. Among the first Goldens shown in Bench competition were Culham Brass and Culham Copper who were first in competition in 1908. These dogs traced their pedigrees directly to Lord Tweedmouth's stock and are behind almost the whole breed today.

In 1911 the Golden Retriever Club of England was formed, and the Kennel Club recognized Goldens as a separate breed—at first called "Yellow or Golden Retrievers." A few years later, the ultimate result of Lord Tweedmouth's breeding program was officially known and designated as "Golden Retrievers," and the "Yellow" was dropped forever from their name.

EARLY GOLDENS IN THE UNITED STATES

Although Goldens were known to have been in the United States as early as the 1890s, there was no serious breeding of them done here at that time as far as can be determined today. In fact, it wasn't until the early 1930s that a real interest in the breed was generated. Interest developed at that time when Col. Samuel Magoffin's import, Speedwell Pluto, was actively shown, arousing much attention. This dog completed his American and Canadian championships and recorded the first Best in Show win for any Golden Retriever in the country when he went Best at Puget Sound, Washington in 1933. American and Canadian Champion Speedwell Pluto was also the first Golden Retriever bench champion, completing his American title in November, 1932. He is an honorary member of the G.R.C.A. Show Dog Hall of Fame and was also named an honorary Outstanding Sire, having produced four champions, a tremendous accomplishment in those early days.

The first Golden ever documented to be in the United States was "Lady," who was owned by Hon. Archie Marjoriebanks, the youngest son of Lord Tweedmouth. There is a photograph of this bitch, taken somewhere in Texas about 1894, in the archives of the Golden Retriever Club of America.

Two Goldens who figure in many of today's top winner's pedigrees are in this 1957 photo at the G.R.C.A. Eastern Regional Specialty. Right, going Best of Breed is Ch. Little Joe of Tigathoe***, a G.R.C.A. Outstanding Sire of eighteen champions owned by Mrs. George H. Flinn, Jr. On the left, going Best of Opposite Sex is Joe's daughter Ch. Golden Pines Bambi's Lady owned by the Golden Pine Kennels of Mrs. Mary Luise Semans. She was a G.R.C.A. Outstanding Dam. Photo: Wm. Brown.

While registrations of the breed were accepted earlier, the Golden Retriever was officially recognized by the American Kennel Club (A.K.C.) in 1932. At that time, Goldens were considered a rare breed —a far cry from today. In 1938 a group of the original Golden owners in this country formed the Golden Retriever Club of America. Today G.R.C.A. is among the largest of all Parent Breed Clubs in the country with a membership of over 4,500. It continues to play a vital role in safeguarding the welfare of the breed today.

15

A most unusual photograph taken in 1948 showing a number of well-known dogs of the time: left to right, Ch. Lorelei's Marshgrass Rebel**, Ch. Lorelei's Golden Anne***, Ch. Duffy's Golden Desire, Ch. Lorelei's Golden Sheen**, Ch. Gold Button of Catawba**, and Ch. Lorelei's Golden Rip***. Rebel and Rip are Outstanding Sires, and Gold Button of Catawba is an Outstanding Dam. Photo courtesy of Mrs. George H. Flinn, Jr.

The first Golden registered by A.K.C. was Lomberdale Blondin, owned by Robert Appleton. This dog, an English import, was registered in November 1925. Since 1932, the popularity of the Golden Retriever has increased dramatically. From a once rare breed, the Golden has grown in numbers to the point where it now occupies sixth place in all-breed A.K.C. registrations. From 1932 to 1956, only 20,376 Goldens were registered. In contrast, during 1982 alone over 51,000 were registered. It is expected that this increase in popularity will continue for the foreseeable future. Fanciers of the breed will have to remain vigilant in order to maintain the quality of the Golden Retriever for future generations.

THE GOLDEN RETRIEVER CLUB OF AMERICA (G.R.C.A.)

G.R.C.A. was formed in 1938. The first president of the club was Samuel S. Magoffin, owner of American and Canadian Champion Speedwell Pluto. The incorporation papers for the club clearly set forth its purpose: To perfect, by selective breeding, the Golden Retriever and to do all in the club's power to ". . .protect and advance the interests of Golden Retrievers in the Field and on the Bench." One method of accomplishing these goals has been education. The club has maintained a newsletter since the beginning and now has an excellent bi-monthly magazine to educate and foster communication between members. It has held yearly National Specialty Shows and Field Trials since 1940. Through its various committees, G.R.C.A. has been instrumental in helping breeders attempt to avoid and control genetic problems associated with the breed. One of these committees was formed to serve as a clearing house for Goldens cleared of hip dysplasia. The work of this committee eventually evolved into the Orthopedic Foundation for Animals, now the central organization for hip clearances for all breeds.

The Golden Retriever News, the magazine published by G.R.C.A., is the club's main format for communication to its members. This informative publication contains many articles of interest to all who are concerned with the welfare of the breed, as well as "how to" articles and reports from committees, the Board of Directors, and regional Golden clubs. The cost of a subscription is included in G.R.C.A. membership dues. The club also publishes a *Yearbook* every two years containing full statistics on the breed for the previous two-year period. This includes new title holders, wins in field, bench and obedience

Another Outstanding Dam from Golden Pine Kennels in Chesapeake, Virginia is Ch. Golden Pine's Punkin' Pi (Ch. Golden Pine's Easy Ace, W.C. ex Ch. Tigathoe's Gold Digger). Shown winning Best of Opposite Sex at the Piedmont Kennel Club in 1972. Owned by the Golden Pine Kennels of Mrs. Mary Luise Semans of Chesapeake, Virginia. Photo: Earl Graham.

Sire of the first two Laurell champions, this is Ch. High Farms Sutters Gold, shown at the Camden County show in December, 1966 with handler William Trainor. He was sired by Ch. High Farms Brassy Gold Braid and out of High Farms Golden Satinwood**, bred by Mrs. Ruth Worrest and owned by Lester A. Browne. Photo: Evelyn Shafer.

competition and up-to-date information on Outstanding Producers and Hall of Fame Dogs. A number of pamphlets on the breed are offered by the club as well.

Anyone seriously interested in Goldens should give strong consideration to becoming a member of G.R.C.A. In addition to receiving the *News*, members have the opportunity to become involved with others who are interested in the breed. Membership also provides a say in matters presented to the membership by committees and the Board through the voting process. Consideration should also be given to joining one of the local Golden clubs if there is one in your area. This will provide face-to-face opportunities to share ideas and concerns and provides good fellowship as well as an excellent opportunity to learn more about the breed. For more information on local clubs, contact the secretary of G.R.C.A. whose address can be obtained from the American Kennel Club, 51 Madison Avenue, New York, NY 10010.

Since 1940, G.R.C.A. has held a National Specialty Show and Field Trial, later adding Obedience Trials and Tracking Tests. Until fairly recently, these shows were held in the Mid-west. Currently and for a number of years, the show has been rotated on a region-by-region basis so that every three years there is a National Specialty in the East, the Mid-west, or the West. This allows breeders from all over the country to exhibit at a National Specialty once every three years without having to travel great distances. In addition, a Regional Specialty is held in each Region every year. Host clubs for both the National and Regional Specialties are local Golden clubs who volunteer to run the show.

One result of many generations of breeding at Golden Pine Kennels, this is Am., Can. Ch. Golden Pine's Remy Martin (Ch. Golden Pine's Shehazarin, U.D.T., W.C. ex Chaparrel V.S.O.P. of Golden Pine, C.D., W.C.). Remy Martin's mother, a daughter of Am., Can. Ch. Golden Pine's Courvoisier, Am., Can. C.D.X., W.C., Am. W.C.X., had twelve championship points to her credit. He was owned by Nancy Kelly Belsaas of San Mateo, California. Photo: Jayne Langdon.

Chapter 2

The Golden Retriever Standard of Perfection

What is it that makes a Golden Retriever a Golden and not, say, a Labrador? At a dog show, how does the judge determine which Golden will be the winner and which the losers? How does the serious Golden Retriever breeder decide which dog to breed to which bitch in order to try to improve the breed?

The answer to each of these questions involves a thorough and complete knowledge of the Breed Standard. The Standard is a complete written description of what the perfect Golden Retriever should look like, how it should act, and how it should move. Every serious breeder is striving to produce the perfect dog. No one has ever succeeded, and it is unlikely that anyone ever will, for there is no such thing as the perfect dog. Rather, this is the goal toward which breeders strive. If each individual breeder had his own idea of what a Golden should look like, the result would be chaos and a wide variation in dogs. In order to keep Goldens looking like Goldens rather than each individual's idea of what a Golden Retriever should be, one Standard of Perfection is used nationwide. The same is true for all breeds of dogs, as well as most purebred animals. The Golden Retriever Standard was prepared and approved by the membership of the Golden Retriever Club of America and then approved by the American Kennel Club. It is the ideal toward which all serious breeders work, and is the basis for the dog show judges' decisions.

Without such a Standard, each breed would quickly lose its identity and there soon would be no such thing as a purebred dog that looked like all other members of its breed. It is adherence to the Standard which separates the serious breeder from the so-called "backyard" breeder, who is often only out to try to make a dollar with no consideration for the welfare of the breed or the quality of the puppies produced from their breedings.

The current American Kennel Club approved Standard for Goldens is a newly revised one that went into effect on the first of January, 1982. It replaced a Standard that had been in effect since 1963. This new Standard reflects the current thinking of the members of G.R.C.A. The process of revision was a long one, spread out over many years, and was very carefully worked out by a committee, with frequent input from the Club membership. This new Standard, which is quite complete and concise, provides the reader with a clear mental image of what it is that makes a good Golden, both in terms of how he looks and, new to the current Standard, how he should behave.

The Standard is presented here in its entirety, followed by the author's additional comments on a section-by-section basis. A study and understanding of the Standard is most important to anyone seriously interested in the breed.

Now let us look at the Standard. The first section tells us what, in general, a Golden Retriever is bred to do and how he should look. The succeeding sections describe specifically the various parts of the dog that together make up the perfect whole. The reader may be aided in developing a mental image of the perfect Golden by looking at the photographs throughout this book. The dogs depicted herein are some of the most important Golden winners and producers in this country over the years.

In studying the Standard, it is important to remember that in real life there is no such thing as the perfect Golden; each has faults that make it less than perfect. However, it is the over-all appearance of the dog that is most important, not his individual parts. In the breed ring, it is the judge's responsibility to sort out the good from the faulty and then to decide which dog comes closest to the perfection described by the Standard. It is the judge's interpretation of the Standard that decides who the winners are in the ring on that day. Outside the dog show ring, it is your decision that counts.

Finally, it is important to bear in mind that each section of the Standard is related to the others. No section stands on its own. It is this interrelationship that makes the whole from the sum of the parts. No one section or one part of the dog should be considered alone, but should be thought of in conjunction with the dog as a whole, and how well that whole fits together. It is not merely that a dog has a beautiful head, but how well that head goes with the rest of his body. What is most important is the total image that the dog presents.

STANDARD FOR GOLDEN RETRIEVERS

GENERAL APPEARANCE: A symmetrical, powerful, active dog, sound and well put together, not clumsy nor long in the leg, displaying a kindly expression and possessing a personality that is eager, alert and self-confident. Primarily a hunting dog, he should be shown in hard working condition. Over-all appearance, balance, gait and purpose to be given more emphasis than any of his component parts.

HEAD: Broad in skull, slightly arched laterally and longitudinally without prominence of frontal bones (forehead) or occipital bones. Stop well defined but not abrupt. Foreface deep and wide, nearly as long as skull. Muzzle straight in profile, blending smoothly and strongly into skull; when viewed in profile or from above, slightly deeper and wider at stop than at tip. No heaviness in flews. Removal of whiskers is permitted but not preferred.

EYES: Friendly and intelligent in expression, medium large with dark, close-fitting rims, set well apart and reasonably deep in sockets. Color preferably dark brown; medium brown acceptable. Slant eyes and narrow, triangular eyes detract from correct expression and are to be faulted. No white or haw visible when looking straight ahead. Dogs showing evidence of functional abnormality of eyelids or eyelashes (such as, but not limited to, trichiasis, entropion, ectropion, or distichiasis) are to be excused from the ring.

TEETH: Scissors bite, in which the outer side of the lower incisors touches the inner side of the upper incisors. Undershot or overshot bite is a disqualification. Misalignment of teeth (irregular placement of incisors) or level bite (incisors meet each other edge to edge) is undesirable, but not to be confused with undershot or overshot. Full dentition. Obvious gaps are serious faults.

NOSE: Black or brownish black, though fading to a lighter shade in cold weather not serious. Pink nose or one seriously lacking in pigmentation to be faulted.

EARS: Rather short with front edge attached well behind and just above the eye and falling close to cheek. When pulled forward, tip of ear should just cover the eye. Low, hound-like ear set to be faulted.

NECK: Medium long, merging gradually into well laid back shoulders, giving sturdy, muscular appearance. Untrimmed natural ruff. No throatiness.

BODY: Well-balanced, short coupled, deep through the chest. Chest between forelegs at least as wide as a man's closed hand including thumb, with well developed forechest. Brisket extends to elbow. Ribs long and well sprung but not barrel shaped, extending well towards hindquarters. Loin short, muscular, wide and deep, with very little tuck-up. Back line strong and level from withers to slightly sloping croup, whether standing or moving. Slabsidedness, narrow chest, lack of depth in brisket, sloping back line, roach or sway back, excessive tuck-up, flat or steep croup to be faulted.

FOREQUARTERS: Muscular, well co-ordinated with hind quarters and capable of free movement. Shoulder blades long and well laid back with upper tips fairly close together at withers. Upper arms appear about the same length as the blades, close to the ribs without looseness. Legs, viewed from the front, straight with good bone, but not to the point of coarseness. Pasterns short and strong, sloping slightly with no suggestion of weakness.

HINDQUARTERS: Broad and strongly muscled. Profile of croup slopes slightly; the pelvic bone slopes at a slightly greater angle (approximately 30 degrees from horizontal). In a natural stance, the femur joins the pelvis at approximately a 90 degree angle; stifles well bent; hocks well let down with short strong rear pasterns. Legs straight when viewed from the rear. Cow hocks, spread hocks, and stickle hocks to be faulted.

FEET: Medium size, round, compact, and well knuckled, with thick pads. Excess hair may be trimmed to show natural size and contour. Dewclaws on forelegs may be removed, but are normally left on. Splayed or hare feet to be faulted.

TAIL: Well set on, thick and muscular at the base, following the natural line of the croup. Tail bones extend to, but not below, the point of hock. Carried with merry action, level or with some moderate upward curve; never curled over back nor between legs.

COAT: Dense and water repellent with good undercoat. Outer coat firm and resilient, neither coarse nor silky, lying close to body; may be straight or wavy. Moderate feathering on back of forelegs and underbody; heavier feathering on front of neck, back of thighs and underside of tail. Coat on head, paws, and front of legs is short and even. Excessive length, open coats, and limp, soft coats are very undesirable. Feet may be trimmed and stray hairs neatened, but the natural appearance of coat and outline should not be altered by cutting or clipping.

COLOR: Rich lustrous golden of various shades. Feathering may be lighter than rest of coat. With the exception of greying or whitening of face or body due to age, any white marking, other than a few white hairs on the chest, should be penalized according to its extent. Allow-

26

able light shadings are not to be confused with white markings. Predominant body color which is either extremely pale or extremely dark is undesirable. Some latitude should be given to the light puppy whose coloring shows promise of deepening with maturity. Any noticeable area of black or other off-color hair is a serious fault.

GAIT: When trotting, gait is free, smooth, powerful, and well coordinated, showing good reach. Viewed from any position, legs turn neither in nor out, nor do feet cross or interfere with each other. As speed increases, feet tend to converge toward center line of balance. It is recommended that dogs be shown on a loose lead to reflect true gait.

SIZE: Males 23-24 inches in height at withers; females 21½-22½ inches. Dogs up to one inch above or below standard size should be proportionately penalized. Deviation in height of more than one inch from the standard shall disqualify. Length from breastbone to point of buttocks slightly greater than height at withers in ratio of 12:11. Weight for dogs 65-75 pounds; bitches 55-65 pounds.

TEMPERAMENT: Friendly, reliable, and trustworthy. Quarrelsomeness or hostility towards other dogs or people in normal situations, or an unwarranted show of timidity or nervousness, is not in keeping with Golden Retriever character.

Such actions should be penalized according to their significance.

FAULTS: Any departure from the described ideal shall be considered faulty to the degree to which it interferes with the breed's purpose or is contrary to breed character.

DISQUALIFICATIONS: 1. Deviation in height of more than one inch from standard either way. 2. Undershot or overshot bite.

Approved by the American Kennel Club,
January 1982

The following comments and interpretations of the Standard are the author's and should not be confused with the requirements of the Standard.

General Appearance—This section tells us, in general, what a Golden is and what he should look like. Important to note is the requirement that the dog be shown ". . .in hard working condition." The Golden is a sporting dog and he needs room to run. He will not be a healthy, happy dog if always confined to an apartment with only short walks outside. He needs to be given the opportunity to have a good run on a daily basis, no matter what the weather, for both his physical and mental well being. When the dog is shown, he should always be well muscled. Never show your Golden when he is not in good physical condition. A soft, overweight dog is not a healthy one. At the same time the Golden is not a dog that can be left outside alone day and night. He wants and needs to be a member of the family and will need to spend a part of the day with people.

Head—Clearly, a Golden should not have a long, narrow head or muzzle, as many poorly bred Goldens seem to have today. At the same time he should not have a heavy, overdone head that makes him look more like a Rottweiler. Nor should there be a prominent bump (occiput) at the back of the skull. In order to be able to pick up game, the length of muzzle should be about the same as the length of his skull, definitely not shorter. He should have a definite stop, but not an abrupt one as found, for example, in a Pointer, nor the gentle stop of a Whippet. The muzzle should be straight when viewed from the side, not with a Roman nose look as is often seen. Above all, the head and the face must exhibit a kindly, soft, trusting and loving expression, never a hard one.

Eyes—The eyes are the key to the typical appealing Golden expression and a window to his intelligence and mood. The darker the color of the eye the better, with dark pigmentation around the eye also most important in contributing to the correct expression. Eyes that are too closely set together detract from this correct expression, as do triangular or slanted eye shapes. The correct eye is an almost but not quite almond-shaped one.

Teeth—This section is self-explanatory. It should be noted that some popular Golden breeding lines today have a potential bite problem in the manner that the two center teeth in the lower jaw are dropped lower than the adjacent teeth. Often this is not evident until the dog has matured—frequently when he is more than two years of age—and may progress with age. While this is currently considered a misalignment of the teeth, it could lead to a more serious problem in years to come and should be avoided where possible when planning breedings.

Nose—Basically, the darker the nose the better, with a really pink or flesh-colored nose being a serious fault. However, not only is it not unusual for the nose to lighten in color during colder weather, but often, in bitches, the nose color will become lighter when the bitch comes into season.

Ears—A low ear set is a common problem with many Goldens. There is also often a problem with ears set too high on the head so that they

A lovely head study of Am., Can. Ch. Golden Pine's Easy Ace* (Ch. Little Joe of Tigathoe*** ex Ch. Wessala Pride of Golden Pine). A G.R.C.A. Outstanding Sire and Show Dog Hall of Fame member, he was owned by Mrs. Mary Luise Semans of Chesapeake, Virginia. Photo: Fausette.

This is one of the early Outstanding Dams at the Golden Pine Kennels, Ch. Wessala Pride of Golden Pine (Ch. Duke of Rochester II, C.D. ex Wessala Tawny). Bred by Dorothy and Grace Rowley, she was owned by Mrs. Josiah T. Semans of Golden Pine Kennels in Chesapeake, Virginia.

appear to be sitting almost on top of the head when erect. Both problems detract from the all-important correct expression. The ears should not be too large nor too small and should be in balance with the size of the head.

Neck—The words "well laid back shoulders" are the key ones here. Many Goldens have poor front-end assemblies with straight shoulders, resulting in a lack of proper angulation and, therefore, inferior movement. (See sections on Forequarters and Gait.) Another common problem is too short a neck. Basically, the neck should appear to the eye as though it flows smoothly into the topline rather than being set onto the back at an abrupt angle. In order for this to happen, the shoulders must be well laid back and the neck reasonably long.

Body—The Golden is a solid dog and should not appear to be weedy nor too long in leg. At the same time, he is not a Newfoundland and should not be so broad or coarse as to look like a draft dog. A problem sometimes seen today is the Golden with a correct body on legs that appear to be too thin to balance the breadth of body. Many others lack proper forechest. A number of judges today seem to miss the requirement for a level topline whether standing or moving, but rather seem to favor the incorrect Setter-like topline. Beware of the puppy whose body looks like that of an adult dog; he will often become coarse and overdone as he matures. A puppy should appear somewhat underdeveloped, as a Golden often does not reach full physical maturity until three to four years of age, especially in terms of rib-spring and skull development.

Forequarters—This is the area which most concerns the author because of the widespread nature of the problems found in Golden Retriever fronts today, especially as it relates to correct movement. The second arm in many Goldens appears to be too short, restricting correct movement. The back of the shoulder blade should point toward the tail, not the ears! Too many Goldens have straight shoulders, poorly laid back, resulting in poor angulation. This, combined with the too short humerus (upper arm), results in an inability of the dog to reach forward fully. The lack of proper front extension has contributed to much up and down motion in the front rather than the forward reach necessary for balance and coordination with rear movement.

Over the past five to ten years, much emphasis has been placed on breeding for substantial rear angulation. Many breeders do not seem to realize that if this rear angulation is not matched by equal front angulation, the dog simply cannot move properly. In terms of movement, balance between the fore and rear quarters is all important. Better a straighter rear end to match the front, than well angulated hindquarters and straight fronts.

The Standard does not say that the dog's feet have to point straight forward when the dog is standing still. Doing so produces an unnatural position for correct balance. Try standing with your feet pointing straight forward for a while, and you will find that it becomes most uncomfortable. Our natural stance is with the feet pointed slightly outward to spread the weight of the body. The same is true of the dog.

Pointing the feet straight forward when stacking (posing) the dog in the ring may also tend to make him appear out at the elbows, when this may not actually be the case.

Note also that good bone is required. The dog should not look as though he is standing on stilts. The leg bone should appear to be in harmony with the rest of the body. At the same time excessive bone is as undesirable as too little bone.

Hindquarters—A problem often seen in the hindquarters is a narrowness of body through the hips. A fully matured dog should be very nearly as broad in the hips as he is at the shoulders. This is particularly important for a bitch, who will need the width here to whelp normally.

As mentioned in the section on Forequarters, many breeders have tried to bring substantial rear angulation into their bloodlines without paying equal attention to front angulation, which must equal that of the rear in order to have balanced, well coordinated movement. The result of this lack of balance often leads to the dog's rear legs overtaking the front legs when the dog is moving. This leads to movement faults such as crabbing and sidewinding, or up and down movement in the front. Most often the result is uncoordinated movement.

While cow hocks was, perhaps, more of a problem in the past, many Goldens today seem to be spread-hocked, where the hocks are pointing away from each other as the dog is viewed from the rear at a trot. It might also be pointed out here that poor movement of the rear is not necessarily the result of hip dysplasia (a partially genetic malformation of the hip joint) as is often thought. The author has seen many sound-moving dogs who, upon radiographic examination, were dysplastic, and just as many poor-moving dogs whose hips showed no radiographic evidence of dysplasia. Most poor movement is the result of other structural faults.

Feet—A cat-like foot is what is wanted here, not one that is long and narrow. In order to maintain a proper foot, regular cutting of the dog's nails is required. They will not wear down naturally, and left untrimmed may lead to splayed feet. Uncut dewclaws will grow in a circle back into the leg. Cutting is a simple matter that can be done by anyone with the proper tool. See the chapter on Grooming Your Golden in this book.

Tail—The true Golden Retriever tail should be fairly wide at the base, becoming narrower as it approaches the tip. The tail should not be carried curled over the back in Husky fashion when gaiting, but it is

Good Goldens haven't changed that much over the years. This photograph taken in 1951 shows (left) Ch. Duke of Rochester II, C.D. (Happy Rochester ex Beauty Valle) owned by Josiah T. Semans, and (right) Ch. Holly of Claymer, U.D.T. (Flyer of Taramar ex Tulachard Merrilass, U.D.) owned by Clayton L. Hare. Photo by E. Shafer courtesy of Mrs. Josiah T. Semans.

proper to be carried somewhat above the topline if relatively straight. Remember, the Golden uses his tail as a rudder when swimming and often when running as well, so correct placement on the body and tail carriage is important. The tail is, of course, the key to every dog's emotions. The normal position for most Goldens' tails seems to be wagging!

Coat—The Golden has a naturally oily coat that is water repellent and should not require frequent bathing. Note that the Standard calls excessive coat undesirable. What is wanted is enough coat to protect the

33

dog from water and brush and to make him look good, but not so much that it will interfere with his ability to work in the field. Too much emphasis on coat could eventually lead to the development of a coat that interferes with the original breed purpose—field work. It would be tragic if the Golden Retriever goes the way of some other Sporting dogs (such as the American Cocker Spaniel and English Springer Spaniel) where the show dogs have so much coat that they could not possibly compete in the field without severely damaging their coat. We do not want to develop two parts of our breed, the "show" Golden and the "field" Golden.

The Golden Retriever is not a Poodle, and should not require a great amount of trimming of the coat. While some grooming is necessary for the show ring, and a regular brushing is a must for all Goldens whether they are pets, field dogs or show dogs, excessive trimming and clipping should not be necessary. All trimming that must be done should be completed in a manner that allows the dog's natural look to remain intact.

Color—The Standard permits a wide range of color in the Golden, so long as it is not so washed out as to appear almost white, or so dark that the color compares with that of an Irish Setter. The color of a young puppy's coat tends to get darker with each succeeding coat shed until the age of three or four years. Thus, the dark puppy will not get lighter in color as he matures. The color of a young pup's ears closely approximates his eventual adult coat color.

Gait—What should be emphasized here is the Standard's requirement for ". . .free, smooth, powerful, and well coordinated (gait) showing good reach." Note the words "showing good reach," something missing from many Goldens today. Even some judges are overlooking this important requirement. In order to move properly, a dog must have balance and coordination; that is, his parts must fit together in a manner that allows him to use his body well and freely. Study dogs in motion. Those who seem to move effortlessly are usually the dogs that are properly built and well balanced.

It is important not to equate speed with correct movement. It is the *efficiency* with which a dog covers ground, not the *speed* at which he must move his legs to accomplish this, that determines whether or not a dog is a good mover and has correct gait. Efficient motion is what allows a dog to work all day in the field without total exhaustion. Note the photograph of the dog in motion on the opposite page. It illustrates proper reach and drive.

Ch. Pepperhill's East Point Airily (Ch. Sir Duncan of Woodbury ex Ch. Pepperhill's Return Ticket). Airily is shown in an informal moving photograph with her handler Elliot More. This beautifully coordinated mover recently became the eighth bitch to qualify for the G.R.C.A. Show Dog Hall of Fame. She is owned by Dan Flavin and Helene Geary of Garrison, New York. Note the matching extension of the front leg and rear leg. Photo: John Ashbey.

Size—The desired size of the Golden is very clearly indicated in the Standard; males 23-24 inches, females 21½-22½ inches at the withers. Important to note also is the ratio of height to length of body, something often overlooked. The Golden Retriever should not be square like the Old English Sheepdog. Rather, he should be slightly longer in body than he is tall at the shoulders. This allows the dog to use the angulation described in the sections on Fore- and Hindquarters without having his legs interfere with each other. Too short a back, without proper length of loin, does not provide the dog with enough space beneath his body to fully extend and withdraw his limbs, therefore leading to movement faults and inefficient movement. A breeder who decides to breed for a shorter back must still give consideration to correct movement. No matter how pretty the dog is, he is not a good Golden if he does not move freely and properly.

Temperament—This is the only section entirely new to the Standard following the recent revision. For many years, the Golden Retriever has been known, above all, for its loving, easy-to-train, outgoing nature. In recent years a problem has begun to develop with temperament and it has reached the point where we can no longer always take good temperament for granted. We now are beginning to hear of Goldens fighting with other dogs, though unprovoked, and of Goldens who are so hyperactive that training becomes difficult for the average dog owner. There have even been rare incidents of Goldens biting people, including their owners. Fortunately, these dogs remain very much the exception rather than the rule. However, to not mention this problem would be a disservice to the breed. This type of temperament must not be allowed to become commonplace, or one of the most important attributes of the breed will be lost. It was with the intention of eliminating this problem before it becomes widespread that this section was added to the Standard. It is the author's feeling that under no circumstances should a Golden Retriever be bred if it shows any temperament qualities other than those typical of the breed, no matter what its other attributes. If this temperament is lost, then one of the most important aspects of the Golden will be lost with it. This must not be allowed to happen.

Faults—This section is an instruction to judges and breeders. Dogs showing any major faults listed anywhere in the Standard probably will not do well if shown in conformation (bench) competition at A.K.C. licensed shows. If you are unsure of the quality of your dog, try to find an experienced, objective breeder or professional handler to evaluate your dog for you (see chapter on Showing Your Golden).

Disqualifications—A male Golden more than 25 inches tall or less than 22 inches tall at the shoulders, or a Golden bitch more than 23½ inches tall or less than 20½ inches tall, is not eligible to be shown in the breed ring. Exceptions are routinely made for puppies, however. It is the responsibility of the judge to determine the height of a dog when in the ring, using an A.K.C. approved measuring device called a wicket. The height of a dog may also be questioned by any exhibitor at the show and, once questioned, must be determined by the judge in the ring. If the dog or bitch is found to be over or under the required height, a note to this effect is made in the judge's book and goes to A.K.C. This is recorded in that dog's permanent file. Should the dog continue to be shown, and is later measured out of the Standard's requirements on two other occasions, it is permanently barred from further competition in the breed ring. The same is true of a dog that has a bad bite as defined by the Standard. A.K.C. further requires that all male dogs have two normally descended testicles. If this is not the case then the dog is disqualified from competition. Dogs with disqualifying faults should not be used for breeding purposes since these faults will most likely be passed on to their produce.

It should be pointed out here that these disqualifications apply only to conformation competition, and have no effect on any dog's eligibility for A.K.C. licensed obedience or field competition.

It is important to reiterate here that one must look at each dog as an entity. While each of its individual parts is important, it is the total picture presented by the dog as a whole that is paramount. Just as the sections of the Standard are interrelated with and interdependent on each other, so are the dog's parts interdependent on each other in forming the aggregate. It would be a gross error to look at a dog with a perfect head but weak front as being better than a dog with a good head and good front. Harmony and balance are crucial. The good Golden Retriever must present a uniform picture, with its parts blending together to form a symmetrical whole. The total picture is much more important than the relative perfection of any one part in relation to the total dog.

Am., Can. Ch. Russo's Pepperhill Poppy relaxes on the beach about one and a half weeks before whelping a litter of fourteen pups, three of which went on to become champions. Poppy is owned by the author. Photo: John Ashbey.

Chapter 3

Purchasing Your Golden Retriever

Careful consideration should be given to what breed of dog you wish to own before purchasing one. If several breeds are attractive to you, and you are undecided which you prefer, learn all you can about the characteristics of each breed before making your decision. As you do this, you are preparing yourself to make an intelligent choice. This is most important since, with reasonable luck, you will be purchasing a dog who will be a member of your household for a dozen years or more. The purchase of a puppy is a decision that never should be made impulsively.

Since you are reading this book, I assume that you are interested in a Golden Retriever. It is never wise to just rush out and buy the first cute Golden puppy that catches your eye. All Golden puppies are cute, even poor quality, unhealthy ones. Whether you wish a dog to show, to compete with in obedience, to hunt with, or just a family pet, the more time and thought you invest as you plan the purchase, the more likely you are to meet with complete satisfaction. The genetic background and early care provided to your pet by the breeder will be reflected in the dog's future health and temperament. Even if you are planning the purchase of a dog who will be only a family pet, it is essential, if the dog is to enjoy a trouble-free future, that you assure yourself a healthy, properly raised puppy or adult from sturdy, well bred stock. If you are planning any kind of show career for the dog, even more care must be exercised since more than health is involved.

Throughout the pages of this book you will find the names and locations of many well-known and well established Golden kennels located in various parts of the country. There are many other good quality breeders who are not mentioned here but who are, nevertheless, recognized breeders. Suggestions of the names of quality breeders in your area may be obtained from the Secretary of G.R.C.A. or from a local Golden Club in your area. A.K.C. can also supply you with the names of breeders who have paid to advertise in the *Pure-Bred Dogs—American Kennel Gazette,* but by no means are all or even most good breeders on this list. I strongly recommend that prospective purchasers follow the suggestions that are outlined here, as this will enable you to locate and select a satisfactory puppy or grown dog no matter what its purpose is to be.

Your first step in searching out your puppy is to make appointments at Golden kennels in your area, where you can visit and inspect their dogs, both those available for sale and those who are the kennel's basic breeding stock. Do not be unwilling to travel a reasonable distance to find the right kennel—the time spent now in finding the right dog will be more than worth the additional effort in the future. Convenience to your home should be one of the *last* factors to consider in deciding where to purchase your puppy—certainly not the first.

You are looking for an active, sturdy puppy with bright eyes and intelligent expression, friendly and alert, neither hyperactive nor dull and listless. The coat should be clean and thick, with no sign of parasites. The premises on which he has been raised should look and smell clean and be tidy, making it obvious that the puppies and their surroundings are in capable and particular hands. The puppies should be eager to greet you with tails wagging. If they all consistently run away from a quiet, friendly greeting, there is reason to suspect that they have not been properly socialized and they should be avoided. Goldens are "people" dogs and this innate characteristic should be present even in young pups over the age of five weeks.

If you are unable to locate a good Golden kennel in your area, do not hesitate to contact others at a distance, so long as they are recognized kennels with good reputations. Shipping a dog today is a relatively common practice, especially with show potential pups, and is accomplished with comparatively few problems considering the number of dogs shipped each year. A reputable, well-known breeder wants the customer to be satisfied, and therefore will present his puppies fairly. A breeder of conscience takes real interest and concern in the puppies they cause to be brought into the world, and he will probably question you to make sure that your home is suitable for a Golden. Should you be displeased with the puppy upon its arrival, the reputable breeder will almost certainly permit its immediate return. This type of breeder is proud of his reputation and wants to maintain it. Thus on two counts, for the sake of the dog's future and the breeder's reputation, purchasing a puppy at a distance presents little risk.

If your puppy is to be a pet only, I feel that the best age at which to start it in your home, with proper care, is about seven to seven and a half weeks. If you take a puppy at this age it is often easier to train it to the routine of your household and your requirements. The older puppy may already be started with habits you might find difficult to change. Puppies should not be brought into a new environment during their eighth week, as studies have shown that they are especially sensitive to new changes during that week of their life. It is better to wait until the pup is nine weeks old if you cannot bring it home before the onset of the eighth week.

The younger pup is usually less costly than an older dog, as it stands to reason the breeder will not have as much money invested in it. Obviously, a puppy that has been raised to five or six months of age represents more in care and cash expenditure on the breeder's part than one sold earlier, and therefore you can expect it to be priced accordingly. A top show prospect puppy of nine months or more will be considerably more expensive since most of the element of chance in purchasing such a dog has been eliminated.

There is an enormous amount of truth in the statement that "bargain" puppies seldom turn out to be a bargain. A puppy that is priced significantly lower than the prices established breeders command is often raised either purely for profit or by people with little knowledge or experience who think they can make an extra dollar. This can, and often does, lead to great heartbreak, temperament problems and high veterinarian's bills which can quickly add up to many times what you thought you "saved" by not purchasing a properly reared dog. On the other hand, just because a puppy is expensive does not assure one that it is healthy, well bred, and well reared. I know of numerous cases where unscrupulous dealers have sold puppies for as much as $600 that were sickly, in poor condition, and such poor specimens that it is difficult to recognize that they are Golden Retrievers. Indeed, in some cases they are not, but are mixed breeds that happen to look like puppy Goldens. No reputable breeder will sell an entire litter to a dealer and this should be kept in mind. Common sense must guide the prospective purchaser, plus the selection of a reliable breeder whom you know to have had well satisfied customers.

One more word on the subject of pets. A question often asked is which sex makes a better pet. Bitches make as good a choice as males. In Goldens, the temperament of the male and female is quite similar. In some lines the males are easier to live with than the females, in

Like most puppies, Goldens love to play. When another dog was temporarily unavailable, this youngster chose a friendly cat for a playmate.

others the reverse is true. If you do select a bitch and have no intention of breeding her, by all means have her spayed both for your sake and for the bitch's. The advantages of a spayed bitch include avoiding the nuisance of "in season" periods, with the inevitable males haunting your premises in an effort to visit that most interesting lady in your house. Also, you will not have to deal with the messiness and spotting of furniture and rugs when she is in season. Your bitch benefits greatly from a health standpoint, being much less likely to contract cancer, for example. Be aware, however, that a spayed bitch can not be shown in the breed ring, though she is eligible for obedience and field competition, so be certain that you are not interested in showing her before spaying.

42

In selecting a pet, never underestimate the advantages of an older dog, perhaps a retired show dog or bitch no longer needed for breeding, or a show potential pup kept by a breeder that just didn't reach its potential. These may be available quite reasonably from a breeder anxious to place such a dog in a loving home. These dogs are settled and can be a delight to own; they are already housebroken and trained and can make wonderful companions, especially in a grown-up household where raising a puppy can sometimes be difficult. Goldens are almost always capable of adapting to new homes even at an older age.

PURCHASING A SHOW POTENTIAL PUPPY

Everything we have said so far about the careful selection of a pet puppy and its place of purchase applies here, but with many further considerations. Now is the time for an in-depth study of Goldens and the Breed Standard, starting with every word in this book and the others you will seek out on Goldens and dogs in general. Purchasing a show dog or foundation stock for a future breeding program requires much care and study. The Standard has now become your guide, and you must learn not only the words in it, but how to interpret them. You must learn how they apply to an actual dog before you are ready to make an intelligent selection of a show dog.

If you are thinking about a show dog, obviously you have learned about dog shows and have attended at least several. Now your activities in this direction should be increased, with your attending every single dog show within a reasonable distance from your home. Pay special attention to any Golden Specialty shows that may be scheduled for your area. Much can be learned about Goldens at ringside at any show. Talk with the breeders who are exhibiting. Study the dogs they are showing and others of their breeding. Watch the judging with concentration, noting each decision made, and attempt to follow the reasoning by which the judge has reached his decision. Note carefully the attributes of the dogs who win and, for later use, the manner in which each is presented. Close your ears to the ringside "know-it-alls," usually novice owners of only one dog or so and very new to the fancy, who have only derogatory remarks to make about all that is taking place—unless they happen to win. This is usually the type of exhibitor who comes and goes through the fancy and whose interest is often of short duration, owing to a lack of knowledge and dissatisfaction caused by their failure to recognize the need to learn. You, as a fancier whom we hope will last and enjoy our sport over many future years, should develop independent thinking at this stage as you learn to draw your own conclusions about the merits, or lack of them, seen before you in the ring. This will sharpen your own judgment in preparation for choosing wisely and well.

Note carefully which breeders campaign winning dogs—not just an occasional isolated good one, but those who bring out home-bred winners consistently. It is from one of these people that you should select your own future star. Be careful not to become "kennel blind"—concentrating on one kennel to the exclusion of all others while overlooking the faults in that kennel's line. This could lead you to miss a good dog.

If you are located in an area where only occasional dog shows take place, or where long travel distances are involved, you will need to find another testing ground for your ability to select a worthy show dog. Become a member of G.R.C.A. and read carefully through the articles and advertisements in each issue of the *Golden Retriever News*, paying special attention to the photographs. If possible, join a local Golden club and talk to its breeder/members. Hopefully, there are some good kennels raising Goldens within a reasonable distance. If so, by all means ask permission of the owners to visit these, and do so when permission is given; not necessarily to buy then and there, as they may not have available what you are seeking, but to see the type of dog being raised there and to discuss dogs with the breeder. Most will be more than willing to spend the time with you if they realize that you are seriously interested in showing. Every time you do this, you will add to your knowledge.

We have already discussed the purchase of a pet puppy. Obviously, this same approach applies to a far greater degree when the purchase involves a future show dog. The only place at which to purchase a show prospect is from a breeder who raises show stock. To do otherwise is to court disappointment and probable failure as the puppy matures. Show and breeding kennels obviously cannot keep all of their fine young stock. Even the most active breeder/exhibitor is, therefore, happy to place promising youngsters in the hands of people who are also interested in showing and winning with them, doing so at a fair price according to the quality, prospects and breeding of the dog involved. Here again, if no kennel in your area has what you are seeking in terms of quality or type, do not hesitate to contact breeders in other areas. This is commonly done today. Ask for pedigrees and a complete description of the dog offered, and a photograph. Heed the breeder's

At a little over four weeks of age, these youngsters are fully aware of the world around them and most are curious to learn about it.

advice and recommendations after telling him truthfully exactly what your expectations are for the dog you purchase. Do you want something to win just a few ribbons now and then? Do you want a dog who can complete his championship? Are you thinking of the big time and a dog you can campaign for Best of Breed, Group wins, and possibly even Best in Show? Consider it all honestly and carefully in advance, then discuss your plans openly with the breeder. You will be most satisfied with the results if you do this, as then the breeder is in the best position to help you choose the dog who is most likely to come through for you. A breeder selling a show dog is just as anxious as the buyer for the dog to succeed, and will present it to you with truth and honesty. This type of breeder will not lose interest in you the moment the sale has been made, but will be right there, ready to assist you with good advice and suggestions based on years of experience, if you just ask.

As you make inquiries of at least several kennels, keep in mind that show prospect puppies are not always readily available. You may well have to make a reservation for a puppy from a future litter, the pedigree of which interests you. You may be asked for a deposit to assure you the reservation. Ask each breeder what they do and do not guarantee in their puppies, as this varies from breeder to breeder. Remember that show prospect pups are more expensive than pet puppies from the same litter, and puppies are less expensive than mature show dogs. The mature show dog almost always has a price tag over $1000, and sometimes more. The reason for this is that with a puppy there is always an element of chance, the possibility of its developing unexpected faults as it matures or failing to develop the excellence and quality that earlier had seemed probable. It may become dysplastic, though born of hip-cleared parents. There is always a risk factor in purchasing a puppy show prospect. With the mature dog, "what you see is what you get," and it is unlikely to change beyond coat and condition which are dependent on your care. The status of hips and eyes, always a concern with an animal destined for breeding, is known. Also an advantage for the novice owner, the mature dog has almost certainly received ring training and at least match show experience, if not point show.

If your dog, when ready, is to be shown by a professional handler, by all means let the handler help you locate and select a good one. Through their numerous clients, handlers have access to a number of breeders and show prospects. With their previous experience showing Goldens, they should be able to assist you in choosing a likely show prospect puppy. With an older dog, your handler will certainly know the quality of the dog.

If you are planning the foundation of a future kennel, concentrate on acquiring one or two really superior bitches. They should represent the finest producing Golden bloodlines from a strain noted for producing quality, generation after generation. A proven brood bitch is, of course, the ideal selection if she has been the dam of show type puppies. However, an O.F.A. cleared, eye cleared, proven brood bitch of show quality is usually quite difficult to obtain since no one is anxious to part with so valuable an asset, and the price for such a bitch would be quite high, probably ranging from $2000 up. If you strike it lucky and find such a bitch for sale, you're off to a flying start.

Great attention should be paid to the pedigree of the bitch that you intend to breed. If you do not already know them, try to see her sire

Ch. Golden Pines Glorybe's Angel (Golden Pines Tiny Tim ex Ch. Golden Pine's Glorybe). A Foundation dam at R. Ann Johnson's Gold-Rush Kennels in Princeton, New Jersey, Angel is a G.R.C.A. Outstanding Dam of twelve champions, including several Show Dog Hall of Fame dogs. Shown here handled by Laura Kling for owners R. Ann and L.C. Johnson. Photo: Booth.

An adolescent Golden
pup, his tail still too
long for his body, races
off to find that elusive
ball.

Goldens often seem to have a special affinity for youngsters, even while they are
watching the photographer!

and dam. It is generally agreed that someone starting with a breed should concentrate on owning fine bitches before considering keeping one's own stud dog. Knowing your bitch's pedigree will assist you in selecting the proper mate when the time comes to breed her. See the chapter on Breeding Your Golden for information on breeding your dog.

When actually choosing your potential show puppy, the *least* amount of your attention should be placed on the color of the puppy— unless it is unusually light or extremely dark. To best gauge the eventual color of the pup when he is mature, look at the color of the pup's ears. His body coat will eventually darken to match the ear color. The lighter puppy will get darker, but the darker pup will not get lighter. If possible, it is ideal that the color of the dog's feathering be somewhat lighter than the body coat color. This is difficult to tell on a young pup, but if the puppy coat is light and the ears are significantly darker, the puppy will often develop lighter colored feathering as it matures.

Your primary focus in choosing your show "star" should be on type and overall balance. At approximately six to nine weeks most pups mirror what they will look like as mature adults. At this age one should look for the same things we look for in an adult—correct angulation both front and rear, good reach and drive when moving, proper type, and others. An outgoing temperament is most important as well, since this often portends good showmanship in the adult. After about twelve weeks of age, most puppies go into an asymmetrical growth stage that continues until they are almost a year old. Thus, it is better to choose your pup before this age where possible, or wait until the pup is nine or ten months old. Finally, if there are two puppies in the litter that you like equally, choose the one with the fuller and straighter coat. A straight coat is much easier to deal with in an adult show dog than the wavy coat. Don't be fooled by large amounts of fuzzy puppy coat on an adolescent Golden. This will not necessarily be the same once the adult coat grows in fully.

To summarize, if you want a family dog strictly as a companion, it is best to buy it young and raise it to the habits of your home. If you are purchasing a show dog, the more mature it is the more certain you can be of its future beauty and quality. If you are buying foundation stock for a kennel, purchase the best you can afford from the finest *producing* bloodline available to you. In beginning a kennel, bitches are better to start with.

While most Golden litters have eight to ten puppies in them, sometimes only one is born. This proud mother poses with her only son, about five weeks of age.

Chapter 4

So You Bought a Puppy— Now What?

Having decided that a Golden Retriever is the dog for you, then carefully selected and made your purchase, you are ready to bring home the cuddly ball of fur that you finally chose. Whether you purchased a dog or a bitch, you will now give your time, love, and attention to this new member of your family. The foundation of trust and training that you build during the pup's first weeks in your home will determine the dog's patterns of behavior for the rest of its life. The extra time and effort you spend now will be rewarded for many years to come. This chapter will help you get off on the right foot, as it answers many of the most frequently asked questions about how to raise your puppy.

When you purchased your puppy, you should have received from the breeder a blue form that was issued by the American Kennel Club especially for your pup's litter. This is the A.K.C. Dog Registration Application form and it contains all of the important information about your new dog. If the breeder was unable to supply this form, then you should be given the identification of the dog consisting of the breed, registered name of the sire and dam, their registration numbers, date of birth and name of the breeder.

The Registration Application is your proof of purchase, since it transfers title of the dog to you. It is the manner in which you will formally name the puppy, and it will be used to register the dog and his new name in the A.K.C. Stud Book. Parts of the form should have been filled in by the breeder when you purchased the dog. You will be responsible for completing the rest of it later. Be careful not to misplace this paper, for you will need it in the future.

On the form, the following information will be pre-printed: Breed; the names and registration numbers of the sire and dam of the litter ("sire" means father and "dam" means mother); the date of birth for the litter; and the name and address of the breeder. There are several spaces that the breeder fills in, including the sex of the puppy, its color, and, on the back, your name and address. Make sure that all the persons listed as breeders have signed the form in the proper places on the upper portion of the back. If, for some reason, you have not purchased the puppy directly from the breeder, the original purchaser's name and address should be on the back of the form and the seller will have to supply you with a gray Supplemental Transfer Statement signed by the original purchaser and endorsed to you as the new owner. If the person who is selling you the dog does not have his name on one of these two forms, then he or she is not following A.K.C. requirements and it is possible that you may encounter difficulty in registering the dog. I suggest that you take great care in purchasing such a puppy.

Many people feel that their new pup must immediately be formally named, and that name entered on the A.K.C. form. This is definitely NOT the case! Rather, I suggest that a name or names be selected and then lived with for a while before completing the papers. There is no rush of any kind in filing the form with A.K.C. Some breeders even wait until the pup is a year or more old before sending the papers in. A dog may even be shown before receiving an individual number simply by filling in his litter number on the entry form. However, a dog cannot earn a title without being individually registered, and once he has earned points towards his championship or a leg toward an obedience degree, you cannot change the name under which you showed him when he won.

Remember to choose a "call" name (the name you will use every day when you refer to the dog) that will be appropriate when the dog is fully grown. "Poopsie" or "Tiny" may seem cute for a young pup, but seems inappropriate for a seventy-five pound adult male Golden. The registered name you choose need not use the dog's call name, although this may be easier. Often, the registered name will begin with or include the kennel name of the breeder. A.K.C. requires that your choice of name consist of no more than 25 letters (dashes, apostrophes, etc., do not count). Try to use an unusual name since A.K.C. will affix a numerical suffix to the name if it has been used before. Your dog may end up permanently named "Golden Bear XXXIII." In selecting the more formal registered name, a look at the pup's pedigree (a listing of his ancestors) may be helpful. If the breeder did not supply you with one, you can obtain a certified pedigree from A.K.C. for a fee.

When you get to filling out the blue form, do so very carefully, as A.K.C. will return it to you for explanation of any changes, cross-outs or erasures. Send the form with the correct fee to A.K.C. You will receive in the mail after about four weeks the dog's Individual Registration form (the famous "papers"), indicating the dog's individual number. Once registered, a dog's name can never be changed with A.K.C.

Before you pick up your puppy, there are a number of steps you can take that will make things easier on the day you do bring him home for the first time. If you have children, this will help them to deal with their impatience and excitement as you wait for the puppy to be ready to leave its littermates. It will also be a good time to help the children to learn what they can and cannot do with the puppy.

First, it is a good idea to purchase your basic equipment in advance. You will need two bowls, one for food and one for water. I strongly advise the weighted ones which will be difficult for the puppy to tip over. Be sure they are large enough for the dog when he is fully grown, as there is no sense in buying dishes more than once. Get the kind that can go into the dishwasher to make things easier. You will also need a pin brush—the best is the type with pins that are about an inch long with rounded ends—and a comb. In addition, you'll need a nail cutter; again, get one that you can use on an adult Golden. Finally, you'll need a leash and collar or something on which to walk the puppy. I suggest starting with a show lead. This is a soft combination lead and collar in one, with the collar part being adjustable. Purchase one that is about 3/8″ wide, or a little wider, so that it will not cut into the puppy's neck if he pulls against it. I have found the flat style works better than the round one. Later you can purchase a separate lead and collar, but wait until the dog is about six months old. (Do not get the chain type of lead as it is hard to hold and will cut into your hands if the dog pulls against you.) This will complete your basic kit for the puppy's care. Have your children help you make the purchases so they feel involved with the puppy from the start.

HOUSEBREAKING

Housebreaking has always been a major concern for those purchasing their first dog. The patterns you set with the dog in the beginning will become lifelong habits for him, so take the time to do it right from the start. While the old method of paper training the dog and then teaching him to do his duty outside will eventually work, there is a

This young dog seems to be saying, "Hummm, what shall we play with next?"

much faster method which has proven to be most satisfactory over the years. This method has the added benefit of protecting your furniture and other belongings from being chewed. This technique involves the use of a wire crate (or cage) which will serve both as the puppy's bedroom, and his dining room. While paper training is fine for a small toy dog who lives in an apartment, it only serves to extend housetraining time for a large dog like a Golden.

A crate is a wire enclosure used, at first, to house the puppy when you or a member of your family cannot actively supervise him. It should be large enough for an adult Golden, since you will probably want to use it until the pup is roughly a year of age—that is about 21 to 22 inches wide, 24 to 26 inches high, and at least 32 inches long. The crate should be well built, with welds that cannot be broken by an active adult dog. Frequently the inexpensive crates are poorly welded and have large spaces between their thin wires. The initial cost of the crate will be more than saved in unchewed furniture and unstained carpets, so do not skimp on this.

The theory behind the use of a crate is a simple one: dogs are den animals and feel safest and most comfortable in a confined space. They have an instinctive need to keep this space—their "house"—clean and therefore will do everything in their power not to mess in it. The puppy confined to a crate will quickly learn to "hold it" until he is outside of his house. This means you will have to take him directly out of the crate and outdoors—with no stops on the way. To help the puppy feel more at home in the crate, I suggest feeding him in it and giving him a toy or two to play with while he is inside. However, it is usually not a good idea to leave water in the crate at first as Goldens are water dogs and young puppies will often try to swim in the water dish!

At first, leave the puppy in the crate whenever you cannot actively supervise him. This means that if you have to leave the room for a while, the very young pup should be put back in his crate. Soon, as he becomes more trustworthy, you will be able to leave him out for longer periods of time. The more trust you can place in the pup, the longer he can stay out. How long this process will take differs with each dog, and you will have to use your own judgment. However, if you do not gradually increase the time he is loose, the puppy will never learn to be out on his own. Remember, he will learn by making mistakes and then being gently corrected. Using a crate is not in any way cruel. The puppy quickly prefers to sleep in his crate and will go into it on his own. Better to use a crate than to have to scold the puppy all the time.

When you first bring the pup home, establish a regular schedule for time out of the crate. Each time you take him out of it, immediately bring him outside so he may do his duty. Wait until he does it before bringing him back inside to play. At a minimum he should be taken outside five times a day: first thing in the morning (yes, before you take your shower—at first he won't be able to wait until you're done), before leaving for the day, around noon or as soon as someone returns home, at dinner time, and last thing before bedtime. More often is fine, less often is not. Try to balance the amount of time in and out of the crate to allow the puppy as much exercise as possible. Increase the time out of the crate as he gets older. You will be able to decrease the number of times out as the pup matures and gains greater physical ability to control his elimination urges. Finally, you should be aware that when there is no one around to play with, most dogs will go to sleep. There is no reason why the dog should not sleep in his crate, where you will not have to worry about him.

As with very young children, everything goes into a puppy's mouth. He won't know not to chew on things that are dangerous to him; so placing the pup in the crate when unsupervised may save his life when you are not around. When he is out of his crate, the door should be left open so that he may go in and take a nap or a bite of food whenever he wants too. Young puppies play hard and then sleep soundly, just as young children do. After awakening from a nap, the puppy should be brought outside to "go" before being allowed loose in the house. The crate will also become a refuge for him when he wants to get away from over-eager children. From the beginning, children should be taught that they must not disturb the puppy when he is in his "house." It is his room, his space, and he should be allowed to have peace when he is in it.

THE FIRST DAY—AT THE BREEDER'S

Everything is set. You are ready to go to pick up your new family member. It will be a good idea to bring along some paper towels in case you have an unexpected clean-up to take care of because of car sickness. If you own a station wagon or van, take your crate so that the pup can ride home in his new house. Place a thick layer of newspaper on the floor of the crate to absorb any liquids. You will need to leave paper in the crate until the puppy is able to stay dry overnight for several nights in a row (he'll also have fun making confetti out of it).

Do not be afraid to ask the breeder questions; most will be more than happy to answer any you have. The good breeder is as concerned about the puppy's welfare as you are. Make sure to get a written record of all the shots the puppy has received as well as any wormings it may have had, noting the dates of the wormings and the type of worms the pup had. You will need this information later for your veterinarian. Be certain that you understand any instructions the breeder has given you and that you understand clearly what the breeder guarantees regarding the puppy. Check to see if you have the right to return the puppy if your veterinarian finds something significantly wrong with it.

Check with the breeder regarding feeding. While some breeders use homemade mixtures, most use commercial preparations. With the careful testing that major dog food manufacturers do today, there is really no need to make your own dog food. In fact, the commercial products are probably better balanced than most homemade concoctions. I recommend using one of the better commercial foods prepared especially for growing puppies. In my own kennel, we feed puppies a dry kibbled puppy food made for the growth stage of a dog's life. The pups seem to like crunching on the dry food, especially when they are teething. Make sure that plenty of fresh cool water is readily available. If he doesn't overeat, you can feed your pup on a free choice basis by just leaving food out for him to snack on. Otherwise, plan to feed three to four times a day at first, decreasing to twice a day when the pup is five to six months old. You may feed an adult dog once a day if you wish.

At first, use the same food that the breeder fed the puppy in order to avoid upsetting his stomach. If you decide to use a different food, wean the pup gradually to the new food by mixing more and more of it with the old food while at the same time decreasing the amount of the old food until he is entirely on the new diet. This process will take several days. Remember that a pup should not be allowed to get too fat, as this is unhealthy and places unnecessary stress on the undeveloped bone structure and muscles of the dog. Again, it is most important to use a high-quality dog food made specifically for puppies since it contains the extra nutrients required by a rapidly growing dog. Do not feed the puppy any "people" food, especially from the table. This can upset the balance of the dog food and can easily lead to bad habits and obesity. Remember that the puppy grows very rapidly and will soon be big enough to help himself from the table, especially once he has acquired a taste for your meals. Manners are as important for a dog as for people, and many people object to dogs begging at the dinner table.

Before you leave the breeder's kennel with your pup, it is a good idea to ask if you may call at a later time if you have any further questions regarding the puppy. It is always a good idea to keep the lines of communication open in case you need them later.

THE FIRST DAY—AT HOME
When he first arrives in your house, the puppy may be unhappy and confused. He has grown accustomed to living with his littermates and has become used to playing, sleeping, and eating with company. He may be lonely for a day or two, but will soon settle into your home and your routines. If he cries the first night after you have let him out for the last time and put him in his crate, do NOT let him out again! If

you do so the first night, puppy will have learned that howling will get him out of the crate and he'll try this new trick every night. Even though it might be difficult to listen to, leave him in the crate. He'll soon settle down to sleeping quietly through the night once he has realized that he must stay in the crate.

At first, it will probably be easier to confine the puppy to one room of the house when he is out of his crate. Usually, the kitchen is best since the family tends to spend considerable time there and the floor is easily cleaned in case of an accident. Also, the puppy will still feel a part of things when he is confined to his crate. Place the crate off to one side of the room and put the puppy's food bowl and a toy or two inside. Put his water bowl on the floor out of the way and keep it filled with fresh, cool water. If possible, place the crate near the door you will be using to take the puppy outside. Try to always use that same door as the pup will quickly associate the door with going out to do his duty. Soon he will go to the door and ask to go out when he needs to.

Allow the puppy to explore his new surroundings. Do not over-whelm him with attention at first, but give him time to get used to his new home and its different sounds and smells. Should the puppy do something wrong, tell him "no" in a tone of voice that tells him you mean it. This is the first command he needs to learn and is the most important one of all. If he persists or has an accident, tell him "no" again and put him in his crate for a while. His punishment for the error is the loss of his freedom for a period of time. NEVER hit the pup-py, either with your hand or an object such as a rolled-up newspaper. All this will accomplish will be to make him hand-shy and afraid of you. A sharp "no," said like you really mean it, is all that should be necessary. Your Golden really wants to please you and will try his best to do what you ask. Your task is to teach him what it is that you want in a way he can understand. The most important thing you can teach a young pup is *how* to learn. Keep his immaturity in mind as you try to train him. Remember, be firm with him, be patient, use common sense, and use your crate.

Start using the puppy's call name as soon as you have decided what it will be. You'll be amazed at how quickly he will learn it. Begin teaching him to immediately come when he is called, as this will save a lot of trouble later on.

Within a day or two after you have your new pup home, it is an ex-cellent idea to take him to your veterinarian both for a check-up and to receive any needed shots. Bring along a fresh stool sample to be

As yet unaware of his surroundings, this week-old puppy sleeps soundly. His eyes will not fully open until he is three weeks of age, about the same time that he will begin to hear everything around him. When it is cool, puppies will pile on top of each other for warmth. On warmer days they will often sleep apart.

checked for worms as well as the record of his previous shots and wormings that you received from the breeder. This first visit is an important way of establishing a good relationship with the vet, one that may last for years. Should you have any questions about the health of the pup, now is the time to find out if there is a problem—before you have formed a strong attachment to the pup. If you have been careful in selecting your breeder, it is unlikely that the veterinarian will find anything significantly wrong with the pup. Check with the vet for instructions regarding feeding and routine medical care that you should plan on for the future. Again, ask as many questions as you need to in order to feel comfortable with any instructions the breeder or veterinarian gave you.

ROUTINE CARE OF YOUR PUPPY

Goldens should be groomed at least once a week. This is not a major task, and involves only a good brushing and perhaps some combing of the hair behind the ears. Always brush in the direction the coat naturally grows. This brushing will help to minimize any shedding. Nails should be cut every two to four weeks, depending on how much they wear down naturally. The establishment of good grooming practices now will make for a happier and healthier dog later.

When grooming, teach the puppy to stand still while you are working. If possible, I suggest the use of a grooming table or other suitable table with a non-slip surface to stand the pup on. This will make the grooming process much easier on your back, and the dog will be less likely to try to walk away from you while on the table. Begin by completely brushing the dog from head to tail following the direction the coat lays. Make sure that the brush goes through the coat rather than just brushing the top layer of hair. Pay attention to the dog's feathering as he grows older. If left unbrushed, it will tend to knot, particularly behind the ears. A comb can be useful in this area especially. Excess hair behind the ears may be trimmed with a thinning shears (see chapter on Grooming Your Golden). Cut the pup's nails by picking up one foot at a time while he is standing and cutting the white tip of each nail. Don't forget the dewclaws on both front legs as they never wear down naturally and can actually grow back into the leg if neglected for too long.

At our kennel, we are often asked how frequently a Golden should be bathed. A Golden Retriever's coat is naturally oily to protect the dog's skin from water, much like a duck's feathers protect the bird. Frequent bathing will remove this natural oil, drying out the skin and hair which could lead to a dandruff-like problem. Therefore, bathing should be avoided unless really necessary. Here, we bathe dogs who are not being shown two to three times a year. Should your dog get muddy, allow the mud to dry and most of it will fall off on its own. The rest can be brushed out of the coat easily. If the puppy goes for a swim (and they love to), just rinse off his coat with fresh water from a hose to remove any dirt. When you must bathe the dog, use a good quality shampoo made specifically for dogs and be sure to rinse the coat completely so as to remove all traces of soap in order to avoid irritating the skin.

The Golden Retriever is a mouthy dog and he loves a good chew. This is especially true of puppies, particularly when they are teething. It is important to make sure that the puppy does not chew on something that might harm him. Many house plants are poisonous and should be moved out of his reach. The puppy will not know at first

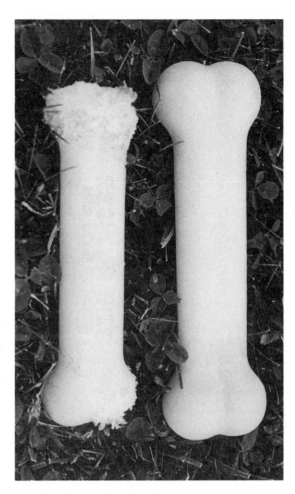

A chewed-up Nylabone® is not potentially dangerous. The frazzled filaments are tough and will not break off easily. Those that occasionally become detached are harmless fibers even when swallowed.

that chewing on electrical cords is dangerous. This is one of the reasons you must watch him carefully when he is loose. He should have time to play and socialize after he has come out of his crate and gone outside, but almost constant supervision is necessary when he is very young, especially during the first few weeks he is in your house. Providing him with toys of his own to chew on will help. Offer him a toy when he starts to chew on something he shouldn't. Use hard nylon bones (Nylabone®), hard rubber toys, and others. Old shoes and socks are definitely *not* recommended since the puppy will not know the difference between the old shoes you gave him and the new ones you just bought for the big party next week.

61

Like young children, puppies play hard and then need a nap. This youngster has found an unusual pillow, but seems quite content.

DISCIPLINE AND TRAINING

There are almost as many methods of discipline and training as there are people who offer advice on the subject. Numerous books are available that deal with all phases of discipline and training, so I shall not deal with this subject at great length here.

A good Golden wants more than anything else to please his master. Proper training is the responsibility of those who own and love the dog, and should begin on the day you first bring him home. A well trained dog is a pleasure to be around and a good citizen. The untrained, unruly dog is a nuisance to everyone and fun for no one.

The first lesson is to teach the pup the meaning of the word "no." Remember that dogs understand tone of voice, so be sure to sound like you really mean it when you say "no." Firm use of "no" is your greatest tool. Be consistent. Do not allow the pup to do something one day and then punish him for the same thing the next. Always reward the puppy with lavish praise when he does what you have asked. Verbal praise is all that is necessary—food rewards are specifically *not* recommended. If your dog expects a cookie every time he does something right, he will not do as you wish when he knows that you have no treat for him—and he will know!

When the young puppy does something wrong (wets the floor, chews a shoe, retrieves a dirty sock, etc.) pick him up, show him what he has done wrong, tell him "NO! BAD BOY!" in no uncertain terms, and put him in his crate for a while. Remember that a young puppy has a very short memory, so if you do not catch him in the act or immediately afterward, forget the punishment until the next time when you see him do it. Be patient. It takes time to learn. Your puppy is sensitive to your feelings and will know when he has displeased you.

Basic obedience training begins immediately. The youngest puppy can learn to come when called, to sit or stand on command, or to walk on a leash. Leash training too should begin immediately. This is fairly easy to accomplish if you will start out by letting the puppy walk you on lead, and then begin to call him to you as you walk along with him in the direction you wish to go. Many puppies have a natural instinct to follow you and this should be encouraged. Do not engage in a tug-of-war with the puppy or pull him along by the neck. This can damage his undeveloped muscles and bone.

From the beginning, teach the puppy to walk on your left side and not to pull you along. Encourage him to stay by your leg and not under your feet. I suggest that you wait until the puppy is at least six months old before beginning formal training in a class situation—unless you are lucky enough to have a "puppy kindergarten" class offered in your area. Once you do begin formal obedience training, a class or group situation is suggested over individual instruction. A class situation will force your puppy to learn to listen to you in distracting circumstances when other dogs and people are around and he is in a strange environment. It is not at all helpful if the dog listens well at home but pays no attention to commands when away from home. Working with your dog will help you to develop a much better relationship with the animal. If someone not in the family does the training, the dog may well listen to the trainer but not to you. Instruction given in the home often does not carry over to other locations. Family members should be involved in the training process, but one person should be the primary trainer. This can be an older child or an adult.

Exercise is an important part of every Golden's life. All dogs love to run, but for a Golden, proper amounts of exercise are also important for his health and physical development. This is especially true for a dog you hope will become a show animal. It is because of this need for exercise that Goldens do not make particularly good apartment dogs, unless their owner is willing to provide *daily* exercise in sufficient amounts no matter what the weather. I am often asked if a young Golden puppy just going to his new home may be allowed outdoors in the winter. Certainly they may, as long as good judgment is used and the pup is not allowed to become overly chilled. In fact, puppies adore playing in the snow! Actually, it is better to allow the puppy to play outdoors than to permit him to run wildly about on slippery floors. Young puppies should be allowed to exercise at their own pace rather than be encouraged to continue running after they have stopped on their own. Like young children, puppies play hard for a while and then need to rest frequently. Do not encourage your young pup to jump up on his hind legs, as this can stress his still pliable bones. Common sense is your best guide in exercising your puppy.

An older puppy can be outside all day long if he is provided with a fenced enclosure, shade, fresh water, and shelter. In fact, he will be just as happy outside when you are not home as he would be locked in his crate indoors. If you need to erect an enclosure, I suggest a strong fence—the chain-link type is best—six feet high, forming an enclosure at least five feet wide and fifteen feet long; bigger is better, smaller is not acceptable. This need not be rectangular in shape, but can conform to the shape of the sides of your house or some natural barrier. The non-rectangular shape is often more interesting to the dog. If you wish, a base of gravel inside the enclosure will help to minimize the mud on the dog. We use a base of about six inches of ¾″ stone topped with about six inches of pea stone. This allows rain to sink in while the surface the dog walks on quickly dries. A layer of chicken wire placed on the ground before the gravel is put in place will help to stop the gravel from sinking into the ground. Boards or railroad ties partially buried at the bottom of the fence will keep the gravel from spilling out and will help deter digging under the fence. A dog house should be provided in case of wet weather while you are away. The house should be large enough for the dog to stretch out in, but not so large that he can not keep it warm with his own body heat in the winter. Have the doorway face away from the prevailing winds. A concrete floor in the fenced area is not recommended for two reasons. First, because concrete is porous, it will absorb the urine odor and eventually become quite odorous unless sealed; and, second, the hardness of the concrete can cause the dog's feet to splay and his pasterns to break down.

On occasion, you should plan to take your puppy out with you when you go shopping or visiting so that he becomes used to riding in the car and becomes comfortable in many different surroundings. Being exposed to strange places and noises as a pup and knowing that you are there if he needs you, will greatly increase his confidence as he grows older. Start with short trips and gradually lengthen them as he becomes more accustomed to riding. If possible, keep the dog in his crate when traveling in the car as this will stop him from getting in your way while you are driving and protect him from being thrown about the vehicle in case of a sudden stop. If this is not possible, teach him immediately that he belongs in the back seat, not in your lap. Do not let the dog ride with his head hanging out of the window since he may get foreign material in his eye and might even jump out. If the pup becomes carsick the first few times out, do not be discouraged. Put newspaper in his crate to absorb any vomit, and do not let him eat or drink for a while before you leave. Take him frequently for short trips until he acclimates to traveling.

When leaving your puppy in the car, extreme care should be taken to allow for proper ventilation. The heat build-up in a closed car is extremely rapid, especially if the car is in the sun. This is true even in cooler weather. Make sure to park in the shade, and remember that the sun moves during the day so that what was in the shade earlier may later be in the full sun. If your puppy is in his crate, you will be able to safely leave the windows wide open. If not, do not leave the windows open so far that the puppy could squeeze out if he sees a passing cat or dog. If you expect to be parked in one place for a long period of time, it is probably better to leave the dog at home.

If you are planning a trip, consider taking the pup with you. He will enjoy a vacation as much as you will, and if you have worked on your training he will be no real problem away from home. If you bring your crate, you may find that many motels will allow the dog in your room if he is kept in his house. When you must leave the dog behind, choose your boarding kennel carefully. Most commercial kennels cannot provide the care and socialization you do at home and should not be expected to do so. It is probably best not to board puppies under six months of age if it can be avoided. If you live reasonably near your puppy's breeder, check and see if they board or can recommend a boarding kennel in your area that is better equipped to handle younger dogs. Older puppies are much more sure of themselves and can handle a boarding experience with little difficulty when in a clean, quality facility. Do make sure your pup's shots are completely up-to-date before boarding him.

In general, raising a young puppy is not really difficult if you use common sense and have some patience. Younger children can share in the responsibilities of caring for a young pup, but should not be expected to have full responsibility. Taking the time to lay the correct foundation with your puppy's early training will lead to years of pleasure from your dog.

Golden Retrievers are generally healthy dogs and have an average lifespan of ten years or more. We currently own a Golden who is still going strong at the age of fourteen and a half years. Fortunately, Goldens are not yet subject to a whole host of genetic problems, although hip dysplasia and certain eye problems do exist in the breed. Goldens are also somewhat prone to a wet eczema skin problem often called "hot spots," the cause of which is not known, although it does seem to be more prevalent in some Golden bloodlines than others. Proper food and exercise combined with regular veterinary care will keep your dog healthy and happy. Some other measures that will help insure good health include: regular immunizations for distemper, rabies, hepatitis, leptospirosis, parainfluenza and parvovivus; regular stool checks for worms; yearly testing for heartworm and daily administration of its preventive medication; and maintenance of the dog in proper weight. Learn to resist those expressive Golden eyes when necessary.

Finally, for those dogs that will not be bred (and most should not) neutering should be strongly considered. This has no negative effect on the personality of the dog or bitch and it will help lengthen his or her lifespan. There is no truth to the old notion that a bitch is improved by having one litter. In fact, it has been proved that her life expectancy is vastly improved by spaying. Nor is there any advantage to allowing a dog to sire one litter—it will only make him want more. Since there are already too many unwanted dogs that are put to death each day, there is no reason to increase this number unless the dog is of outstanding quality as shown by competitive experience in the ring or in the field.

Two Golden senior citizens relax in the shade. They are (left) Am., Can. Ch. Kyrie London by Diel, Am., Can. C.D.X., Am. W.C., age thirteen and (right) Pippin's Merry Maid of Kyrie, W.C. Am., Can. C.D., age eleven and a half. Photo by Marcia Schlehr of Kyrie Goldens, Clinton, Michigan.

Am., Can. Ch. Russo's Pepperhill Poppy (Am., Can., Bda. Ch. Cummings Gold-Rush Charlie ex Russo's Wildwood Flower). A trendsetter, Poppy was the first bitch in twenty-five years to qualify for the G.R.C.A. Show Dog Hall of Fame. She is shown winning the Sporting Group under Judge Bernard McGiven thus completing the minimum number of points required for Hall of Fame status. Handler is Elliot More. Poppy is owned by the author and his wife. Photo: John Ashbey.

Chapter 5

Grooming the Golden Retriever

by Elliot More

One of the appeals of the Golden Retriever is that it is a natural breed requiring a minimum of trimming to look its best both in and out of the show ring. We will deal here primarily with the preparation of your Golden for the show ring; however, this will also serve as a useful guide to maintaining your pet Golden in top shape.

A complete list of equipment to be used for trimming appears below. As all of these items are not absolutely necessary, it is recommended that the reader understand their individual uses before purchasing those desired.

> Pin brush
> Slicker brush
> Comb
> Fine comb
> Tapering shears (single-edge thinning shears)
> Straight shears
> Nail clippers
> Styptic powder or pencil
> Tooth scalers
> Ear cleaners
> Electric clippers

Keeping your Golden in good condition is a simple task. Besides giving your dog the proper food and exercise, the following things should be done about once every two weeks. Done regularly, the whole procedure will take only half an hour or so.

Start with a thorough brushing. Obviously this can be done more frequently if needed. Very often a walk in the woods will result in your Golden bringing home burrs and other debris in his feathering. These should be picked and brushed out right away. A pin brush is recommended for the longer feathering on the front legs, chest, pants and tail, and a slicker brush for the remaining areas.

After brushing, a comb can be used to remove more loose coat. Brushing first serves to untangle the longer hair and make combing easier. Close attention should be given to your dog's skin while brushing. If there is any evidence of fleas or ticks, the dog should be sprayed, powdered, or dipped as soon as possible to avoid having these annoying parasites become permanent house guests. Furthermore if any kind of skin irritation is noticed it can be attended to before a serious problem develops.

Goldens seem to be especially prone to develop so-called "hot spots" (sometimes called moist eczema), particularly during damp weather. Many remedies exist for this and it is recommended that your veterinarian be contacted for advice on appropriate treatment. Hot spots can spread rapidly (even overnight) if left untreated.

Your Golden's nails, teeth and ears should also receive attention when you have brushed your dog. Any accumulated tartar on the teeth should be scraped off with a tooth scaler; this will help prevent gum deterioration and premature loss of teeth. The ears should be cleaned if needed with an appropriate cleaning solution obtainable from your vet. Using a few drops on a cotton ball you can clean the ear canal as far as you can reach with your finger. A few drops of the ear cleaner can be dripped directly into the ear for safe deeper cleaning. It is not recommended that you try scrubbing out the ear any deeper than you can reach with your finger; if your dog's ears are really bothering him, or are full of matter, you should make an appointment to see your vet.

If your dog's nails are cut on a regular basis from the time he is a puppy, this task will remain a simple, routine event. This is because the longer a nail grows, the further its interior blood vessel, or "quick" will grow out. Thus if a nail is left to grow for months at a time, it is very difficult to cut it back to a respectable and comfortable length without cutting into the quick. This causes pain to the dog, resulting naturally enough in a struggle to get the remaining nails cut. If the nails are kept short, the quick will stay short and nail clipping will not become a traumatic event for both dog and owner.

70

Try to cut the nail as close to the quick as possible without causing much bleeding. Do keep a container of some sort of styptic powder (such as Quik-Stop) or styptic pencil handy to stop bleeding from a nail cut too short.

The preceding is really all that is needed to keep your Golden healthy. If the occasional bath is required, a good quality dog shampoo is recommended. If skin problems exist you might need a medicated shampoo, which your vet can provide. After shampooing and a thorough rinsing (it is essential to get all the soap rinsed out to prevent irritation), a light cream rinse can be applied if desired to give the coat more body or manageability.

The dog should be towelled dry and brushed when he comes out of the tub. If you are bathing your dog to show, you may wish to pin a large towel around him so the hair on his body will dry straighter and flatter. Although a wavy coat is acceptable according to the Standard, too much wave can detract from the dog's outline. To towel your Golden properly, first brush the coat (which should still be quite wet from his bath) flat in the direction it naturally grows. Then, with the dog standing perfectly still, place the towel over him lengthwise (a bath sheet size is suggested), folding it back at the neck to make a "collar." The towel should reach just a little past the base of the tail in the rear. Pin the towel firmly under the chin, under the body, and under the base of the tail; leave it on until the dog is dry.

Goldens are double-coated and since frequent bathing tends to encourage the undercoat to shed, it is suggested that you give full baths only when you feel it necessary. If the dog's legs or underside are dirty they can be washed without giving the entire Golden a bath.

There is relatively little trimming to do on the Golden Retriever compared to Spaniels and Setters. Due to the nature of the Golden's coat, however, some trimming is in order. If it is done properly there should be no evidence of scissor marks on a dog about to be presented in the show ring.

Trimming the Golden's whiskers is optional, according to the Standard. If you wish to remove the whiskers, a pair of straight shears can be used. Cut the whiskers as close as possible without leaving gouges in the short hair that grows on the muzzle. An electric clipper fitted with a #15 blade can also be used. It is easier to trim along the lip line with a clipper and also to clear the whiskers out in the fold of the lower lip.

The only other area a clipper may be used is on the undersides of the Golden's feet. Using a #15 blade, the hair that grows between the pads can be "scooped" out. This not only serves to decrease the chance of infection in this area in damp weather, but also improves the dog's traction in indoor show rings.

Some Goldens grow a tremendous amount of soft hair on and around their ears, and this can be neatened to enhance the appearance of the head and expression. The hair at the opening of the ear canal under the flap of the ear can be shortened using tapering shears (46 tooth single-edge thinning shears). If the hair growing along the edge of the ear leather is long or straggly it too can be neatened by trimming around the natural outline of the ear with the tapering shears. The correct use of tapering shears should result in no scissor marks being left. Excessive hair on the top of the ear leather can be reduced using a stripping knife to pull out much of the longer fluff. This method is somewhat tedious compared to thinning the hair with shears, but the end result is more natural looking and stays that way for a longer time.

The Standard asks that Golden Retrievers have an untrimmed natural ruff, so there should be no evidence of trimming in this area. If the ruff is so abundant that it makes your dog's neck appear shorter, or if your dog simply has a short neck, you might wish to do some subtle work on it. Again, the hair should be pulled in preference to cutting it off. Use a fine tooth comb (flea comb) and a coarse stripping knife to pull out as much coat as desired along the edge of the ruff directly beneath the ear. Very often there is a cowlick of hair growing out the wrong way in the throat area, which can be thinned with the tapering shears to help outline the neck.

The Golden is supposed to be a double-coated breed, but very heavy undercoat through the shoulder and neck area can detract from the dog's outline. Some of this undercoat can be removed by just combing through with the fine comb. This can also be done on the dog's rump if he appears a little high behind. For the same reason it is wise not to comb too much in the area directly behind the withers where there is often a slight dip. The topline should appear straight and level from withers to croup.

The tail bone should extend to the hock joint. If the tail is left untrimmed, it will often appear longer and detract from the dog's outline. Use tapering shears to gently trim the tail to the appropriate length, remembering that a properly trimmed Golden's tail should in no way resemble a Setter tail. Setter tails are tapered right to the tip, while the tip of a Golden's tail should have at least an inch of feathering on it. The feathering at the tail end should curve gently rather than appear chopped off, and should then lengthen gradually toward the base of the tail. The length of the feathering at its longest should be in proportion to the coat on the rest of the dog. Excessive tail feathering detracts from the overall functional appearance and balance of the Golden.

You may also wish to separate the feathering at the base of the tail from the rear of the dog. Holding the tail out straight, trim the feathering underneath the root of the tail with tapering shears until the desired effect is achieved. This makes it easier to distinguish the natural line of the rear assembly and tail set.

The feet should appear round and compact. If the nails have been kept short and the hair on the bottom of the feet cut, further trimming is simple. With the dog standing, use straight shears to trim around the bottom edge of the foot, with the shears held almost parallel to the ground. Then, with the tapering shears pointed toward the surface on which the dog is standing, thin around the foot from the top in the direction the hair grows. This should shape a round, neat foot without any apparent scissor marks. Hair between the toes on the upper side of the foot should be combed to remove small mats that might be present. This hair, however should not be cut out as it will just result in gaps between the toes and spoil the compact look.

If the feathering on the front legs down near the feet is long, you may wish to taper it to the rear pad of the foot with fine thinning shears. This enhances a strong pastern. Again, the hair should not look chopped. Then, looking at the dog head on, any hair at the elbows that sticks out can be pulled or thinned to prevent the dog from appearing to be out at the elbows.

The hair on the back of the rear legs below the hock joint can be neatened with the tapering shears if it is very long or straggly. When viewed from behind, the hair should not stick out significantly on either side of the leg as it will distort the appearance of the dog's rear movement.

Your Golden should now be ready for the ring!

Shown going Best of Breed is Ch. Sun Dance's Alexander (Ch. Wochica's Okeechobee Jake ex Ch. Sun Dance's Contessa). Like both his parents, this dog is a G.R.C.A. Outstanding Sire. He is owned by Shirley and William Worley.

Chapter 6

Breeding Your Golden Retriever

THE GOLDEN BROOD BITCH

In an earlier chapter we discussed the selection of a bitch you plan to use for breeding. In making this most important purchase, you will be choosing a bitch whom you hope will become the foundation of your kennel. Thus, she must be of the finest producing bloodlines, excellent in temperament, of good type, and free of major faults. Her sire and dam should be free of inherited defects such as hip dysplasia and juvenile cataract, and the prospective mother must also be cleared of these serious problems. If you have been offered a "bargain" brood bitch, be wary, because for this purchase you should not settle for less than the best. You should expect the price of the brood bitch to be in accordance with her age, quality, and bloodlines.

Conscientious breeders feel quite strongly that the only possible reason for producing puppies is the ambition to improve and uphold the quality and temperament of the breed. It is definitely *not* because one hopes to make a quick profit on a mediocre litter, (the profit part never seems to work out anyway in the long run) and which accomplishes little beyond perhaps adding to the nation's heartbreaking number of unwanted canines. The only reason, ever, for breeding a litter, with conscientious people, is a desire to improve the quality of dogs in their kennel or because an individual dog is a truly outstanding specimen as shown by competitive accomplishments in the field, breed ring, or obedience trial. In any case, it should not be done unless one has a definite list of prospective owners for as many puppies as the litter may contain, often more than ten with a Golden Retriever, lest you find yourself with several fast-growing young dogs and no homes in which to place them.

There is a myth among many pet owners that every bitch should be bred at least once "for her own good." There is no truth to this assumption at all. In fact, producing a litter can sometimes actually be harmful to the bitch's health and can, occasionally, lead to the death of the animal. From a health standpoint, the best thing you can do for your bitch is to spay her.

Once you have decided to breed your bitch, she should not be mated earlier than her second season, when she is fifteen to eighteen months old, so that she herself has had adequate time to mature before dealing with the stress of a litter of puppies. Many breeders prefer to wait and complete their show bitch's championship first and then breed her as pregnancy is almost always a disaster for the coat, and getting the bitch back into shape again takes at least six months and often a year or more. Also, the bitch's topline can suffer permanent sagging from the stress of carrying and nursing a large litter. It is important to realize that the average Golden litter is eight or nine puppies—fourteen is not an unusual a number of pups in one Golden litter.

Whenever you decide will be the proper time to breed your bitch, plan ahead. Start watching for what you feel will be the perfect mate at least several months in advance. Look for a dog that complements your bitch's bloodlines, does not carry the same faults as she, and who is strong where she is weak. Subscribe to magazines which feature Retrievers and to the G.R.C.A. *News* to familiarize yourself with outstanding stud dogs in areas other than your own. There is no necessity nowadays to limit your choice to a dog nearby unless you truly like him and feel he is the most suitable. It is quite usual to ship a bitch to a stud dog a distance away, and this generally works out with no ill effects. The important thing is that you need a stud dog that is strong in those features where your bitch is weak or lacking. Compare seriously the background of both your bitch and the stud dog under consideration, paying particular attention to the quality of the puppies this dog has produced when bred to other bitches whose breeding is similar to yours. If they are of a type and quality you admire, then this dog would seem to be a sensible choice for your bitch too.

Stud fees today usually run from $300 to $500, sometimes even more under special situations for a particularly successful sire. The average stud fee for a quality stud is based on the price of a show potential puppy in the area. It is money well spent, however. Do not, ever, breed to a dog because he is less expensive than others unless you really, honestly, believe that he can sire the kind of puppies who will be a credit to your kennel and to the breed.

Am., Can. Ch. Beckwith's Chianti, Am., Can. C.D. (Am., Can. Ch. Beckwith's Xciting Fellow ex Am., Can. Ch. Beckwith's Nutmeg, C.D.X., Can. C.D.). Representing five generations of Beckwith breeding, Chianti recently qualified for the G.R.C.A. Show Dog Hall of Fame, only the seventh bitch to achieve this honor. Her father's pedigree goes back to Ch. Misty Morn's Sunset, C.D., T.D., W.C. on one side and Am., Can., Bda., Mex., Col. Ch. Beckwith's Copper Coin on the other. Her mother's pedigree also goes back to Copper Ingot and Copper Coin. Chianti is owned by Richard and Luddell Beckwith of Snohomish, Washington. Photo: Carl Lindemaier.

Contacting the owners of the stud dogs you find interesting will bring you pedigrees and, sometimes, pictures which you can then study in relation to your bitch's pedigree and conformation. Discuss your plans with other breeders who are knowledgeable—including the breeder of your own bitch. While you may not always receive unbiased opinions (particularly if the person giving the opinion also has an available stud dog), one learns by discussion, so listen to what they say, consider the options, and then you may be better qualified to make your own decision.

As soon as you have made a choice, contact the owner of the stud dog you wish to use to find out if this is agreeable to him. You will be asked about the bitch's health, soundness, temperament and freedom from serious faults. A copy of her O.F.A. clearance and eye clearance, along with her pedigree and, perhaps a photo of her, may be requested. Most stud dog owners will not breed to a bitch who is not hip and eye cleared. In some cases just a discussion of the bitch's background over the telephone may be sufficient to assure the stud's owner that she is suitable to be bred to the stud and of type, breeding and quality herself to produce puppies of the quality for which the dog is noted. The owner of a top quality stud is often extremely selective in the bitches permitted to breed to the dog in an effort to keep the standard of his puppies a high one. The owner of a stud dog will often require that the bitch be tested for brucellosis, which should be done not more than a month before the breeding.

Check out which airport will be most convenient for the person meeting and returning the bitch if she is to be shipped, and find out which airlines serve that one and which, if any, have direct non-stop flights. You will find that the airlines are apt to have special requirements on acceptance of animals for shipping. These include weather limitations based on temperature, and types of crates that are acceptable. The weather limits concern extreme heat and extreme cold not only at the point of departure but at the destination as well. The crate problem is a simple one. If your own is not suitable (which very often is the case), most airlines have crates available for purchase at a moderate price that are designed for airline shipping. It is a good idea to purchase one if you intend to be shipping dogs with any frequency. They are made of fiber glass and are the safest type to be used for shipping. When purchased new, however, they often have only a cardboard bottom. This should be replaced with one of wood or other solid material to provide more comfort for the dog.

Winning the Brood Bitch Class at the 1981 Fort Detroit Golden Retriever Club Specialty is Ch. Laurell's Killimanjaro with her children Ch. Laurell's York and Ch. Laurell Travellin' Too Far. "Killer" is owned and bred by Tom and Laura Ellis Kling of Cincinnati, Ohio. Photo: Booth.

Normally, you must notify the airline several days in advance of your planned shipping date to make a reservation, as they are only able to accommodate a certain number of dogs on each flight. Plan to ship the dog on her sixth or seventh day of season, as arranged with the stud dog owner, but try not to ship her on a weekend, if possible, as the schedules often vary then and some freight offices are not open at all on weekends. Whenever you can, ship the dog on a direct flight. Changing planes always carries a certain risk of a dog being overlooked or wrongly routed at the middle stop, so avoid this danger if at all possible. The bitch must be accompanied by an up-to-date health certificate which you must obtain from your veterinarian before taking her to the airport. Usually it will be necessary to have the bitch at the

Am., Can. Ch. Pepperhill's Basically Bear (Ch. Gold-Rush's Great Teddy Bear ex Ch. Cummings Dame Pepperhill) winning the Stud Dog Class at the 1982 G.R.C.A. National Specialty. With him are two of his seven champion get: Ch. Pepperhill's Bonni Valentine, C.D.X. and Ch. Pepperhill Yankee O'Goldtrak who had won the 12-18-Month Dog Class earlier. Bear is a G.R.C.A. Outstanding Sire. Photo: Tom Morrissette.

airport about two hours prior to flight time. Check with your carrier. Before finalizing the arrangements, find out from the stud's owner at what time of day it will be most convenient to have the bitch picked up promptly on arrival.

If you live fairly near the stud, then it is simpler to bring the bitch yourself for the breeding. Some people feel that the stress of the flight might cause the bitch not to conceive, and, of course, there is a slight risk in shipping her which can be avoided if you provide her transportation yourself. Be sure to leave yourself enough time to assure your arrival at the right time for her breeding (normally on the ninth to fourteenth day following the first signs of color), and remember that if you want the bitch bred twice, it is best to allow a day between the two matings. Do not expect the stud's owner to house you while you are there. Locate a motel nearby that takes dogs and make that your headquarters.

Just prior to the time your bitch is due in season, you should take her to visit your veterinarian. She should be checked for worms and should receive all booster shots for which she is due as well as a parvo shot if she has not had one recently. Some breeders also like to have a vaginal smear taken and cultured at this time to insure that the bitch has no vaginal infections. The brucellosis test can also be done at this time, and a health certificate can be obtained for shipping if she is to travel by air. Should the bitch be at all overweight, now is the time for a diet. She should be in good condition, neither underweight nor overweight, at the time of breeding.

The moment you notice the swelling of the vulva, for which you should be checking on a daily basis as the time of her season approaches, and the appearance of color, immediately contact the stud's owner and settle on the day for shipping, or make the appointment for your arrival with the bitch for breeding. If you are shipping, the stud fee check should be mailed immediately so that it will have ample time to arrive before the bitch does and the mating takes place. Be sure to call the airline and make the reservation at this time too.

Do not feed the bitch within a few hours of shipping her. Be certain she has a drink of water and has been well exercised before closing her in her crate. Make sure that the name, address and phone number of the stud dog owner is written on the shipping label as well as your own name, address and phone number. Remember that the bitch should be brought to the airport on time, as the airlines sometimes refuse to accept late arrivals.

If you are taking your bitch by car, be certain that you will arrive at a reasonable time of day. Do not appear late in the evening. If your arrival in town is not until late, get a good night's sleep at your motel and contact the stud's owner first thing in the morning. If possible, leave the children and relatives at home, as they will only be in the way and perhaps unwelcome to the stud's owner. Most stud dogs' owners prefer not to have an audience of unnecessary people around during the actual mating.

Once the breeding has taken place, if you wish to sit and visit for a while with the stud's owner and he has the time, return the bitch to her crate in your car. She should not be permitted to urinate for about a half hour following the breeding. This is the time when you get the business part of the transaction completed. Pay the stud fee, upon which you should receive your breeding certificate and, if you do not already have it, a copy of the stud's pedigree. The owner of the stud does not sign or furnish a litter registration application until the puppies have been born.

When you return home, settle down to planning for the puppies in anticipation of a wonderful litter. A word of caution. Remember that although she has been bred, your bitch is still an interesting target for all male dogs, so guard her carefully for the next week or so until you are absolutely certain that she is out of season.

THE GOLDEN STUD DOG

Choosing the correct stud dog to complement your bitch is often very difficult. The two principal factors to be considered are the stud's conformation and his pedigree. Conformation is fairly obvious. You want a dog that is typically Golden in the words of the Standard and, remembering that there is no such thing as the perfect dog, one who does not have faults in common with your bitch. Understanding pedigrees is a bit more difficult since the pedigree lists the ancestry of the dog and there may well be individuals and bloodlines involved with which you are not familiar.

Thus, to a novice in Goldens, the correct interpretation of a pedigree may be difficult to grasp at first. Study the pictures you will find in this book since they include many names you may recognize from the pedigree. Make an effort to discuss the various dogs behind the proposed stud and your bitch with some of the veteran breeders in your area. Start with the breeder of your own bitch. Frequently, these people will be personally familiar with at least many of the dogs in question, can offer opinions on them, and may have access to additional pictures which you would benefit from seeing. They may also know of other dogs produced by some of the dogs in the pedigree which will provide you with some basis for comparison.

It is very important that the stud's pedigree be harmonious with that of the bitch you plan to breed to him. Do not run out and breed to the latest winner with no thought of whether or not he can produce quality. By no means are all winners great stud dogs or great producers. It is the producing record of the dog in question that you are interested in, not his record of wins. His pedigree must blend well with your bitch's and should show good depth of quality in the dogs behind him. This is the basis upon which you should make your ultimate choice.

Breeding dogs is never a money-making operation. By the time you pay a stud fee, transportation expenses, care for the bitch during pregnancy, whelp the litter and rear the puppies through their early shots, worming, etc., you will be fortunate to break even financially. If you figure in the amount of time you have spent in producing the litter, it is almost always a financially losing situation. Your chances of making a small profit are greatly enhanced if you are breeding for a show quality litter which will bring higher prices as some of the pups are sold as show prospects. Therefore, the wisest investment is to use the best dog available for your bitch, regardless of the cost, since you then should wind up with more valuable puppies. Remember, it is equally costly to raise a litter of mediocre puppies as a litter of top ones, and your chances of financial return are better with the latter. To breed to the most excellent, most suitable stud dog you can find is the only way that makes sense, both in terms of economics and the welfare of the breed. It is poor economy to quibble over what you are paying for a stud fee.

Once you have decided to breed an animal, there are three basic options available to you: linebreeding, inbreeding, and outcrossing. Each of these methods has its adherents and its detractors. Linebreeding is breeding a bitch to a dog belonging originally to the same canine family, being descended from the same ancestors; for example, half-brother to half-sister, niece to uncle, cousin to cousin. Inbreeding is breeding father to daughter, mother to son or brother to sister. Outcross breeding is breeding a dog to a bitch with no mutual ancestors. In all these cases, we are talking in terms of a four- or five-generation pedigree.

Linebreeding is probably the safest course, and the most likely to bring good results, for the novice breeder. The more sophisticated inbreeding should be left only to the experienced, long-time breeders who intimately know and understand the line involved over time, and who know its risks and possibilities. Inbreeding is usually done in an effort to intensify some ideal feature of the strain. Outcrossing is the reverse, being an effort to introduce some improvement in a specific feature needing correction in a line, such as shorter backs, better movement, more correct head, better angulation, coat, etc.

It is the ambition of all serious breeders to develop a strain or bloodline of their own, one strong in qualities for which their dogs will become distinguished. However, it must be realized that this will involve time, patience, and at least several generations before the achievement may be claimed. The road to success is marked by periodic failures, and one must be willing to accept these setbacks as well. The safest way to embark on this plan is by the selection of one or two bitches of the best quality you can buy from top producing kennels. These will become your foundation brood bitches. In the beginning, you really do not have to own a stud dog. In the long run it is less expensive and wiser to pay a stud fee when you are ready to breed a bitch than to purchase a stud dog and feed him all year. A stud dog will not be used by others until he has at least become a champion, has been bred successfully, "specialed" for a while, and has been at least moderately advertised—all of which adds up to quite a large investment. It should go without saying that stud dogs and brood bitches *must* be clear of genetic problems, especially hip dysplasia and eye problems.

So, the new breeder's wisest course is to start out as I have outlined above. Keep the best bitch puppy from each of the first several litters and perhaps breed them to sound quality producing stud dogs and retain the best from these litters. After this, if you wish to keep your own stud dog or if there has been one especially good male in one of your litters that you feel has great potential, by all means do so. Remember that experienced breeders feel that a kennel is only as good as its bitches. By this time, with several litters already whelped, your eye should be developing to a point that enables you to make a wise choice, either from one of your own litters or from among dogs you have selected elsewhere that appear suitable.

When you make the decision to acquire your own stud dog, the greatest care should be taken in his selection. He must be true to type and the highest quality, as he may be responsible for siring many puppies each year. He should be clear of genetic faults. Ideally, he should

Ch. Sun Dance's Bronze (Ch. Indian Knoll's Roc-Cloud, U.D. ex Sidram Kapering Korky, C.D.). A two-time winner of Best of Breed at G.R.C.A. National Specialties in 1959 and 1965, Bronze was a G.R.C.A. Outstanding Sire as well. He was owned by Opal Horton and bred by Alice and William Worley. Bronze is shown winning the Veteran Dog Class at the 1965 National Specialty under judge Mrs. R. Gilman Smith.

come from a line of excellent dogs, on both sides of his pedigree, which are themselves descended from successful producers. This dog should have no glaring faults in conformation, being of a quality to hold his own in keenest competition within his area of exhibition, be it the breed ring, the field, or the obedience trial. He should be in good health, virile, and a keen stud dog. If you are purchasing an older dog, he should be a proven sire able to transmit his best qualities to his puppies. Need I say that such a dog would be enormously expensive unless you have the good fortune to produce him in one of your own litters! But, to purchase a lesser stud dog is to downgrade your breeding program unnecessarily since there are many dogs who fit this description who are available to you for use at the payment of a stud fee.

Never, never breed to an unsound dog, one with serious faults, or one with genetic problems. Not all champions, by any means, pass along their best features. Occasionally, you will find a good dog that never gained its title because of unusual circumstances. The information you need about a stud dog is: what type of puppies he has produced; with what bloodlines; and whether he possesses the characteristics of a good Golden Retriever.

Most exciting of all is when a young male you have kept from one of your own litters, due to his tremendous potential, turns out to be the stud dog we have described above. In that case, he should be managed with great care and bred only to worthy bitches since he is a valuable property that can contribute tremendously to the breed as a whole and to your own kennel. Careful use of your stud dog will only enhance the reputation of your kennel and the dogs it produces.

Do not permit your young dog to be used at stud until he is about one year old and has been hip and eye cleared. Even then he should be bred to a mature, proven brood bitch accustomed to being bred so as to make this first experience a pleasant and easy one for the dog. A young dog can be turned off breeding forever by a maiden bitch who fights and resists his advances. Never allow this to happen. Always start out a stud dog on a bitch who is mature, has been bred before and who is willing to be bred now. The first breeding should be done in quiet surroundings with only you and one other person to hold the bitch present. Do not make a circus out of it. This first experience will determine the dog's outlook for future breedings. If he does not enjoy the first time, or associates it with any unpleasantness, you may have a problem to contend with in the future.

Your new stud must permit help with the breeding, as later there will be bitches who will not be co-operative. If right from the beginning you are helping him and praising him, he will come to expect and welcome your assistance. In some cases, where the dog is bred to a particularly large or small bitch, the only way a "tie" can be accomplished is with assistance.

Things to keep handy before you introduce your dog to the bitch are K-Y jelly or Vaseline, to be used as a lubricant on the bitch and to hold the feathering away from the vulva, and either an old stocking or a length of gauze with which to tie the bitch's muzzle should it become necessary to keep her from biting your dog. Some bitches put up a fight; others can't wait to be bred. Since you often do not know in advance, it is better to be prepared.

At the time of breeding, the stud fee becomes due, and it is expected that it be paid immediately, unless other arrangements have been made in advance. Normally a return service is given only if the bitch fails to conceive or does not produce at least one live puppy. The conditions of the service are what the stud dog owner makes them and there is no standard rule covering this. Thus, it is better to discuss this in advance. The stud fee is paid for the service, not the result. If the bitch fails to conceive, it is customary for the owner to offer a free repeat service on the bitch's next season, but this is a courtesy, and should not be considered a right, especially in the case of a proven stud who is siring consistently and whose fault the failure obviously is *not*. Stud owners are always anxious to see their clients get good value and to have winning puppies produced by their dog; therefore very few refuse a second mating, but it is wise for both parties to have the terms of the transaction clearly understood before the time of the breeding.

If a return service has been provided and the bitch has missed a second time, that is considered to be the end of the matter and the owner of the bitch would be expected to pay a further fee if it is felt that the bitch should be given a third chance with the stud dog. The management of a stud dog and his visiting bitches is quite a task, and a stud fee has usually been well earned when one service has been achieved—let alone repeated services to the same bitch.

Occasionally, other arrangements are made for the payment of a stud fee, such as the stud owner taking pick of the litter instead of money. This does not happen as often as it once did. When such arrangements are made, almost always at the choice of the stud owner, then the terms should be clearly spelled out in writing on the breeding certificate, including at what age the stud owner will select the puppy, whether it is to be specifically of a stated sex, etc.

The price of a stud fee varies according to circumstances. Usually, to prove a young stud dog, his owner will allow the first breeding to be quite inexpensive. Then, once a bitch has become pregnant by him, he becomes a "proven stud" and the fee rises accordingly for the bitches that follow. The sire of championship quality puppies, or top obedience or field puppies, will bring a fee of at least the purchase price of one show potential puppy from the litter. Until at least one champion or advanced title holder is produced by a dog, the stud fee is usually equal to the price of a pet puppy. As the list of winners grows, so does the stud fee. For example, a G.R.C.A. Outstanding Sire can be expected to command the highest stud fees.

Almost invariably, it is the bitch who comes to the stud dog for breeding. Immediately after you have selected the stud you wish to use, you should contact the dog's owner to discuss details. It is the prerogative of the stud dog owner's to refuse to breed to any bitch deemed unsuitable for this dog. If the owner of the stud dog must travel to an airport to meet the bitch and ship her for the flight home, an additional charge will often be made for the time, gas and tolls involved. The stud fee includes board for the bitch for a day or two prior to the breeding and a day or two after. If it is necessary that the bitch remain longer, additional board will probably be charged at the normal rate for boarding in the area.

Be sure to immediately advise the owner of the stud when you know that your bitch is in season. This is especially true if the dog is being campaigned since he or the owner may be out of the area at shows if the owner is not fully aware of when you'll be needing him. Occasionally, arrangements can be made to have a bitch bred at a show, but this is often not the case and must be planned for in advance.

Going into the actual management of a mating here is a bit superfluous. If you have had experience previously in breeding a dog and bitch you will know how. If not, you should not attempt to follow a book, but should turn to someone experienced in this. Ask a breeder friend (of any breed—this part is the same for all) or a professional handler to assist you the first few times. In many cases, you can not rely on your veterinarian in this, as most have had little or no experience in actually doing breedings either. You DO NOT just turn the dog and the bitch loose together and await developments, as too many things can go wrong and you may miss getting the bitch bred altogether. Someone should hold the dog and another person the bitch until the tie is accomplished, and should stay with them for the entire time they are tied.

If you get a complete tie, then probably only one breeding is really necessary. However, most breeders will try for two matings about 24 hours apart to try to insure a good breeding and pregnancy. If a bitch has come a long way for the breeding, it is to the stud's advantage to produce a litter from her. Since the sperm live for at least 24 hours inside the bitch, providing two breedings a day apart actually covers four possible days of the bitch's ovulation.

Once the tie has been completed and they release, be certain that the dog's penis goes completely back into its sheath. He should be allowed a drink of water and then be put into his crate or somewhere alone so he can settle down. Do not allow him to be with other males for a while as they will notice the bitch's odor on him and this may lead to a fight.

There is no more valuable dog than one who is a proven sire of top quality dogs. Once you have such an animal, you have a responsibility to him, and to the breed, to allow him to be mated only with the best quality females. DO NOT allow him to be bred to just any bitch that comes along. It takes two to make puppies, and even the most dominant dog cannot do it all himself. Remember that when the puppies arrive, your stud will be blamed for any lack of quality, while the shortcomings of the bitch will be quickly and conveniently overlooked. It is to your advantage to protect the reputation of your dog and your kennel by allowing only the best bitches to be bred to your dog.

PREGNANCY, WHELPING AND THE LITTER

Once a bitch has been bred and is back home and you are certain that she is completely out of season (past her 23rd or 24th day at least), she should be treated normally. Controlled exercise is important, as, if she is in top physical condition, she will have an easier time whelping (giving birth). Bitches rarely, if ever, get morning sickness, by the way. After about the seventh week, cut back on the exercise so as to not stress her while her body is off balance due to the weight of the puppies. Be especially careful to avoid asking the bitch to jump or play roughly.

The theory that a pregnant bitch should be overstuffed with food is a poor one. A fat bitch is never an easy whelper, so the overfeeding you consider good may actually be the opposite. During the first few weeks of pregnancy your bitch should be fed her normal diet. At four to five weeks along, some breeders supplement the diet with extra calcium and vitamins. Others rely on the special diets produced by some of the better dog food companies specifically for bitches in whelp. If you are using a top quality food, neither is absolutely necessary. If using extra calcium, you should use caution as too much can create serious problems for the bitch. If during the seventh, eighth and ninth weeks she seems to crave more food, you may increase her rations. This might best be done by adding a second meal if you are feeding once a day. This is the time of the unborn puppies' most active growth and more food may be necessary.

A week before the pups are due, your bitch should be introduced to her whelping box so that she will become accustomed to it and feel at

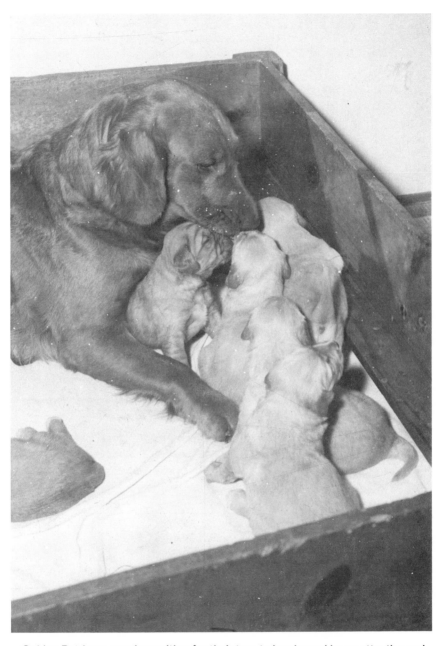

Golden Retriever puppies waiting for their turn to be cleaned by an attentive and loving mother.

home there when the puppies arrive. She should be encouraged to sleep there, but be permitted to come and go as she wishes. The box should be roomy enough for her to lie down and stretch out, but not so large that the pups might tend to get too far from her and get chilled. Be sure that there is a "pig rail" for the box so that the pups can get under it and avoid being crushed against the side of the box. Here, we use a box about four by five feet in size with sides 16 inches high. The height is accomplished by using one piece of 1″ x 12″ lumber, a 1″ x 3″ piece laid flat so that the wide side faces the floor forming the pig rail, and a 1″ x 3″ piece beneath this. All the boards are screwed together to provide maximum strength. If you choose to make your own box and plan to paint the sides, be sure to use paint or stain that is lead-free since both the pups and, occasionally, the mother may chew on the wood.

The room in which the box is placed should be in a quiet part of your home, away from normal household traffic—the kitchen is not a good place—or your kennel. It should be kept at about 75 to 80 degrees Fahrenheit at least for the first week, after which the puppies will be able to maintain their own body temperature. In cool weather, it may be necessary to have a heat lamp over the whelping box in order to keep the pups warm enough. Be certain that the lamp is not too close to the box by placing a thermometer on the floor of the box for a while when the lamp is on and checking the temperature. If it is too warm or cold in the box, the puppies will scream to alert you.

Newspapers will become very important and you should start saving them as soon as you have decided to breed your bitch. Keep a pile of them near the box so that you can keep placing fresh papers inside as you remove the wet, soiled ones. Other necessities for whelping time are clean, soft turkish towels, and perhaps some clean scissors and a bottle of alcohol.

You will know that the time for whelping is near when your bitch becomes restless, wandering in and out of her box and the room. She may refuse food and may try to create a nest for her pups by ripping up the paper you have already placed on the floor of the box. She will shiver and generally look uncomfortable. Within 24 hours of her whelping time, her body temperature will usually drop to about 99 degrees and then begin to climb again just before she actually whelps. Only you should be with your bitch at this time. She does not need an audience, even though they may be family members she knows. Young children should be kept out of the room as their antics may worry the mother-to-be. Do not hover over her since she may find this unusual behavior on your part to be upsetting. You should stay quietly watchful nearby, speak quietly to her frequently to help calm her, and if she needs it, pet her gently. Eventually she will settle down in her box and begin panting, followed eventually by visible contractions. Soon, the first puppy will appear at the vulva and will begin to emerge, sliding out with the contractions. The mother may yelp as she gives birth to the first puppy since this will stretch open the birth canal. Once the pup is fully out, the mother immediately should open the sack with her teeth and sever the cord by shredding it. Make certain she leaves several inches attached to the pup's body to avoid any damage to the pup. It will dry up and fall off in several days. She will then begin to clean the puppy. If she does not start with the puppy's head, turn it to her so that she cleans it first, thus clearing the nose and breathing passages. You should allow her to eat the placenta as this will encourage further labor for the next puppy and promote the production of milk. If it does not upset the mother or if she is not doing her job of licking the puppy, you may take it from her, wrap it in a turkish towel and rub it briskly to dry it and help stimulate breathing, making sure to remove all traces of the membrane from around the pup's nose. Once the puppy is cleaned and dried, it should be placed next to the mother unless she is showing signs of having the next one immediately. Almost at once, the puppy will start searching for a nipple on which to nurse, and you should make sure that it latches on successfully.

If the puppy is a breech (i.e., born feet first) you should watch carefully for it to be delivered as quickly as possible and remove the sack rapidly so that the puppy does not drown in its own fluids. It is possible to help the puppy out by gently and carefully pulling the pup out *as the mother contracts and pushes,* thus speeding up the birth process. Sometimes even a normally positioned puppy will seem extremely slow in coming out and you can assist in the same manner. If, once a puppy is delivered, it shows little signs of life, take a towel and rub the puppy quite briskly back and forth along the chest after making sure that its mouth is cleared of any mucus or other obstruction. Keep this up for about fifteen minutes. If there appears to be fluid in the lungs, or the puppy is wheezing badly, place the pup in a towel and, supporting its head carefully, swing it in an arc from your head to your knees to force the fluids out. Do not be alarmed if the pup cries out; this is actually a good sign as it means that there is air getting to the lungs.

Sometimes it may be necessary to try mouth to mouth breathing in order to revive a seemingly dead pup. This is done by pressing the pup's jaws open using a finger, depressing the tongue, which may be stuck to the roof of the mouth, and blowing gently down the pup's throat. Bubbles may pop out of its nose, but keep on blowing until the pup appears to be breathing on its own. Keep trying one method or another for at least 20 minutes before giving up. You may be rewarded with a live puppy who would not have otherwise made it.

If you are successful in bringing the puppy around, do not immediately put it back with the mother. Put it in a box with a heating pad to keep it warm. As soon as it seems recovered or the rest of the litter is born, place it with the bitch and make sure it has a good chance to nurse.

An hour or more may elapse between puppies, which is fine so long as the bitch seems comfortable and is neither straining or actively contracting. She should not be permitted to remain unassisted for more than an hour if she is straining or contracting without any results. Now is the time to call your veterinarian, who you have already alerted to the whelping, and tell him of the problem. He will probably want to examine her and perhaps give her a shot to stimulate her labor. In some cases, a Caesarean section may be necessary. If the bitch does require a section, the puppies already born must be kept warm in a box lined with towels and a heating pad.

Should the mother lack milk at this time, the puppies will have to be fed by hand, kept very warm (about 85 degrees Fahrenheit) and held to the mother's teats several times daily in order to stimulate and encourage the secretion of milk, which should start shortly.

Assuming that there has been no problem and that the bitch has whelped naturally, you should insist that she go outside to exercise when she seems to be finished. She will probably be very reluctant to leave her pups at this time, and a lead and collar may be necessary. As soon as she is finished outside, allow her to return to her pups. You may wish to feed her some broth mixed with honey to replenish her energy at this time. While she is outside, remove all of the wet newspapers and replace them with a thick layer of clean ones. The bitch will probably be quite tired now from the work of being in labor, and will probably want to cuddle with her pups and sleep.

As we said before, the average Golden litter is eight to ten puppies, with as many as thirteen or fourteen not that unusual. Most bitches have only ten teats so that you will have to make sure that each pup has its turn to nurse. The colostrum, or first milk, contains all of the immunity factors that the bitch passes on to her pups, so it is most important that all the pups drink this.

Actually, unless there is some problem, there is little that you must do about the puppies until they are three to four weeks old. For the first day or so, the mother may need some help in arranging the puppies so that they do not get under her body where she might accidentally crush them, but she will soon get the hang of it. Keep the box clean and supplied with fresh dry newspaper. After the first week, when the bitch will be discharging heavily, you may wish to place a piece of indoor/outdoor carpeting on top of the newspaper to give the puppies a dry surface to lie on and good footing. Make sure that you use the kind without any rubber backing so that the liquids can soak through to the newspaper underneath. Buy enough for two pieces so that you can clean one as you replace it with the other.

If the bitch has difficulties with her milk supply, or if you should be so unfortunate as to lose her, then you must be prepared to either bottle feed or tube feed the pups if they are to survive. Personally, I prefer tube feeding as it is so much faster and easier. Your veterinarian can teach you this easy procedure. If the bitch is available, it is best that she continue to clean and care for the puppies in the normal manner—except for the feeding—as long as she will. You will have to feed the pups on a four-hour basis around the clock until they are about three to four weeks old when they can be weaned to solid food. If it is impossible for the bitch to do this, or if she refuses to clean the puppies, then you must learn to gently rub each pup's abdomen with wet cotton to make it urinate, and the rectum should be gently rubbed to open the bowels. This must be done after each feeding since the puppies cannot eliminate on their own at this age.

After a normal whelping the bitch will require additional food to enable her to provide sufficient milk. She can be fed as much as she wishes to eat at this stage. Her food should be a top quality product, preferably one made for lactating bitches. If supplements are used, care should be taken not to over-supplement as this can create more problems than it solves.

Most bitches tend to develop diarrhea after whelping because of all the placentas they have eaten. In order to help control this natural reaction, we often add yogurt with active cultures to the food we feed. This often helps bind the bitch's stool sooner and is an excellent source of extra protein and natural calcium.

Weaning the pups can begin any time after the third week. Each breeder has his favorite method of doing this. Some prefer to mix a special concoction using meat and cereal. Many use the commercial puppy foods, which is by far the easiest method. In our kennel, we use a top quality commercial food made specifically for puppies and soften it with hot water at first, then gradually decrease the water until the pups are eating dry food. This process takes about a week and a half to two weeks. This also gives the pups something to crunch on as they are teething. At first, you will have to feed the pups at least four times a day, or, if you are using a dry food, on a free-feeding basis. By the time the puppies are five to six weeks old they should be completely weaned from the mother. At twelve weeks, you may reduce feedings to three times a day. As the puppies grow you will find that you have to increase the amount of food you give them.

The mother's maternal antibodies can last anywhere up to twelve weeks in the puppies. Until it is gone, vaccinations will not "take" and provide the puppy with longer lasting protection from disease. Since it is very difficult to know when the mother's protection ends without a special blood test, most veterinarians recommend a series of temporary shots beginning at six weeks of age. This will include, at various ages, at least a D.H.L.P. (distemper, hepatitis, leptospirosis, parainfluenza) shot and a parvovirus shot. New studies on parvovirus seem to indicate that these shots probably should not be given at the same time that the D.H.L.P. shot is administered. Check with your own veterinarian for the most current information on this and the schedule he prefers for puppy shots. At the same time you are doing the first shots, or before if possible, bring a few stool samples from the puppies to be checked for worms. Most puppies have round worms that they received from their mother and some have other types of worms as well. Untreated, the worms can have serious harmful effects on young puppies. If worming is needed, administer the worming medication as directed by your veterinarian. Each time you take the puppies for shots, take a new set of stool samples along even if the previous samples had been negative. Worms go through various stages of development and may be present in the puppy even though their eggs do not appear in the stool sample. The second or third check may show worms to be present even though the first did not.

Continue to feed the puppies four times a day until they are about three months old when you can cut down to three feedings a day. At

Most Goldens are quite tolerant of other animals. Nursing a week-old litter, Am., Can. Ch. Russo's Pepperhill Poppy shares her whelping box with a friendly female cat who shared the chores of cleaning the puppies. At weaning time, these pups accepted cats as a normal part of their environment. Photo: John Ashbey.

At about five weeks of age, this youngster is very much aware of his environment, even if the grass is almost as tall as he is! Shown is the author's Pepperhill's Lonesome Trav'ler (Am., Can. Ch. Southern's Gold-Rush Traveler ex Am., Can. Ch. Russo's Pepperhill Poppy).

about six months, this can be reduced to twice a day. Some people feed their dogs twice a day throughout their lives; others go to one meal a day when the dog is about one year old.

The ideal age for puppies to leave their littermates for new homes is about seven to seven and a half weeks. Studies have shown that puppies are best able to adapt to new surroundings at this age. If this is not possible, it is suggested that you wait until they are nine weeks old before letting them go. Research has shown that during the eighth week puppies are extremely sensitive to new situations and the fear response they develop at this time can have a permanent effect on the dog. As they leave, each puppy should be accompanied by a written set of instructions for feeding and housebreaking, as well as additional shots and wormings needed. A list of shots and wormings already provided should be given to the new owners as well. Finally, the blue Individual Registration Application and a pedigree also should be provided to the new owners.

The socialization you will have provided the puppies during their third to seventh weeks is crucial for their correct emotional development. They should be accustomed to handling and grooming. They should have been played with on a regular basis by both adults and children. If you do not have any young children in your family, to play with the pups, "borrow" your neighbor's so that the puppies will become used to children as well as adults. Allow the pups to explore, under close supervision, both in the house and outdoors. Expose them to normal household noises like vacuum cleaners and other appliances so that they become used to these sounds. The more time and care you provide your pups, the better they will be able to develop confidence in themselves and in humans, thus making them the best kind of canine citizens and a joy to live with.

Chapter 7

Choosing the Right Mate for Your Dog or Bitch

**(Based on an article first published in the
Golden Retriever News, Vol. XXXIX,
No. 6. Used by permission.)**

The art of breeding dogs is also a science, though an inexact one. The more a breeder knows about what makes good dogs, the better the chances that the products of a breeding program will be an improvement over what has come before. The goal of every serious breeder is to produce the best possible puppies, hopefully each generation being better than what came before. Every show breeder would like to produce a Best in Show winner, the obedience breeder a top-winning Obedience Trial Champion, and the field oriented breeder a National winner. The methods used in striving to reach this goal vary somewhat from breeder to breeder, but all breeding programs follow similar basic patterns over the years.

Choosing the right mate for your dog is never an easy task. There is, unfortunately, no easy recipe that one can follow with guaranteed results. Please remember this as you read this chapter: there is no one "right" way of doing things, and there is no way that one can eliminate the element of chance, for we are dealing with living things. What might look good on paper in the form of a pedigree, or what looks like a correct physical matching of a dog and bitch based on observation, just might not work out. It is usually not a good idea to rely on photographs either, since many do not present a true picture. It is possible, however, to improve the odds in your favor for producing good puppies by utilizing a number of proven techniques.

Before going any further, we must examine our reasons for wanting to do a breeding, for our motives play a large role in all of this. If the intent is to produce some outstanding competitors in the field, on the bench, or in obedience trials then one will have to choose dogs who

Ch. Pekay's Deliverance, U.D.T., W.C.X. (Ch. Misty Morn's Sunset, C.D., T.D., W.C. ex Honor's High Stakes). Owned by Pekay Goldens, Alpharetta, Georgia.

Am., Can. Ch. Beckwith's Malagold Cherub, U.D.T., Can. C.D.X. (Ch. Malagold Beckwith Big Buff ex Am., Can. Ch. Beckwith's Frolic of Yeo). A granddaughter of Ch. Beckwith's Copper Coin, is G.R.C.A. Outstanding Dam, the mother of seven champions. Bred and owned by Dick and Luddell Beckwith of Snohomish, Washington. Photo: Martin Booth.

Am., Can., Mex. Ch. Cal-Vo's Happy Ambassador, C.D. winning his first Best of Breed at the age of ten months at the Oakland Kennel Club in 1971. "Adolph" was sired by Ch. Footprint of Yeo, C.D. out of Ch. Beckwith's Malagold Starfarm. He was owned by Bill and Joan Young of Concord, California. Judge is Dr. James Harrison.

have already proven their worth in that area of competition. If the intent, however, is simply to produce puppies, this may be a problem. In my opinion, the world does not need another litter of puppies that do not possess the potential to be excellent representatives of their breed.

So many times I hear people say that they want to breed their bitch or dog because she or he has a "wonderful temperament." I'm glad this is true, but it is hardly unique for a Golden Retriever. This wonderful temperament is, after all, what first attracted so many of us to the breed. No, there has to be more than this as a reason to bring more dogs into the world. Occasionally, we hear people say that they want to breed their bitch "just once" before it is spayed, because this will somehow "improve" the bitch. This is nothing but an old folk tale, having no validity at all. The fact is that having a litter does nothing for the bitch and might, in some cases, even be harmful to her. Giving a male one "fling" is another reason often heard. A dog does not have a sex drive in the way people do. If he is being bothersome by mounting other dogs, or even people, breeding him will not stop this behavior—in fact it often makes it worse! What you are dealing with in this case is a dominance problem, not the dog's unfulfilled need for sex. Providing the children with a lesson in sex education is another reason often offered. If breeding your bitch is the only way you can do this, you have a problem. It is not fair to use your dog to help you in teaching your children that subject.

The ultimate reason many people offer for breeding their animal is the thought that it is a way to make some "easy" money. Dealing properly with a litter of puppies is anything but easy. Further, in most cases you will be lucky to break even, especially if you calculate in your expenses the value of your time that must be spent cleaning up after puppies, socializing them, and finding good homes for the entire litter. In some cases, it is quite possible to actually lose money.

No, breeding will not meet any of these needs. Rather, the conscientious breeder thinks only of trying to improve the breed, often breeding a litter in order to have a good pup or two of their own. A truly good breeding is one that is chosen as a method to enhance the quality of the breeder's bloodline, and is based on careful thought and planning, and the investment of a good deal of time, energy, and money.

PLANNING QUALITY MATINGS

So, how do we plan a quality breeding? First, the potential breeder absolutely *must* have a complete understanding of the breed standard, and must be capable of using this knowledge in a practical way. He must be able to fault his own dogs based on this knowledge of the standard. As has been said so many times, there is no such thing as a "perfect dog." Each dog has its own set of faults, and a failure to recognize this fact can lead to disaster, and to poor quality puppies.

One basic rule of breeding is that one should avoid breeding a dog to a bitch if they have faults in common. For example, if both are lacking in proper front angulation and shoulder layback, one can almost guarantee that the puppies that are the result of this mating will have the same fault, perhaps even amplified. If, in evaluating your bitch, you feel she is weak in the forequarters, then you should seek a stud dog that has an excellent front in order to try to compensate for the bitch's fault. If you are not sure of the difference between a good front and a weak front, then it's back to the books to find out. The same is true for any fault. You must first recognize the problem and then attempt to compensate for it. As a conscientious breeder, you should try to improve your knowledge by reading, by attending educational seminars sometimes offered by Kennel Clubs, by talking to other breeders who have more experience than you do, and by constantly striving to be objective about your own dogs. There is nothing sadder than a breeder who is "kennel blind," feeling that his own dogs have no faults. This person is incapable of being objective and will experience difficulty in improving his bloodline.

Part of being objective is realizing that we really don't know it all. We must constantly strive to gain new knowledge and at the same time make sure that we really know what we think we know. Do you *really* understand what makes good shoulders? Do you fully comprehend what correct gait with proper reach and drive is? Do you understand what the breed standard calls for in terms of conformation? You owe it to yourself and your breed to be sure that you understand as much as possible about what you are doing. It is this knowledge that makes the difference between a breeder who is successful over the long term and one who is not.

TYPE

Another area of consideration in breeding is *type*. This is an often misunderstood word that may be defined, simply, as those characteristics which make a dog of one breed look like all other dogs of the same breed. Within a breed, type refers to the characteristics that

Am., Can. Ch. Sadie's Sundance Kidd, C.D.X. (Ch. Brandywine's Dusty Dandy, C.D.X. ex Aurora's Sunshine Sadie), G.R.C.A. Show Dog Hall of Fame dog from California, owned by Jamie and Jack Warren.

Opposite page: (*Above*) O.T. Ch. Meadowpond Fem De Fortune, W.C. (Ch. Bardfield Boomer, U.D.T. ex Ch. Meadowpond Dazzle's Sparkle, C.D.). Winner of the 1981 Gaines Super Dog National title, "Charo" has 23 High in Trial awards (four perfect and nine scores of 199½). She is a member of the G.R.C.A. Obedience Hall of Fame. Owned by Diane Bauman. (*Below*) F.C., A.F.C. Misty's Sungold Lad, C.D.X. (Sherrydan Tag, W.C.ex Luke's Golden Misty). This outstanding High Point Field Trial Golden owned by Ken and Valerie Walker, a Field Trial Hall of Fame member and G.R.C.A. Outstanding Sire, earned 212½ Open and Amateur points before he died.

make one line different from another. Too much variation within a breed leads to a loss of type. Many of the more experienced Golden breeders today talk about a loss of type. While most Golden Retrievers look like Goldens, they do not look alike. The differences within the breed are the result of breeders looking for different types. The variations within Goldens seem to center primarily around head structure and body conformation. For instance, there is a generally accepted "English" type of head in our Goldens that is clearly different from the so-called "American" head type. The English version has, in general, more stop, a rounder eye and a broader somewhat more rounded skull than its American counterpart. The question of which is the "correct" head type is the subject of debate. So long as the general structure of the head conforms to the requirements of the standard, the type that each individual breeder prefers becomes a matter of personal choice. What is important here is that you, as a breeder, be aware of the differences, decide what you think the perfect head type is, and then breed for it consistently over a number of generations until it has firmly established itself as "your" type.

While a mixture of types is certainly permissible and often is desirable in order to gain the desired results, your ultimate goal should be to establish one head type in all of the dogs of your line. This will, of course, take a number of generations to establish firmly.

These same principles are true for body type, though there is much more variation here because the structure is more complex. Conformity to the standard is paramount, but there is a good amount of leeway and flexibility within the desired range.

When making your decision regarding the proper mate for your dog or bitch, type has to enter into your consideration. If you are less than totally pleased with the type of your dog (and who isn't), then it is important that you choose a mate with the type that you desire in order to attempt to improve on your animal. In the author's opinion, there is too wide a divergence of type within the breed, and we breeders need to work toward correcting this problem. A look at photographs of Goldens of years past points to the differences in show and field stock over the years. A more critical problem exists with many of the so-called "pet quality" Goldens that are found in pet stores and from "backyard breeders" who are not concerned with maintaining the quality of the breed but only with making a dollar. These dogs are often so very long in leg, light in bone, and narrow in muzzle and chest.

Differences can even be seen in our show stock over the past fifteen years or so. A look at some of the older pictures in this book in comparison with the most recent ones will show this difference. Color has lightened. Forechest seems to be decreasing markedly while overall size, both in height and breadth, has increased.

What may be less obvious to some is the divergence in type found in dogs produced by serious breeders specializing in the various areas of competition. The dogs produced for, and winning in, the show ring look different than those bred for the obedience ring who, in turn look different from those bred primarily for field trials. Some Sporting Breeds have already reached a point where the field dogs look quite different from the dogs bred for the show ring. While there remains a good deal of overlapping between the types today, further divergence in type would be a detriment to the breed and should be avoided.

TEMPERAMENT

Temperament, too, has to be considered when planning breedings. We are not just talking here of those dogs whose temperament is so bad that they are given to unwarranted fighting, or those few that have actually bitten a person. Clearly, that temperament is a major detriment to the breed, and Goldens displaying that kind of temperament should never be bred—no matter what other attributes they might possess. It is, after all, the Golden's temperament, more than any other feature, that makes the breed so desirable to own.

There are other temperament considerations which are less obvious and less frequently dealt with when planning a breeding. For example, a quiet, extremely mellow dog with a low energy level probably should not be bred to a bitch with a similar temperament, especially if the desired result is puppies to be used for any kind of competition. At the same time, an extremely exuberant "up" dog that is stubborn and difficult to control and has a very high energy level, probably should not be bred to a bitch of similar behavior either, especially since at least some (if not most) of the pups from the litter will go to pet homes. These owners often have little or no experience in working with difficult dogs. The results of such a breeding might well be pups who are nearly impossible to control and they would be a disaster in the average pet home. This is the kind of dog who eventually winds up in the pound, unwanted and unhappy. As with physical problems, thought must be given to complementing the dog's temperament so as to improve the breed. Too often, the temperament of dogs to be used

Since 1970, only three dogs have completed both a field and conformation championship. The only one still living in 1983 was Dual Ch. A.F.C. Tigathoe's Funky Farquar (F.C., A.F.C., Can. F.C. Bonnie Brook's Elmer ex Tigathoe's Chickasaw***). Bred by Mrs. George H. Flinn, Jr. and Mrs. Robert R. Sadler, this remarkable Golden is owned by Dorothy Ramsay and Elinor L. Tribon.

With generations of top field dogs behind her, this is F.C., A.F.C. Topbrass Mandy, the High Point living field trial bitch in the United States. Sired by A.F.C. Holway Barty, an English import, and out of Ch. Sunstream Gypsy of Topbrass who traces her pedigree back to Dual Ch. A.F.C. Ronakers Novato Cain and F.C., A.F.C. Can. F.C. Bonnie Brooks Elmer. She is owned by Jackie Mertens of Topbrass Goldens, Elgin, Illinois.

O.T. Ch. Goldenloe's Just Ducky (Ch. Golden Pine's Courvoisier, C.D.X., W.C.X. ex Ch. Goldenloe's Tawny Tiger, U.D.). A top-winning obedience dog, "Puppy" retired with 52 High in Trial awards. He comes from a litter of five champions, two of whom also had U.D. titles. Breeder/owner Anne Couttet Shannon of Evergreen, Colorado. Photo: Feinberg.

for breeding is given little if any consideration; yet, temperament is a major aspect of the breed and should not be neglected.

BREEDING BY PEDIGREE

One of the ways of decreasing variation in type is to follow a plan of line-breeding. If your dog was purchased from a reputable breeder, you probably received a written four or five generation pedigree for him. If not, a three or four generation pedigree on your dog may be obtained for a fee from the American Kennel Club. The information found in a pedigree can be the most valuable tool of all in planning breedings, if it is used properly and with good knowledge of the dogs contained in it. Far too many people look at a pedigree simply to see what titles the dog's ancestors had earned, and are satisfied with this alone if there are a number of, say, champions in it. While titles certainly are important and are an indication of the quality of the dogs, they tell only a part of the story. A title will not, by itself, tell you how difficult it was for the holder to earn it (a C.D. in three shows or 23, a Championship in ten shows or 110, etc.). The title will not tell you what the holder looked like, whether he was clear of genetic problems or was affected by one or more. It will not tell you if the dog had good shoulders or bad, a good head or a poor one, a strong topline or a weak one or anything else about the dog. For this kind of important information, it is necessary to know more about the individual dogs whose names appear in the pedigree.

You might ask, "Why do I need to know more than the titles? After all, if the dog was a champion, he must have been good." Unfortunately, this is not necessarily true. While the majority of champions are worthy representatives of their breed, there are some dogs who managed to obtain their championship title despite the fact that they were really not good dogs. Some champions are of a quality that just barely meets that expected of a champion, and took 100 or more shows to complete their title. Is this the kind of dog you want to breed your bitch to? There are many more dogs, some champions, who are decent quality animals but who have genetic problems. The Championship title will not tell you this.

For example, hip dysplasia is one problem affecting Goldens that has received much attention. There are many champions who are dysplastic. Some breeders feel that a particular dysplastic dog has other qualities that are desirable enough that he should be bred anyway. This is a decision that individual breeders must make, but it is

110

one that must be made from a basis of knowledge. On the other hand, it should be remembered that just using a dog that has clear hips, without knowing anything about his siblings and parents, is really not having enough information either. A dog that is the only one in its litter to clear O.F.A. is less likely to produce clear hips than one whose entire litter has cleared. Further, breeding clear hipped dogs to clear hipped dogs in no way guarantees that the product of such a breeding will have clear hips. What about the dogs in the third and fourth generations of the pedigree? Are you aware of the faults they possessed? If you knew that more than half of them were dysplastic, this might have an effect on your decision, especially if you knew that your bitch's ancestors had similar problems. To reverse this, you might well decide to use a specific stud dog who has many good qualities despite his dysplasia, if you were aware that his siblings and most of his ancestors were free of the disease.

When dealing with dysplasia or eye problems, we have the advantage of a relatively easy method of checking whether or not the dogs in a pedigree were clear of these problems—the use of O.F.A. (Orthopedic Foundation for Animals) normal listings and C.E.R.F. (Canine Eye Registry Foundation) listings. Unfortunately, there are numerous other genetic problems that are not so easily checked. These include monorchidism, cryptorchidism, thyroid problems, epilepsy, and blood disorders, to name some of the major ones. Certainly one would not wish to breed a dog and a bitch who have one of these problems in common in their respective pedigrees; but the only way to know this information is to be thoroughly familiar with the dogs in a pedigree beyond just knowing their names and titles. In fact, this information is quite difficult to learn, and it will take a lot of conscientious digging to find, since people are reluctant to share information of this kind for reasons we will discuss later.

There are three basic forms of long-term breeding plans which utilize the information that can be provided by a complete knowledge of a dog's pedigree. These are: outcrossing, linebreeding, and inbreeding. The study of genetics is a complicated one, and any kind of complete explanation of its intricacies requires much more space than is available here. To boil the genetic methods of breeding down to simple terms: *Outcrossing* means breeding a dog and a bitch that are unrelated in at least four generations; that is, no dog's name that appears in the sire's side of the pedigree also appears in the dam's side; they have no ancestors in common. *Linebreeding* is a mating in which

Amberac's Reeva Rustelle is G.R.C.A. Outstanding Dam of five champions and a foundation bitch at Amberac. Owned by Ellen Manke of Hartland, Wisconsin.

Can. Dual Ch., A.F.C. Carolee's Something Special, Am., Can. C.D., W.C.X. (Can. Ch. HGL's Golden Pine Gibson Solo ex Can. Ch. Carolee's Cafe Au Lait, Am., Can. C.D., W.C.). Canada's only living Golden Retriever Dual Champion, "Bumper" was bred by Shirley Goodman and is owned by George Stewart. He is the sire of four Canadian champions.

In harness and ready to work, a Golden sits for his portrait. This dog has been through extensive training to prepare it for a lifetime of usefulness. Photo courtesy of Guiding Eyes for the Blind, Yorktown Heights, New York.

the sire and dam have a number of common ancestors within the first three generations of the pedigree. Linebreeding on one dog, sometimes done with an outstanding dog, means that the dog's name appears several times in the pedigree. *Inbreeding* (best left to those breeders who are fully aware of the genetic and conformation faults of each dog and its ancestors), is breeding father to daughter, mother to son, brother to sister, grandparent to grandchild. A sound understanding of the basic principles of genetics is helpful in understanding the uses of each of these methods, and the reader is referred to one of the many good books on the subject.

Generally, the more unrelated the dogs, the larger the gene pool available to the puppies from a mating. The more related the dogs, the smaller the number of genes available, so the puppies should be more similar to each other. With an inbreeding, the gene pool is relatively small and the puppies should look very much the same within the litter. Some stud dogs who are linebred are prepotent in some areas, and will tend to dominate the genetic input of the bitch in these areas; and viceversa for a bitch who is the product of a linebreeding. If you need, for example, better head structure in your puppies, you might wish to choose a stud dog that, when bred previously, has proven to be prepotent in throwing good heads. The same would be true of any problem area needing improvement. Unfortunately, some dogs can be prepotent in undesirable characteristics as well.

Folklore tells us that close breeding, such as those we consider linebreedings or inbreedings, should be avoided. The reason for this is the fact that the potential for recessive genetic problems increases as the size of the gene pool decreases. In these types of breeding, we are "doubling up," or intensifying, the "bad" genes. But, as much as this is true, so is its converse; we are also intensifying the "good" genes so that if two top quality animals who are closely related are bred to each other we have the potential for producing some really superior puppies. Because of this intensification, breeders must be aware of the potential genetic problems in a pedigree so that the puppies can be checked carefully to see if they have inherited an illness. If they have not, they may, in theory, be free of the problem and, because their "blood" is pure, not pass it on to future generations. Remember, though, that even if some of the puppies in the litter are clear, it does not necessarily follow that all of them are. It also should be remembered that some genetic problems do not show up until a dog is older.

Only really superior quality dogs should be linebred on their own lines, since poor quality dogs bred to poor quality dogs of the same lines are certain to produce even poorer quality puppies. On the other hand, superior quality dogs linebred to superior quality dogs are likely to produce superior quality puppies, especially if their ancestors were free of genetic problems and were of top quality themselves.

Inbreeding is really the ultimate form of linebreeding, but, because the animals are so closely related great care must be taken to avoid producing puppies who are riddled with genetic problems, some of which they might well pass on to succeeding generations. This problem can only be avoided through knowledge of the dog's ancestors and luck. It is through the careful use of linebreeding and inbreeding, with occasional outcrosses, that the quality of livestock such as horses and cows has been dramatically improved over the years. We dog breeders can learn much from the experience these live-stock breeders have gained.

There is much to be said for outcross breeding, and it has its proponents. This is one way to attempt to avoid the occurrence of genetically based problems. Those breeders who rely primarily on linebreeding also must occasionally outcross in order to bring some "new blood" into their lines to avoid weakening it as the gene pool shrinks. The outcross is used to enlarge the gene pool and, therefore, reduce the chance of genetic problems. It is also used to bring into the established bloodline a quality that it is lacking or is weak. An outcross breeding of two dogs that were linebred on different lines will often produce some excellent puppies (especially if both parents were themselves excellent representatives of their respective lines). The puppies from such a breeding are then bred back into the original line, thus establishing the "new blood" within the line. Here again, a complete knowledge of both sides of the pedigree will be extremely helpful, as the breeder will be aware of the depth of both strong and weak points within the pedigree. An example: if your own line is lacking in a quality, say typey heads, but another line has the good heads you need firmly established, you might decide to breed your bitch to a dog from that line, using one who has proven to be prepotent in throwing these good heads. One or two of the puppies that are the result of this breeding, assuming that they have the desired head, might later be bred back to dogs of your own line as a method of introducing the more desired head into your line.

It should be pointed out that breeding two dogs, each with their individual gene pool, is not like mixing two solutions together. Mixing two colors of paint, for example, will produce a third color that is a

Am., Can. Ch. O.T. Ch. Sunstreak of Culynwood, T.D., W.C.X., CAN. C.D. (Ch. Sabakas Alexander of Cal-Vo, C.D. ex Ch. Tangelo's End Of The Rainbo, C.D., W.C.). An outstanding bench and obedience dog, "Streaker" is shown with some of his trophies, these from the G.R.C.A. National Specialty in 1977 when he was Highest-Scoring Dog in Trial. He was owned by David and Susan Bluford, of Carmel, California. He died March 2, 1982.

O.T. Ch. Amberac's Sunrise Duke, winner of Super Dog title at 1982 Gaines Central Competition. He is out of Amberac's Sunburst Sunbrave, W.C. and was bred by Ellen Manke.

Valentine Torch of Topbrass (Ch. Rockgold Chug's Ric O Shay ex Ch. Goldenloe's Bronze Lustre), already retrieving from water at the age of four months, is the foundation of the successful Topbrass Goldens of Mr. & Mrs. Joseph Mertens of Elgin, Illinois.

Having completed her retrieve, Ch. Topbrass Ad-Lib's Bangor*** (Dual Ch. A.F.C. Ronaker's Novato Cain ex Valentine Torch of Topbrass*) awaits her handler, bird in mouth. This dual purpose bitch is bred and owned by Joe and Jackie Mertens of Elgin, Illinois.

homogenous result of the blending of the original two. Combining genes is more like mixing together two batches of dissimilar sized beads. The result will be mixtures of various kinds, some piles having more big beads than others, for example. For instance, breeding a long-bodied dog to a short-bodied bitch is likely to result in some puppies that are long in body, some that are short in body, and some that are neither too long nor too short. It is probably one of the latter puppies we are looking for, but all will not be the same. When breeding dogs, we are dealing with living animals with a complex set of genes. The ways that these genes combine and work together is not fully understood, so there is still a strong element of luck in any mating. It is for this reason that breeding dogs is such a challenge and so fascinating.

As we have seen, it is most important to serious breeders that they know more about the individuals in their own dog's pedigrees than just the names and titles. A good working knowledge of what these dogs produced can be an invaluable method of improving one's own breeding stock. But from whom does one obtain this information? Unfortunately, the kinds of things we need to know are quite specific and can not be found in any book (and probably never will be). It would be nice to have a committee of G.R.C.A. serve as a responsible depository for this information so it could be available to serious breeders, but this is not the case and it is unlikely that it ever will be. So where can this information be found?

The very best method of obtaining this most important knowledge is through experience. If you have personally known all or even many of the dogs in a pedigree, then you are probably in an excellent position to use pedigree information. This kind of experience, obviously, takes many years to collect. Since this is impractical for many people, other methods must sometimes be relied on. One way is to learn by talking with others who have more experience in the breed than you do. This too will take some time and effort, since it will usually be necessary for you to first establish and build a trusting relationship with these people before they will begin to share the really salient information with you. This reluctance to share is the result of experience. Many times people have misused this kind of information. Beware, also, of the know-it-alls; often they do not really know as much as they want you to think they do. Beware, too, of the person who has an axe to grind because their dogs are not as highly spoken of as those of others.

Because dogs are so frequently the family pets of breeders, their owners become very emotionally involved with them. In many ways, the dogs often become, in their owner's minds, an extension of themselves. In many cases, an owner's feelings about his dogs can be just as strong as his feelings about his children. Just as many of us would like others to think we are perfect, or our children are perfect (even though we know they are not), so do many of us feel that others should consider our dogs perfect. Because of this, we are often reluctant to admit that our dogs have any faults, or might pass on a genetic defect to their offspring. Further, while we might admit in private to our close friends and family that faults exist, we are reluctant to let the "public" know about them. We certainly do not want some stranger bad-mouthing our children or dogs and we get defensive about this. . .even if what they say is the truth. This very human quality has made the sharing of knowledge regarding individual dogs' problems very difficult. The result is that, often, very little is known about a dog other than his winning record.

While some people are willing to praise another's dog in public, they are often reluctant to criticize them, lest an enemy be made, or worse yet something bad be said about their own dogs. Others are all too willing to criticize, but do so out of jealousy, often without having any real knowledge of the problems they allege a dog has. This is how false rumors start. Because of this, remember that once you have earned the trust of those with the knowledge you seek, do not violate their confidence by sharing the information with those who might misuse it. Do not embellish what you know with what you *think* might be true unless you know it for a fact. Breeders who share the information you need will probably be willing to do so only when they are certain that what is shared will be used properly. They have the right to expect you to do the same.

BALANCE

There is one other area of breeding that some breeders seem to lose sight of, and that is the critical area of balance. When we talk of *balance* in dogs, we are discussing symmetry and proportion. A well balanced dog is one in which all of his parts appear to be in correct proportion to one another: height to length of body, head to body, neck to head and topline, skull to foreface, etc. Balance is a look of harmony in the dog, both when it is standing still and when it is moving. A dog with a large head needs a large body to lend this sense of balance. The neck must be in proportion to the head and to length of

This is Ch. Goldenrod's Lark of Trowsnest, U.D., W.C. (Ch. Alstone's Sutter Creek Charade, U.D., W.C. ex Sansue Rebecca, C.D.) owned by Marjorie Trowbridge of Madison, Connecticut. Lark earned all three obedience degrees in just six months, and all were earned with Dog World Awards, meaning that all were completed in three straight trials with scores of 195 or better out of a possible score of 200 points. Lark helped to repay her owner by using this obedience training in doing television commercials and magazine ads. Photo: M & R.

Opposite page: (*Above*) Shown with their new owners at a Match Show is half of a litter sired by Am., Can. Ch. Golden Pine's Courvoisier Am., Can. C.D.X., W.C., Am. W.C.X. The dam is Ch. Pepperhill Golden Pine Irish. Breeders are Nancy K. Belsaas, Gail Cortesia, Margaret Flynn and Pepperhill Kennels. Photo: Vicky Fox. (*Below*) Ch. Sun Dance's Rarue (Ch. Misty Morn's Sunset, C.D., T.D., W.C. ex Ch. Sun Dance's Susie Q) winning his first Group First placement under judge Gerhard Plaga, handled by Lisa Schultz. A Best in Show winner, Rarue is a G.R.C.A. Show Dog Hall of Fame member and an Outstanding Sire. Owners are Shirley and William Worley of Sun Dance Kennels. Photo: Klein.

body, and this can only occur when the length of body is adequate for the length of neck. Correct angulation, both in the forequarters and hind-quarters, combined with proper shoulder lay-back and correct length of the second arm is crucial. All must fit together.

Balance involves all parts of the body. The croup must be at the correct angle for the rear-end assembly to be used properly. The length of the dog's muzzle must be in proportion to the depth of muzzle for the dog to be able to carry a bird. Indeed, correct balance covers all parts of the dog's body from the tip of his nose to the tip of his tail. No one part can be emphasized without making corresponding allowances for equal emphasis on other parts of the dog. All parts must be harmonious to be in correct balance.

The concept of balance is one of the more important things that a breeder must learn. An understanding of good balance can help make the difference between a successful breeding program and one that only occasionally manages to produce a decent dog, and this often by luck. The Standard says that overall appearance and balance is what should be given emphasis. The good Golden must present a uniform, balanced picture. Breeding plans must keep this concept in mind along with the others we have discussed here.

A successful top-quality breeding program, then, is not just a matter of putting a dog and a bitch together and awaiting the outcome. It goes beyond obtaining hip and eye clearances (though these are important) for the prospective breeding pair. Rather, it is the culmination of a carefully thought-out plan of action formulated from a firm basis of knowledge. Carefully planned breedings are not just the result of breeding to the current big winner, for he may not have the qualities that your bitch needs in order to produce superior puppies. Big winners are not necessarily good producers, and even those who produce well may not have what is needed to improve what you already have.

As stated at the beginning of this chapter, the serious breeder must be willing to admit that his dogs have faults, and must be ready to acknowledge these faults to themselves and others when it is appropriate. Only by having a real understanding of a dog's faults, and then breeding to correct them, can we really hope to improve the breed.

A carefully planned breeding is one in which the breeder takes into account an honest evaluation of the conformation, type, temperament, and pedigree needs of his own dogs and those that he plans to breed to. This is a necessary part of any breeding program that the breeder hopes will be successful and have a long-term impact on the breed.

Chapter 8

Eye Diseases Inherent in the Golden Retriever

by David Covitz, D.V.M.
Diplomate, American College of Veterinary Ophthalmologists

There are a number of ocular defects which appear to be hereditary in the Golden Retriever. The exact genetic basis for most or perhaps all of these defects has not been proved. It might be more accurate to simply acknowledge that we have a number of ocular defects which seem to be much more common in Goldens than chance alone would predict.

A number of variables may influence the manifestation of a given ocular defect. One or more of these variables might precipitate the defect in an animal that carried a pre-existing tendency, whereas the same circumstances would not affect a litter mate. It is this predisposition to develop a defect that we are speaking about and a genetic discussion of a predisposition with multiple variables is difficult or impossible.

The incidence of ocular defects may vary from area to area and my assessment of the significance of a given disease may differ with the experience of another veterinary ophthalmologist. The following description is based on Goldens primarily from New York State and Connecticut.

ENTROPION

In my experience, entropion is the most common ocular defect present in the breed. Entropion is an inrolling of an eyelid, usually the lower lid. The inrolling brings lashes or skin hairs into direct contact with the cornea.

Am., Can. Ch. Jolly Jack Daniels (Ch. Golden Pine's Gradene's J D, C.D.X., W.C. ex Ch. Indanda Thembalisha) at three years of age with his breeder and owner, Dr. John Lounsbury and judge Alan Stern. "Jack" is a G.R.C.A. Outstanding Sire. Photo: Steve Klein.

Opposite page: (*Above*) Ch. Brandywine's Sparkling Wind, C.D. (Ch. Wochica's Okeechobee Jake ex Ch. Brandywine Tansu D'oro). Best of Winners at the 1980 G.R.C.A. Western Regional Specialty and winner of a number of Best of Breed awards, "Sparkle" is bred and owned by Ben and Bonnie Gikis. (*Below*) Can. Ch. Meadowlake Carolee's Miss Magic, Can. C.D., a daughter of Dual Ch. A.F.C. Carolee's Something Special II, winning Junior Sweepstakes at the Golden Retriever Club of Canada 1981 National Specialty under American breeder/judge Marcia Schlehr. She went on to be Top Show Puppy of 1981 for G.R.C.C. "Tia" is shown with her breeder/owner Shirley Goodman.

There are a number of variables associated with the manifestation of entropion in a predisposed animal. In most cases affected animals are not born with the defect. Most acquire it between one and four months of age.

One variable in the manifestation of entropion is the rate of skeletal development. If the skull develops rapidly, the globes can sink deeper within the orbit, a state called enophthalmia. The lids can follow an enophthalmic globe to a point where they flip into an entropic position. The dog has a muscle behind the eye, the retractor oculi muscle, which pulls the globe backward into the orbit. It is a protective mechanism triggered by actual or anticipated corneal pain. (We do not have this muscle and do not possess this ability.) The deeper placement of the globe results in additional inrolling of the lids and more hair contacting the cornea. This produces more pain, more retraction of the globe, more entropion, etc. Sometimes the relief of pain can stop the cycle long enough to allow the passage of time to correct the enophthalmic state and the problem can correct without surgery. Most of the time, the discomfort can not be handled medically and eventually the cornea will show evidence of pathology unless surgical correction is elected.

Another variable which may influence the manifestation of entropion is conjunctivitis. Conjunctivitis is a common, usually non-infectious inflammation of the conjunctiva, the membrane which lines the inside of the lids and covers the white portion of the eye. Conjunctivitis can result in enough discomfort to cause squinting of the lids. This can result in a spastic inrolling of the lids in an animal predisposed to the development of entropion.

A third factor which can result in the manifestation of entropion is distichiasis, a defect in which extra eye lashes grow at the lid margin and contact the cornea. The discomfort can be insignificant or can cause enough squinting to trigger spastic entropion.

Other factors include any anatomic feature which places the lower lid into contact with the eye in a position which favors inrolling. The pup which seems to have more skin than his head can carry is a prime candidate. A loose ligament at the lateral aspect of the lid margin would be another example. Given a predisposing anatomy, anything which causes corneal pain can result in spastic entropion.

Since the terminology is confusing, it might be of value to summarize the various conditions which result in hair contacting the eye. Trichiasis is the overall term which includes any condition in which hair contacts the eye. Trichiasis would include entropion as well as distichiasis and ectopic cilia.

ECTOPIC CILIA

An ectopic cilia is a misplaced eye lash or an ingrown skin hair that exits through the under surface of the lid. In my experience, these have always involved the upper lid, 1/8″ to 1/4″ back from the lid margin. They are perpendicular to the eye and friction keeps them short and bristly. Ectopic cilia are much more irritating than distichiasis which exit at the lid margin and contact the cornea at a gentle tangent. They are relatively rare in the general canine population: however, most of the cases I see are in the Golden Retriever.

Ectopic cilia produce the signs of a painful foreign body. Even when suspected, they are very difficult to observe without special lighting and magnification. Once an ectopic cilia has been located, treatment can be either direct surgical excision or electrocautery. In either case, the goal is to remove or destroy the follicle which produces the hair.

DISTICHIASIS

Distichiasis has been mentioned as a trigger mechanism in entropion. It should also be mentioned as a separate entity since the incidence is increasing in the Golden Retriever. In my experience, the Golden is second only to the Cocker Spaniel in breed incidence.

In most cases, there are only a few extra lashes and these are soft enough and long enough to float on the tear layer covering the cornea without any noticeable irritation. In some cases there will be a complete row of extra cilia involving all four lids. Occasionally, there is noticeable foreign body sensation manifesting as frequent squinting, excessive tearing and conjunctivitis. In cases where corneal irritation can be demonstrated or where foreign body sensation is obvious, surgery is advised.

Surgical procedures designed to handle the problem have included electrolysis, lid splitting and, the latest approach, direct electrocautery of the producing follicles approached through the conjunctiva covering the inside of the lids. (By Dr. Ron Riis, Veterinary Ophthalmologist at the N.Y. State College of Veterinary Medicine at Cornell University).

In my hands, the last approach has resulted in the least post-operative complications and the lowest incidence of recurrence.

Nancy Kelly Belsaas with Golden Pine Jameson (Am., Can. Ch. Golden Pine's Courvoisier Am., Can. C.D.X., W.C., Am. W.C.X. ex Ch. Pepperhill Golden Pine Irish). A one-time winner of the Limited Junior Showmanship Competition at the Westminster Kennel Club in New York City, Nancy has been working with Goldens ever since. Photo: Warren Cook.

Ch. HGL's Golden West Coquette (Am., Can. Ch. Cal-Vo's Happy Ambassador, C.D. ex Goldenloe's Golden Aspen) winning Best of Breed on her way to a Sporting Group Second at Tucson Kennel Club in 1978. Owners are Vicki Beran and John and Lynne Lounsbury.

Although no one has suggested a genetic basis for distichiasis, it does seem to have a predilection for certain lines of Goldens. Considering the potential problems it can produce, it would be a good idea to breed away from it.

CATARACTS

Cataracts are the most common intraocular defects I observe in Golden Retrievers. These generally appear as triangle-shaped opacities at the center of the posterior aspect of the lens. They are usually bilaterally symmetrical, although an occasional unilateral case will present itself. The terms which are most commonly used to describe these lens opacities are posterior polar cataracts and posterior subcapsular cataracts. On rare occasions they progress to other parts of the lens. When this occurs, it tends to be a rapid event and not a gradual development. Most of the time, the condition remains stable with no apparent vision loss.

The typical hereditary type cataract in this breed is rarely present at birth (rarely congenital). Most appear within the first year of life. The terms developmental cataract or juvenile cataract would be appropriate for most of the cases we see. A few show up between one and two years of age and there have been a few unwelcomed surprises in five- and six-year-olds.

The mode of inheritance has not been determined. It has been suggested that a dominant trait is involved and that an animal with one abnormal gene (heterozygotes) will show triangular opacities, whereas one with two abnormal genes (homozygotes) will manifest complete cataracts. Another theory is a dominant gene that does not always manifest itself (incomplete penetration).

In my experience, the incidence of these cataracts has decreased since the first cases were reviewed in the literature nine years ago. (Reference: Rubin, L.F. 1974. Cataracts in Golden Retrievers; Journal Am. Vet. Med. Assoc. 165:457.)

PROGRESSIVE RETINAL ATROPHY (PRA)

PRA has been documented in the Golden Retriever. It is a progressive degeneration of the retina which leads to complete blindness. Genetic studies in other breeds has always pointed toward a simple recessive mode of inheritance. As far as I know, the exact genetic basis has not been worked out in the Golden.

In my experience, PRA is very rare in the breed.

CENTRAL PROGRESSIVE RETINAL ATROPHY (CPRA)

CPRA has been reported in Golden Retrievers in England. This entity involves the central area of the retina initially and progresses to involve the periphery. Vision is impaired in the day and improved at night. These features are the reverse of PRA. As the disease progresses, visual impairment occurs in any illumination, although some cases stop progressing prior to total blindness.

I have never diagnosed a case of CPRA in the breed.

IRIS CYSTS

Benign cysts produced by the posterior lining of the iris are occasionally observed in dogs. In my experience, the Golden Retriever has a much higher incidence of these cysts than other breeds. Most of them stay attached to the iris and are hidden from view until the pupil is widely dilated. They are observed as an incidental finding during routine ocular clearing examinations.

Iris cysts can break free of their iris attachment and float within the anterior chamber. They rarely get larger than a small pea. They are benign and in my experience have never produced any symptoms. Perhaps the only significance of iris cysts is that they have to be distinguished from ocular tumors.

SUMMARY

The eye problems which seem to generate the most concern are the intraocular defects. In my experience, the extraocular problems (especially entropion) are of primary concern in the Golden Retriever breed today.

Ch. Sun Dance's April Fool (Ch. Kyrie Daemon, C.D.X. ex Ch. Sun Dance's Contessa) is an Outstanding Dam from Sun Dance Kennels. Owned by Shirley and William Worley. Photo: Martin Booth.

Winner of Best of Opposite Sex at the 1981 G.R.C.A. National Specialty and a multiple Best of Breed winner with a number of Group placements, Ch. Sutter Creek Cloverdale Erin, owned by Jane Zimmerman and Susan Breakell and bred by S. Breakell and Pamela Tillitson, is shown here winning the Sporting Group under judge Mrs. Virginia Hampton at the Tidewater Kennel Club in 1980, handled by S. Breakell.

A delightful head study of Valentine Torch of Topbrass (Ch. Rockgold Chug's Ric O Shay ex Ch. Goldenloe's Bronze Lustre). This is G.R.C.A. Outstanding Dam of eleven champions is owned by Joe and Jackie Mertens of Elgin, Illinois.

Chapter 9

Showing Your Golden

THE MAKING OF A SHOW DOG

If you have decided to become a show dog exhibitor, you have accepted a very real challenge. The groundwork has been accomplished with the selection of your future show prospect. If you have purchased your puppy, I assume that you have chosen him with care and purchased him from a top show kennel. The basic care you will give your potential champion is the same that you would provide for your beloved pet, with a few added precautions.

Remember the importance of keeping your future winner in trim, top condition. Since you want him neither too fat nor too thin, it is important to feed him only quality food in proper amounts. Avoid feeding him treats since they may spoil his appetite for proper food. Allowing the pup to become too fat can also place extra stress on his hips, leading perhaps to an unnecessarily dysplastic dog. Proper exercise is also important in building good muscle and condition.

It is impossible to over-estimate the importance of showmanship. Many a mediocre dog has defeated a better specimen because of superior showmanship and temperament. From the day the dog joins your family, socialize him. Encourage your friends and relatives to gently "go over" him as the judges will do later in the ring, so that this will not seem strange to him. Practice showing his bite (the manner in which his teeth meet) quickly and deftly. It is quite a simple matter to slip your fingers inside his lips and pull them apart to show the teeth up front. Also practice showing the side teeth to show the judge that no molars are missing. Teach him to permit his jaws to be opened to examine the teeth since some judges are now doing this.

Some judges prefer that exhibitors themselves display the dog's bite and these are the considerate ones who do not wish to chance the spreading of disease as they go from dog to dog. Others prefer to look at the bite themselves, so the dog should be ready for either experience.

Do not overly shelter your future show dog. Instinctively, you may want to keep him home where it is safe from germs and danger. This

G.R.C.A. Outstanding Dam Ch. Brandywine Tansu D'oro is shown with two of her champion children, Ch. Brandywine's Dusty Dandy, C.D.X. and Brandywine's Princess D'oro, C.D. Owned by Ben and Bonnie Gikis of Los Altos Hills, California.

Am., Can., Ch. Amberac's Asterling Aruba (Ch. Gold Coast Here Comes the Sun, C.D. ex Sunahaven's Amberac's Aruba). A Best in Show bitch and mother of a Best in Show bitch, Aruba is a member of the G.R.C.A. Show Dog Hall of Fame, one of only eight to achieve this honor. Owned by Mary Wuestenberg.

Ch. Pepperhill Yankee O'Goldtrak (Am., Can. Ch. Pepperhill's Basically Bear ex Goldtrak Charlie's L'il Angel, C.D.). One of the most recent Pepperhill champions, "Yankee" is shown winning his fourth "major" under judge Mrs. Bernard Ziessow. Owned and handled by the author and Ann T. Hall of Agawam, Massachusetts. Photo: Steven Klein.

137

can be unwise on two counts. First, a puppy kept away from other dogs does not build up a natural immunity against all the things with which he will come in contact at dog shows, so it is actually wiser to keep his vaccinations up to date and then let him grow used to being with other dogs and dog owners. Second, a dog who never goes among strangers and unknown places or unfamiliar dogs may grow up with a shyness or timidity of spirit in unfamiliar places that will cause you real problems as his show career grows near.

Keep your dog's coat in immaculate condition with frequent brushing and, if he gets dirty, occasional bathing. When you do bathe the dog, follow the instructions given in earlier chapters in this book. Remember to keep the nails short to avoid splaying the toes. Don't forget to trim the dewclaws. Be especially careful to comb out any knots that may develop in your dog's feathering before they get so large that they can be removed only by cutting.

Assuming that you will be handling the dog yourself, or even if he will be handled by a professional, spend a few moments of each day practicing stacking, or posing, your dog as you have seen the exhibitors do at shows. Teach him to hold this position once you have set him up to your satisfaction. Make this learning period as pleasant as you can by being firm yet providing lavish praise when he responds correctly. Teach your dog to gait at your left side, trotting at a moderate speed on a loose lead as the Standard suggests. When he has mastered these basics at home, seek a show-handling class in your area (usually run by a local kennel club) and continue your work. With the younger puppy, the special "puppy kindergarten" classes offered by some clubs can be an excellent help in the learning process for both you and the dog.

If you haven't done so already, accustom your dog to being in his crate. He should learn to relax when in it no matter what is going on outside of it. If you have used your crate for house training, then this will be no problem at all.

A show dog's teeth must be kept clean and white, free of tartar. Hard dog biscuits or dry, kibbled dog food can help in this and will not upset the nutritional balance of his regular food. If there is a yellow tartar accumulation on your dog's teeth, see that it is removed either by your veterinarian or, if you know how to do it and have the proper tools, by yourself. Meat bones are not suitable for a show dog as they tend to wear down and damage tooth enamel and may splinter and become lodged in his throat.

Shown going Best of Breed at the 1979 Central Regional Specialty is Ch. Sun Dance's Rainmaker (Ch. Wochica's Okeechobee Jake ex Ch. Sun Dance's Contessa). This G.R.C.A. Show Dog Hall of Fame dog is owned by Tony and Penny D'Alessandro of Paradise, Pennsylvania. He was Best of Opposite Sex at the 1979 G.R.C.A. National Specialty. Photo: Thacker.

Remember to make each training session with the younger puppy short and fun. You want your dog to love to be shown, which means that it should be a fun game for him at all times, so long as he is behaving. The difference between the big winner and the dog who just does well is often one of the dog's attitude. Leash train the puppy gently. Teach him to trot alongside or just ahead of your left leg. Keep him happy so that his tail is wagging as he moves. When he becomes tired or bored, stop for the day. Try to stop when he has done something right so that you can end each work session with praise rather than punishment. If you are getting frustrated with the dog's behavior, stop immediately before you get angry with him and yourself. At first, work the puppy on a soft show lead at least 3/8″ wide. Remember, when you stop gaiting, the dog should stand at your side, not sit, unless you have given him the command to sit.

The Standard calls for Goldens to be shown in "...hard working condition..." This cannot be accomplished in one day or week, but requires regular exercise on a daily basis. Do not over-tax a young puppy, but do not allow the older dog to become soft either, as it can take months to get a really soft dog in proper muscular condition. When you practice your grooming, remember that the Standard requires the coat to have a "natural appearance." This means that when you have finished any necessary trimming, the dog should not show any scissor marks on his coat and should not be over-trimmed. Ideally, when you are finished, the dog should look like he was never touched with a scissors. See the chapter on grooming for specifics.

Ch. Pepperhill Golden Pine Irish (Am., Can. Ch Pepperhill's Basically Bear ex Am., Can. Ch. Russo's Pepperhill Poppy). A Best of Breed winner, Irish was bred by the author. She is shown with co-owner, Nancy Kelly Belsaas.

Opposite page: *(Above)* Am., Can., Bda. Ch. Cummings Gold-Rush Charlie winning the Stud Dog Class at the G.R.C.A. National Specialty with two of his children, Ch. Gold-Rush's Great Teddy Bear, and Am., Can. Ch. Russo's Pepperhill Poppy. Charlie was owned by R. Ann and Larry Johnson. *(Below)* Ch. Sir Duncan of Woodbury at the 1981 Garden State Golden Retriever Club Specialty with two of his puppies, Ch. Jolly Speculator owned by Joyce Pederzini and John Lounsbury, and Rock Hill's Ramblin' Rose owned by Clarie Firestone. Duncan was owned by Lynne Lounsbury.

DOG SHOWS

A dog show is just a huge elimination contest. By paying your entry fee, you are asking to have the judge evaluate your dog based on the Standard. The judge will award placements to the dogs in the order of their overall quality (in his or her opinion) in relation to the other dogs in the ring. The dogs which, (again, in his or her opinion) come closest to the perfection called for in the Standard in comparison to the other dogs actually in the ring, will be placed highest.

There are three types of conformation shows that are approved by the American Kennel Club: the Match Show—the least formal of the three—; the All Breed Show; and the Independent Specialty Show. At various times in a dog's show career, he will probably be entered in all three of these kinds of shows. Let's see what each show is and how it works.

THE MATCH SHOW

Your show dog's first experience in the ring (other than at a training class) should be in match show competition for several reasons. First, this type of event is intended as a learning experience for both the dog and the exhibitor. You will not feel embarrased or out of place no matter how poorly your puppy may behave or how inept your initial efforts at handling may be, as you will find others there with the same problems. The important thing is that you get the puppy out and into a show ring where the two of you can practice and learn together.

Only on rare occasions, usually at "A" matches, is it necessary to make show entries in advance, and even those "B" matches that have a pre-entry policy will usually accept them at the door as well. Therefore, you need not plan several weeks ahead, as you must with a point show, but can go when the mood strikes you. There is also a vast difference in cost. Match show entry fees normally run from three to four dollars, while entry fees at point shows today average between thirteen and fifteen dollars. There is no sense in spending this amount of money until we have some idea of how the puppy will behave or how much more "pre-show" training is needed.

Match shows are frequently judged by professional handlers and experienced breeder/exhibitors who, in addition to making the awards, are happy to help new exhibitors with comments and advice on their puppies and their presentation of them. So, avail yourself of all these opportunities before heading out to the sophisticated world of the point shows.

ENTERING YOUR DOG AT A POINT SHOW

As previously mentioned, entries for American Kennel Club point shows must be made in advance. This must be done on an official entry blank of the show-giving club or an A.K.C. approved entry form. The entry must then be filed either personally or by mail with the show superintendent or show secretary (if the event is being run by the club members alone and a superintendent has not been hired) in time to reach its destination prior to the published closing date and time, or the filling of the quota. These entries must be completed carefully, must be signed by the owner of the dog or the owner's agent (usually a professional handler), and must be accompanied by the entry fee. Otherwise, it will not be accepted and you will not be entered in the show. Remember, it is not *when* the entry leaves your hands that counts, but the *time and date of its arrival* at the superintendent's or show secretary's office. If you are relying on the mail, remember to allow ample time in order to avoid disappointment.

A dog must be entered at a dog show in the name of the actual owner at the time of the entry closing. If a previously registered dog has been acquired by a new owner, it must be entered in that person's name regardless of whether the new owner has or has not actually received the registration certificate from A.K.C. indicating the change of ownership. On the entry form, state whether or not the transfer has been submitted to A.K.C. It goes without saying that you should submit this form promptly to A.K.C.

In filling out the entry form, print or type all the required information clearly, paying special attention to correct spelling of names, registration numbers, etc. If you are showing a puppy, be careful to indicate which puppy class the dog is eligible for, if the puppy classes are divided by age. Use carbon paper to make the task easier when you are filling out a number of forms, but be sure to sign each blank individually.

POINT SHOWS

The following are the classes offered at point shows. Consider entering the classes other than Open until your dog has had sufficient ring experience to look really good.

The Puppy Class is for dogs or bitches who are at least six months of age and are under twelve months, were whelped (born) in the U.S.A., and are not champions. The age of the dog is calculated up to and including the first day of the show. For example, a dog whelped on

Winning the Brood Bitch class at the 1973 Central Regional Specialty of G.R.C.A. under judge Virgil Johnson is Am., Can. Ch. Kyrie Jaen Cobi, U.D., W.C., Can. C.D.X., W.C. (left) with her children Am., Can., Bda. Ch. Kyrie Loch Cambeauly, Am., Can. C.D.X., Bda. C.D., Am. W.C. (center) and Am., Can. Ch. Kyrie London by Diel, Am., Can. C.D.X., Am. W.C. (right). Photo: Martin Booth.

January 1st is eligible to compete in the Puppy Class at a show the first day of which is July 1st of the same year, and may continue to compete in the Puppy Class up to and including a show the first day of which is December 31st, but is NOT eligible to compete in a Puppy Class at a show starting on or after January 1st of the following year.

This is the class you should enter your puppy in at first. In it, a certain allowance will be made for the fact that these are puppies. An immature dog or one displaying less than perfect showmanship will be less severely penalized in this class than in, for instance, Open. Quite likely the others in the class will be suffering from the same problems too. In entering a Puppy Class, be sure to check the premium list carefully as some shows offer a reduced entry fee for puppies and some divide the Puppy Class into two sections, one for six- to nine-month old-dogs and one for nine- to twelve-month-olds.

The Novice Class is for dogs six months old and older, whelped in the United States or Canada, who, prior to the official closing date for entries, had NOT won three first prizes in the Novice Class or any first prize in any class other than Puppy, or one or more points towards championship. The provisions for this class are confusing to many people, which may be one reason that more exhibitors do not enter in it. A dog may win any number of first prizes in a Puppy Class and still compete in Novice. He may place second, third, or fourth not only in Novice on an unlimited number of occasions, but in any other class as well, and still remain eligible for Novice.

In determining whether or not a dog may be entered in the Novice Class, keep in mind the fact that previous wins are calculated according to the published official closing date for acceptance of entries. If in the interim between the time you made the entry and the official closing date your dog makes a win that causes him to become ineligible for Novice, you must change your class immediately to another by contacting the superintendent or show secretary, first by phone and then in writing to confirm the change. The Novice Class always seems to have the least entries of any, and is therefore a splendid practice ground for you and your young dog while you are gaining a feel for being in the ring.

Bred-By-Exhibitor Class is for dogs whelped in the United States or, if individually registered by A.K.C., for dogs whelped in Canada, that are six months of age or older, are not champions, and that are wholly owned or co-owned by the person or spouse of the person who was the breeder or one of the breeders of record for the dog. Dogs entered in this class must be handled in the class by an owner or a member of the immediate family of an owner. A.K.C. defines members of the immediate family as husband, wife, mother, father, son, daughter, sister or brother. This class is really the breeder's showcase and the one which breeders should enter with particular pride to show off their achievements. At Specialty shows it is often the most hotly contested class.

American-Bred Class is for all dogs, excepting champions, six months of age or older that were whelped in the United States by reason of a mating which took place in the United States. Dogs bred or whelped in Canada are not eligible.

The Open Class is for any dog six months of age or older, and has no further restrictions. Dogs with championship points compete in it, as do dogs who are imported, as well as any other dog. Dogs who have completed their championship requirements may also be shown in this class, but rarely are. For some reason, this class is the favorite of exhibitors who are out to win. Competition in Open is, therefore, usually the stiffest, making it the most difficult class to win. There is something to be said for entering one of the other classes where there is less competition, winning it and thus earning a second opportunity of gaining the judge's approval by returning to the ring in the Winners Class. This can sometimes be the more effective strategy, especially at a Specialty show.

You cannot enter the Winners Class. You must earn the right to compete in it by first winning one of the other classes. No dog which has been defeated in any one of these classes is eligible to compete for winners, and every dog which has been awarded a blue ribbon in one of them and who has not been defeated in another *must* be shown. This is one reason that it is not a good idea to enter a dog in more than one regular class at the same show. Following the selection of Winners Dog or Winners Bitch, that dog leaves the ring and the dog or bitch awarded second in that class, unless previously defeated by another dog or bitch in another class, re-enters the ring to compete for Reserve Winners. This award means that the dog or bitch selected is standing in reserve should, through any technicality when the awards are checked at A.K.C., the dog awarded Winners be disqualified or declared ineligible. In that case, the dog placed Reserve is moved up to Winners and receives the championship points.

Winners Dog and Winners Bitch are the only awards which carry points towards championship. The number of points awarded is based

Winners Bitch at the 1975 G.R.C.A. National Specialty and later a multiple Best of Breed winner, this is Ch. Cloverdale's Sweet Sadie (Ch. Misty Morn's Sunset, C.D., T.D., W.C. ex High Farms Beau Brittany). Handled here by Bob Stebbins, she is a G.R.C.A. Outstanding Dam and owned by Richard and Jane Zimmerman and Bob Stebbins. Photo: John Ashbey.

Opposite page: *(Above)* Ch. Amberac's Sherza Q.T. (Ch. Amberac Ramala Rambling Rogue ex Ch. Amberac Yul B Ritzi). A Specialty Best of Winners bitch who completed her championship in just seven shows, is shown going Best of Winners at the White River G.R.C.A. Specialty in 1982. Owned by Ellen and Leon Manke of Hartland, Wisconsin. Photo: Martin Booth. *(Below)* Ch. Copper Lee Gold-Rush Apollo (Ch. Gold-Rush Skyrocket ex Gold-Rush Sara Lee). Apollo is a Show Dog Hall of Fame member. Bred and co-owned by Judy Breuer of Glen Mills, Pennsylvania and R. Ann Johnson of Princeton, New Jersey. He is handled by Janet Bunce. Photo: John Ashbey.

on the number of dogs or bitches actually in competition (rather than the number entered for competition) and is scaled from one to five points, the latter being the most awarded at any one show. For example, in the Northeast in 1982, points were based on the following numbers of Goldens actually shown: one point, at least four dogs or three bitches; two points, 11 dogs or 11 bitches, three points (a "major") 18 dogs or 20 bitches; four points, 26 dogs or 27 bitches; five points, 41 dogs or 42 bitches. Points are based on the number of dogs defeated of the winner's *own sex*. Three-, four-, or five-point wins are considered "majors." In order to complete its championship, a Golden must have won two majors under two different judges, plus at least one point from a third judge, and a total of fifteen points from all its wins. When your dog has gained a total of fifteen points as described above, a Championship Certificate will be issued to you and your dog's name will be published in the Champions of Record list in the *American Kennel Gazette Pure-Bred Dogs*, the official publication of the American Kennel Club. It will also be published in an issue of the G.R.C.A. *Yearbook*, which lists all new title holders in each bi-annual issue.

The scale of points for each breed is worked out by A.K.C. and reviewed annually, at which time the numbers required in competition for a given number of points may be raised or lowered (or remain the same) based on the numbers of Goldens shown in the previous year in the states covered by each zone. The new scale of points is published annually in the April issue of the *Gazette*, and the current ratings for every breed within the area of the show are always published in the front of every show catalogue.

When a dog or bitch is awarded Best of Winners, its championship points are, for that show, calculated on the basis of which sex had the greater number of points. For example, if there are two points in dogs and three points in bitches, and the dog goes Best of Winners, then both the dog and the bitch receive three points. Should the Best of Winners also be awarded Best of Breed, additional points may be available if there were champions shown as well. This works as follows: if your dog or bitch is awarded Best of Breed and in so doing defeats enough additional dogs and bitches to increase the number of dogs defeated high enough to raise that number to the next highest point category, he will receive those extra points. In other words, if the Winners dog defeated seventeen dogs in the classes and there were two champions present when he won Best of Breed, he has now defeated nineteen dogs. In the Northeast, this would be enough dogs to raise the number of points awarded from two to three—a major.

If your dog goes Best of Opposite Sex after going Winners, and in so doing defeats champions of his or her own sex, these additional dogs are credited as dogs defeated and may be enough to raise the number of points awarded to him at the show.

Moving further along, should your dog win the Sporting Group from the classes (that is, won either Winners Dog or Winners Bitch prior to winning Best of Breed), he will receive points based on the greatest number awarded to any Sporting Dog that day. And, should you have the kind of day that every exhibitor dreams of, and your dog goes Best in Show, the dog will receive the highest number of points awarded in any breed at the show.

Best of Breed competition consists of Winners Dog and the Winners Bitch, who automatically compete on the strength of these awards, plus any dogs and bitches entered specifically for this class, for which Champions of Record (dogs whose championships have been confirmed by A.K.C.) and dogs who, according to their owner's records, have completed the requirements for their championship but have not yet received confirmation from A.K.C., are eligible. Since July, 1980, dogs which, according to their owner's records, have completed the championship requirements after the closing of entries for the show but whose championships are unconfirmed, may be transferred from one of the regular classes to Best of Breed competition—provided this transfer is made by the show superintendent or show secretary at least one half hour prior to the start of *any* judging at that show.

At Specialty Shows, where dogs of only one breed are shown, the highest award offered is Best of Breed. This is considered a most prestigious award and is coveted by most breeders. At an All Breed Show, your dog continues in competition until he is defeated. Best of Breed winners are entitled to compete in group competition. Goldens go into the Sporting Group. Unlike in Canada, this is not required, but is a privilege that exhibitors value. Your Best of Breed Golden is the only Golden who can represent the breed in the Group at that show. Missing this opportunity of taking your dog in for Group competition is foolish, as it is there that the general public is most likely to notice Goldens and become interested in our breed and learning about it. If your dog is the winner of the Sporting Group, he is required to compete in Best in Show competition. Should you have the great fortune of winning Best in Show, your dog will be the only dog undefeat-

Ch. Malagold Summer Encore (Ch. Hunt's Finnegan ex Ch. Malagold Svea) is shown winning the Sporting Group. A full brother to Ch. Malagold Summer Chant, both dogs are Top Ten Goldens.

Ch. Krishna-HGL Ragtime Rhythm (Ch. Wochica's Okeechobee Jake ex Ch. Krishna's Klassic Melody of HGL) shown going Best of Winners in 1979. "Rags" is owned by Joan Young of Concord, California. He is a "Top Ten" dog and Specialty winner and a grandson of Am., Can., Mex. Ch. Cal-Vo's Happy Ambassador, CD.

Sitting amid some of his trophies with his proud owners is Ch. Camelot's Noble
Fella, C.D.X. (Ch. Wochica's Okeechobee Jake ex Hammerlock's Amber Topaz,
C.D.X.). A G.R.C.A. Show Dog Hall of Fame member, Fella recently qualified as an
Outstanding Sire as well when his fifth puppy completed its title. Fella is owned
by Margaret Zonghetti of South Salem, New York and Kay Bickford of Arizona.
Photo: Stephen Klein.

ed on that day, a tremendous honor and the goal of every exhibitor's dreams.

Non-regular classes are sometimes included at All Breed Shows and are nearly always offered at Specialties. These include the Veterans Classes. These are for dogs and bitches of a stipulated age (eight years in Golden Specialties) on the day day of the show. This class is judged on the quality of the dogs and the winners compete for Best of Breed. Any dog or bitch who is old enough may compete in this class, including Champions of Record. A number of dogs have won this class and then gone on to win Best of Breed at a Specialty. The point is not to pick the oldest dog, as some judges seem to believe, but to pick the best Golden Retriever, just as in the regular classes.

Another non-regular class included at Specialty Shows for Goldens is the Field Trial Class. This is for dogs or bitches who have earned at least a Working Certificate or placed in a licensed Field Trial. Champions of Record who meet the field qualifications may enter this class. As with the Veterans Class, dogs who win this class are not eligible to compete for Winners, but are eligible for Best of Breed.

The winners of other non-regular classes are not eligible to compete for Best of Breed. At Specialty Shows, these include the Stud Dog and Brood Bitch Classes, which are judged on the quality of the puppies produced by and accompanying the sire or dam. Two puppies follow their parent and they must be entered in another class at the show or entered just for the Stud Dog or Brood Bitch Class. Here the quality of the Stud Dog or Brood Bitch is beside the point—it is the quality of their youngsters that counts, and the quality of both are averaged to decide which sire or dam is the most consistent producer. Then there is the Brace Class (which at All-Breed shows moves up to Best Brace in Group and Best Brace in Show), this being judged on the similarity and evenness of appearance of the two members of the brace. In other words, the two dogs should look like identical twins in size, color, and conformation and should move together almost like a single dog. One person handles a brace and the dogs comprising the brace must be of *identical* ownership. The same applies to the Team Class, which is occasionally offered, except that four dogs are involved and, if necessary, two handlers.

Finally, some Specialties offer Sweepstakes Classes. These classes are judged by a different judge than the ones doing all the other breed classes at the show. Often a breeder or professional handler is invited to officiate a Sweepstakes. Prize money is offered to the winners, but

Shown winning Best of Breed at the 1968 G.R.C.A. National Specialty is Am., Can. Ch. Sun Dance's Vagabond Lover, C.D.X. (Ch. Sun Dance's Bronze, C.D. ex Ch. Sprucewood's Glamour Girl, C.D.X.). Bred by Violet Topmiller, this dog was a G.R.C.A. Show Dog Hall of Fame member and an Outstanding Sire. He was owned by his breeder and Laura Ellis Kling, now of Laurell Kennels. The judge is the late Percy Roberts. Photo: E.H. Frank.

Jermac's Autumn Mist (Ch. Misty Morn's Sunset, C.D., T.D., W.C. ex Gold Cloud's Apricot Brandy, C.D.), Hawaii's only G.R.C.A. Outstanding Dam. "Misty" was bred to Ch. Wochica's Okeechobee Jake and two pups from her litter completed their championship requirements. A third pup from a litter sired by Ch. Jake's Hanalei Valey Jem completed its championship to make Misty an Outstanding Dam. She is owned by Joan Luria of Kailua, Hawaii and Susan Taylor.

Can. Ch. HGL's Golden Pine Gibson Solo, Am., Can. C.D., W.C. (Am., Can. Ch. Golden Pine's Courvoisier, Am., Can. C.D.X., W.C., Am. W.C.X. ex Ch. HGL's Happy Charisma of Cal-Vo, C.D., W.C.). A top Canadian Stud Dog, he is the sire of the only living Canadian Dual Champion, Ch. Carolee's Something Special II. He was owned by Shirley Goodman of Ambercroft Kennels, Streetsville, Ontario, Canada.

Ch. Gold-Rush's Lightnin' (Ch. Gold-Rush's Great Teddy Bear ex Ch. Wochica's Gold-Rush Bonanza). A G.R.C.A. Outstanding Sire and multiple Specialty winner owned by R. Ann Johnson, Gold-Rush Kennels, Princeton, New Jersey. Photo: John Ashbey.

Ch. Southern's Gold-Rush Traveler (Am., Can., Bda. Ch. Cummings Gold-Rush Charlie ex Ch. Golden Pines Glorybe's Angel). Traveler is shown finishing his championship with a Sporting Group First. He is a member of the G.R.C.A. Show Dogs Hall of Fame and an Outstanding Sire. Owned by Clark and Colleen Williams of Spartanburg, South Carolina.

wins do not carry championship points. Entries are limited to dogs over six months of age and under eighteen months, and are usually divided into three classes for each sex: six to nine months, nine to twelve months and twelve to eighteen months. Sometimes this latter class is further divided into twelve to fifteen months and fifteen to eighteen months to reflect the great amount of maturing a Golden does between the ages of twelve and eighteen months. Entries are made, for an additional fee, at the same time and on the same form as for regular classes at the show.

Specialing (showing your dog once he or she has completed its championship) is not for every dog who completes his title. Only those very few dogs who are really outstanding both in terms of their conformation and their showmanship will do well. Your dog must love to be in the ring. Although there has been some change over the past four years or so, it is primarily the male Golden who does well in this competition. With a very few notable exceptions, the ladies (unfairly) seem to usually be considered by the judge only for Best of Opposite Sex awards. A look at the Show Dog Hall of Fame list at the end of this book will prove the point. Between the time Goldens were first eligible to be shown in 1932 and 1981, only three bitches were able to achieve this honor; they were Champion Des Lacs Lassie in 1949, Champion Chee-Chee of Sprucewood in 1952, and Champion Russo's Pepperhill Poppy in 1979. During the same time period, well over 100 male Goldens achieved this honor. However, this may be changing a bit since four more bitches qualified during 1982 alone and at least one more in 1983. Still, should you decide to campaign your bitch in Specials, she will truly have to be a one-in-a-million bitch in order to do well.

PRE-SHOW PREPARATIONS FOR YOUR DOG AND YOU

The preparation of the items you will need as a dog show exhibitor should not be left for the last moment. They should be planned and arranged at least several days in advance of the big one, in order for you to remain calm and relaxed as the countdown starts.

The importance of a crate has already been mentioned, and I hope it is already a part of your equipment. Of almost equal importance is the grooming table, which very possibly you have already purchased for use at home. You should take it along with you to the show since your Golden will need last minute touches before entering the ring. If you do not already own one, folding tables with rubber tops are made

A G.R.C.A. Outstanding Dam, this is Ch. Malagold Svea (Ch. Appolo of Yeo ex Malagold Beckwith Bootes) owned by Connie Gerstner of Malagold Kennels in DeForest, Wisconsin. Svea is shown going Best of Breed at the 1975 Badger Kennel Club show. Photo: Olson.

Ch. Sun Dance's Taffeta Doll, C.D.X. (Sun Dance's Sand Piper ex Sun Dance's Fancy Pants). A G.R.C.A. Outstanding Dam shown with Lisa Schultz. Photo: E.H. Frank.

Ch. Nordly's Australis. The first Australian-bred and whelped Golden to attain an American Championship, this dog is of pure English bloodlines, combining Camrose and Westley lines. He is owned by Karl and Lei Taft of Kailua, Hawaii.

Am., Can. Ch. Kyrie Daemon, C.D.X., W.C., Can. C.D. (Des Lacs Delaware ex Ch. Gayhaven Harmony). A grandson of the top-winning Golden bitch, Ch. Chee-Chee of Sprucewood, Daemon was a G.R.C.A. Outstanding Sire of fourteen champions owned by Patricia and Joan Nazark and bred by Marcia Schlehr.

specifically for this purpose and are available, as is most grooming equipment, from vendors at dog shows. You will also need a sturdy tack box in which to carry your equipment and grooming tools. This should include brushes, combs, scissors, nail cutters, whatever you use for last minute clean-ups, first aid equipment for both you and your dog, any medications you might need, and anything else that you are in the habit of using on your dog, including a leash and collar or two of the type you prefer, some well cooked and dried out liver or a small package of commercial dog treats to use for bait, a spray bottle of coat spray or water to dampen the dog's coat as you brush it out, etc. It is also a good idea to carry an absorbent towel or two in case your dog gets wet and you need to dry him.

Take a large thermos or cooler with ice and water, the largest you can accommodate, for your use and the dog's. Also take an extra jug of water and a water dish. If you plan to feed your dog at the show or will be away from home for more than a day, bring food with you so he can eat what he is used to.

You may or may not have a portable exercise pen. Personally, I think one is a must even if you have only one dog. While the shows do provide public ex-pen areas for the use of dogs, these are among the most likely places to have your dog come in contact with any illnesses which may be going around, and I feel that having your own ex-pen which is used only by your own dog is excellent protection. Your ex-pen can be useful in other ways as well. For example, it is an excellent place to put your dog when you are with him and wish to allow him more space than is available in his crate; when you are travelling, the ex-pen is a real convenience at motels and rest areas. These pens, too, are available at show concession stands and come in a variety of sizes and heights. Make sure to purchase one that is high enough to deter the dog from jumping out but not so high as to make cleaning up inside it difficult. A set of "pooper scoopers" should also be a part of your equipment for cleaning up after your dog, as well as a supply of plastic bags.

For yourself and members of your party, bring along folding chairs unless you enjoy standing, as these are rarely provided by show-giving clubs any more. Write your name on the chairs so that if you forget them they can be returned to you. Bring along food and drinks in a cooler since dog show food is expensive, usually not great, and often indigestible (although there are some exceptions to this). See that boots and raincoats are always with you as well as warm clothes and a change of shoes since the weather is often unpredictable.

In your car or van you should carry maps of the area. Have everything prepared the night before the show to expedite your departure and to help avoid forgetting anything in the rush to leave in the morning. In preparing your clothing, keep it simple and something that will not detract from your dog. Remember that you do not want your dog to blend into your clothing, making it harder for the judge to see him. Men are expected to wear a jacket and tie. In choosing your wardrobe remember that it is the dog you want to be the center of attention, not you. What you wear on your feet is most important since many types of footing may be encountered, including slippery floors or wet grass. Wear something that is comfortable and provides good traction, such as rubber-soled shoes. Women should always wear either flats or shoes with low heels for their own safety, especially if your dog likes to move out.

Finally, leave yourself plenty of time to get to the show site. If you have early judging, beware of heavy commuting traffic on the way to the show. The number of cars waiting to get into a show site can get amazingly heavy at the opening of a show and finding parking in the immediate area can be difficult. Without the added pressures, you'll be in a better humor to enjoy the day if your trip to the show is not fraught with panic over fear of not arriving in time!

IN THE RING

From the moment of your arrival at the show until after your dog has been judged, keep foremost in your mind the fact that he is your reason for being there and, therefore, he should be the center of your attention. Although you will have done all of your heavy grooming before the show, arrive early enough to have ample time for all those last minute touches that can make the difference in a dog's looking all right or great as he enters the ring. Be sure that he has had enough time to exercise, and that he has used the time to "go." A dog arriving in the ring and immediately using it as an ex-pen hardly makes a good impression on the judge. Further, a dog who has not been exercised often will not move properly when gaited.

When you reach ringside, ask the steward for your arm band and anchor it firmly in place on your left arm. Make sure that you are there when your class is called into the ring. The fact that you have picked up your arm band does not guarantee that the judge will wait for you. He has a full schedule of judging that he would like to complete on

162

Lined up practicing for future careers as show dogs, seven of thirteen pups whelped by Ch. Pepperhill Golden Pine Irish. The litter was sired by Am., Can. Ch. Golden Pine's Courvoisier, C.D.X., W.C., owned by Nancy and Dean Belsaas. This is not an abnormally large litter for a Golden. Photo: Warren Cook.

A good example of a bitch that can do well in the breed ring and in the field, this is Ch. Topbrass Ad-Libs Bangor*** (Dual Ch. A.F.C. Ronaker's Novato Cain ex Valentine Torch of Topbrass, W.C.) winning the Field Trial Bitch Class at the 1976 G.R.C.A. National Specialty. Owners, Joseph and Jackie Mertens, Elgin, Illinois.

time. Even though you may be nervous, try to assume an air of self-confidence. Remember that this is a hobby to be enjoyed! Your feelings will be telegraphed down the lead to the dog, so the calmer you feel the better your dog is apt to do.

Always show your dog with an air of pride. If you make mistakes in presenting him, don't worry about it. Next time you will do better. Do not permit the presence of more experienced handlers to intimidate you. After all, they too were once newcomers.

Usually, judging routine starts when the judge asks that all the dogs in the class be gaited in a circle around the ring. During this period the judge is watching each dog as it moves, noting style, top line, reach and drive, head and tail carriage, and, most importantly, general balance and co-ordination. Keep your mind and your eye on your dog, moving him at his most becoming gait (which, of course, you have practiced extensively at home), keeping your place in line without coming too close to the exhibitor in front of you. Always keep your dog on the inside of the circle, between you and the judge, so that the judge's view of the dog is unobstructed. If the dog in front of you is moving too slowly, make the circle larger to give your dog more space to move or hold your dog back to slow him down when the judge is not looking at you, giving your dog room to move when the judge is looking.

Pose your dog calmly when it is your turn for the judge to go over him. If you are at the front of the line, go all the way to the end of the ring before starting to stack your dog, leaving sufficient room for those behind you to line up their dogs as requested by the judge. If you have watched previous classes, you will have an idea of where to start the line. If you are not at the head of the line but between other exhibitors, leave enough space ahead of your dog for the judge to examine him. The dogs should be spaced so that there is room for the judge to move about among them to see the dogs from all angles. In practicing to set up, or "stack" your dog, bear in mind the importance of doing so quickly and with dexterity. The judge has a schedule to meet and therefore will have only a few moments in which to evaluate your dog. You will help yours immeasurably to make a favorable impression if you are able to get him together in a minimum of time. Practicing in front of a mirror at home can be a big help in reaching this goal.

Listen carefully as the judge instructs you in the manner in which the dog is to be gaited. This may be straight down and back; down the ring, across and back in the shape of an upsidedown "L"; or in a tri-

Can. Ch. Goldenquest's Lucky Charm. Sired by Am., Can., Mex. Ch. Cal-Vo's Happy Ambassador, C.D., this dog is shown winning the Sporting Group, having previously won Best of Breed from the Open Class over an entry of 71 Goldens. Judge is the late Winifred Heckman. Photo: Roberts.

angle. The latter is the most popular pattern with the majority of judges, and requires that the dog be moved down the outer side of the ring to the first corner, across that end of the ring to the second corner, then back to the judge using the center of the ring in a diagonal line. Do this smoothly, without breaking the dog's stride by not making a circle in each corner if at all possible. Always pick yourself a marker at the far side of the ring and run toward it so that you will move your dog in a straight line.

It is impossible to overemphasize that the speed at which you gait your dog is tremendously important. Considerable thought and study, plus experimentation at home, should be given to the matter. The dog should move at a trot, and it is well to remember that gaiting correctly is *not* a matter of who can move the fastest, but which dog can move the best. Speed does not necessarily give the best movement. At home, have someone move the dog for you at different speeds so that you can tell which shows him off to best advantage. The most becoming action, almost invariably, is seen at a moderate speed, head up and top line holding. Teach your dog to move correctly on a loose lead as the Standard suggests. Stringing him up by keeping the lead tight can throw off an otherwise correct gait. Again, remember to move the dog in a straight line so that he does not appear to sidewind.

As you bring the dog back to the judge, stop him a few feet away and be certain that he is standing in a becoming position. Use your bait to have the dog show the judge an alert expression. A reminder: take your unused liver or treats out of the ring with you. Don't just drop them on the floor where some other dog will try to get to it. Also, if you use a ball or squeaky toy to bait your dog, do not use it near another dog who is being examined by the judge. To distract the other dog's attention is unfair.

When the awards are made, accept yours graciously, no matter how you may actually feel about it. What's done is done, and arguing with a judge or stomping out of the ring is not only useless, but is a reflection on your lack of sportsmanship. If you don't agree with the judge, then don't show under him again. Be courteous, congratulate the winner if your dog was defeated, and try not to show your disappointment. By the same token, please be a gracious winner, which somehow seems to be more difficult for some people. Remember, there will be another day and another show. Perhaps next time will be your turn.

Finally, remember that not every Golden should be shown. The competition in Goldens in most parts of the country is quite keen, and

A recent Top Ten Golden, this is Ch. Malagold Summer Chant (Ch. Hunt's Fin-negan ex Ch. Malagold Svea). Chant represents several generations of Malagold breeding. Owned by Malagold Kennels of DeForest, Wisconsin. Shown here winning Best of Breed, handled by Connie Gerstner. Photo: Ritter.

only the best specimens stand a chance of doing well. If you purchased your dog as a pet, even from a top-flight show kennel, the odds are that he is not of a quality that will do well in the show ring. If you are unsure of the quality of your dog, there are a number of ways that you can ascertain the potential your dog has as a show dog. First, ask a few experienced breeders to independently evaluate your dog for you, making sure that they understand that you truly want an honest opinion (if you don't, do not ask!). Second, you can ask a reputable and experienced professional handler who has successfully shown a number of Goldens for their opinion. Finally, you can try showing your dog at match shows. If you do well, then try point shows; if not, then take your dog home and love him, for he still is a wonderful pet!

Goldens and children seem to go naturally together. . . even if they're interested in different things at times.

Chapter 10

The Junior and the Golden

by Nancy Kelly Belsaas and Dean Belsaas

This chapter is about young people and Golden Retrievers. It is partly about Junior Handling, but is mostly about the many activities available for the junior and the Golden. Although both young and old desire a companion dog when they select a Golden as their breed, beyond that common desire other motives often differ between the two.

An adult may have already decided that the dog is to be a hunting companion, or that the suspense of conformation competition is the most enjoyable. Others favor the training and discipline of obedience and tracking. Usually, the adult preference is based on past experiences and a desire to continue or expand on that pleasure, sometimes to take advantage of the multipurpose characteristics of the Golden.

The junior often just wants a dog as a diversion or companion without the benefit of experience to know why a Golden Retriever has been the choice, wise though it may be. What follows is advice from a Junior Handler who chose Goldens, who succeeded in competition by winning the title Champion Junior Handler of the United States; and one who since has enjoyed other breeds but still remains dedicated to training and exhibiting that she first chose and showed to the title of Champion Junior Handler at Westminster Kennel Club.

Conformation Junior Handling is but one of the possibilities open to juniors interested in working with their dogs. There are age limits on Junior Handling, but the junior this chapter is about could be from ten years to sixteen, or from four to twenty-four. This is about learning regardless of age, for there are no limits to learning. For a start, let us consider the multipurpose nature of the Golden Retriever. The activities described are in a sequence beginning with that in which the role of the handler is of greatest significance, and ending with the dog's role being superior.

Junior Handling in the conformation ring is a unique endeavor in dog competition, for it is the handler who is judged, and the dog is merely a stage prop. Competition is within an age group (and is sometimes further divided by gender) and is divided into inexperienced (Novice) and experienced (Open) categories. The Junior Handler is judged on presentation of the dog in a manner to knowledgeably emphasize the dog's better characteristics. He or she must know the Breed Standard well, not only to display the dog's better aspects, but to be able to answer specific questions the judge might ask concerning that Standard and dogs in general. The judge will select those handlers whose presentation and knowledge are better.

In Obedience, the dog and the handler are more a team than in any other form of competition. Judging is according to strict performance standards, which is the reason that a high premium is placed on teamwork. Training of this team of dog and handler is rigorous in order to achieve a competitive edge. While I shall not comment on specific training methods, much of what follows on how to compete in any discipline applies more to the area of obedience than any other. In the obedience contest of training and performance, the Golden Retriever has no equal.

Conformation judging differs from Obedience in that the dog is judged rather than the performance of a team of dog and handler. If there has been previous experience in Junior Handling, the junior may have an advantage over many adult handlers, and better knowledge of the Breed Standard can lead to a better presentation. The dog is compared to the breed standard, not to other dogs, which is why knowing the standard and presenting the dog accordingly is so important to handling the dog, no matter what your age. The popularity of Goldens results in a large number of competitors, but it is quality in the dog supported by quality handling that earns the judge's selection.

Field Trials are a natural development from the original purpose of the breed, that of a hunting dog. Tests are designed to resemble a hunting situation, and the dog should demonstrate trained natural talent in the tests, which are graded by the judge. The dogs are in competition, but subtle handling techniques and handler knowledge will help the Golden if training of dog and handler has been thorough, and if they are a confident team able to communicate. To be really competitive in trials requires the most rigorous training, dedication, and a great amount of time. Rather than licensed trials, it is the Working Certificate and Working Certificate Excellent tests sanctioned by the Golden Retriever Club of America which attract more juniors and handlers training Goldens in other areas of competition. These tests are intended to determine whether the dog has retained the basic retriever aptitude for which he was originally bred. The training it requires is the basic work for a hunting dog prior to each hunting season and for a young Golden before learning more formalized hunting methods.

Tracking completes the progression from events which rely on the handler's ability and talent for this event, which is a test of the dog's ability alone, with the handler just following the dog's lead. All the elements common to preparation for all the previously mentioned activities are also necessary to Tracking, but when the test time arrives, the dog is solely responsible for the results of the competition. The handler is only there to hold the trailing end of the tracking line. The test is similar for all breeds and although hounds may have a sensory advantage, no retriever breed can match the Golden's record.

One can conclude that, for a junior handler, there is no more versatile breed than a Golden Retriever. The opportunities usually exceed the amount of available time, and the first step is to choose those activities that are preferred. Junior Handling and Conformation exhibiting are so similar that they may be attempted simultaneously as a single activity, for the preparation is very similar for both. Tracking is complementary to Obedience, but since training differs, they are usually approached as separate endeavors. Basic field work and its training methods will complement most other activities without difficulty. The choice made will, however, have a bearing on the choice of a Golden puppy, and it is wise to choose your preference before being forced to accept the preference of a dog you already have.

Choosing a dog before deciding what you wish to do with it is just one example of taking things out of order. Remember that competing with a Golden is a learning process, and the most successful competitors have followed a logical sequence in that process. The junior must learn and the Golden must learn, each at its own pace, so that the experience is enjoyable for both. Be aware that the Golden Retriever is very quick to learn, and that the handler must be ahead of the dog, or the dog will be training the handler!

Once you have some preference for competitive activity in mind, the best way to start is by attending the events previously described. The purpose of this is twofold: OBSERVE the handlers and Goldens in the competitive routine in order to learn that routine. DISCUSS the event with exhibitors or knowledgeable observers in the gallery, asking questions about what you have observed and the reasons for a specific routine. Finally, the serious junior competitor will get a reading list of material about the breed and about training methods in the area of competition chosen.

It is wise to attend an event of every type of activity possible. Preferably, the junior will have the opportunity to witness all types, for the prospect of competition will thus be improved, and the scope of expert advice available will be much broader. During this time of exploration, the reading material is also studied, not just for retained knowledge, but also to determine the best sources of information such as training methods, which can be reconsulted and followed later.

Gradually, decisions will be made on the activities that the junior prefers. By going back and observing more of these events, friendships are naturally formed, and this is a most important part of juniors competition. Fellowship within the group of juniors and with Golden fanciers is good, and the mutual enjoyment of our breed is more than a side benefit; it is the cement of the group of breeder/exhibitors who are dedicated to maintaining and improving a breed they cherish. Although breeder/exhibitors are in competition with one another and their opinions and directions therefore vary, their goals are usually similar and the junior will find their help invaluable. It is a fortunate junior indeed who discovers a breeder/exhibitor who quickly becomes a friend, who is eager to coach and advise, who shares a preference for the same activities that the junior is interested in, who lives locally, and who has sufficient expertise to challenge the junior to accomplishments others will recognize.

Few juniors have achieved significant success without the help of experience. The experience borrowed from an accomplished breeder/exhibitor should be used to help planning. The help of such a person can be invaluable in assisting the selection of a puppy.

A borrowed dog is an advantage to seize. It may be the mentor described above or another breeder/exhibitor who has too many dogs to train adequately or who needs help in training who provides the dog. So much can be learned in helping another trainer of Goldens that it is often wise to postpone selecting your own puppy in order to gain the advantage of additional experience. Any offer to assist in training should be accepted eagerly, and if competitive handling is possible, a gift has been given to the junior that should not be undervalued. Even if a competitive environment does not exist, this is the time to place your hands on other dogs to rehearse handling techniques before training of your own puppy is attempted—and great emphasis is implied in this statement.

If you are unable to find the perfect mentor, which is not unlikely, a combination of advisors can be sought. An experienced trainer close to home is desirable. Training together is a significant advantage. Training classes are desirable even for the experienced trainer, for the young dog is exposed to a mock environment of the competitive scene in this way.

It is now time to choose your puppy. Rushing into this decision, departing from good sequence, or the failure to plan well can affect your future progress, so take your time. Choosing a Golden puppy is a subject in which every advisor will wish to assist. The choice is complex, and the advice should be carefully evaluated. Since specific goals are involved in making the selection, the only advice offered here is that the temperament of the dog for the activities planned is paramount.

Once you have made your selection, the training of the handler and the dog will follow. No specific suggestions are made here because no one technique works for everyone. The well-prepared junior will be ready to adapt those techniques already learned to suit the dog involved in the training process.

The only element lacking in the process described here is the setting of goals. Winning at Westminster, or earning a Dual Championship are dreams. Goals are realistic and attainable, and a timetable is included. Goals should also be flexible to allow for early achievement in one activity and training delays in another. Goals are part of the plan for development of the Golden and the Junior Handler.

Several comments have been made here concerning the learning experience and the fellowship and friendship with Golden fanciers that develops over time. To some, that is a sacred institution, for they cherish the Golden Retriever to that extent. To place it all in adequate perspective, however, all this activity is a sport, and the rules of Good Sportsmanship should govern all. A good winner, a good loser, a good sport, is going to enjoy a lifelong experience with Golden Retrievers.

Even with the ultimate in portable jumps, Am., Can. Ch. Laurell's Especial Jason, U.D.T., W.C. (Ch. Major Gregory of High Farms ex Ch. Laurell's Amiable Caboose) sails over with ease. Pictured with his owner Cherie Berger of Meadowpond Goldens in Romeo, Michigan, Jason is a G.R.C.A. Show Dog Hall of Fame member and an Outstanding Sire.

174

Chapter 11

The Golden in the Obedience Ring

There is one area of competition that has been dominated by the Golden Retriever for a number of years. The breed excels in the obedience ring, and Goldens have been winning top obedience honors in numbers well out of proportion to their total number in relation to all dogs registered with the American Kennel Club. For example, from January 1 to November 6, 1982, there were 810 All Breed Obedience Trials held throughout the United States. Of these licensed trials, 205 (or more than 25%) were won by Goldens, that is, a Golden Retriever was Highest Scoring Dog in Trial. At that time, Goldens constituted only 4.9% of all breeds registered with A.K.C. Top obedience dogs compete regularly in the Gaines Obedience Competition all over the country and these trials have been similarly dominated by Goldens. The title of Obedience Trial Champion is a relatively new one. The first dog of any breed to earn it was a Golden, O.T. Champion Moreland's Golden Tonka, and the first conformation Champion to also hold the O.T. Champion title was another Golden Champion, O.T. Champion Russo's Gold-Rush Sensation. Interestingly, both were bitches, although both male and female Goldens have done equally well in the sport of Obedience.

The first Golden to earn a U.D. (Utility Dog) title was Goldwood Toby, owned and trained by Rachael Page Elliott, in 1947. Since that time, hundreds of other Goldens have completed this title and nearly one hundred have qualified for the G.R.C.A. Obedience Dog Hall of Fame by winning five or more High in Trial awards. The methods used for such successful training require much more space than is available here and there are a number of excellent books dealing with this subject. Therefore we shall not attempt to provide that information. The specifics of training are best left to these sources or a good local obedience training class in your area.

Am., Can. Ch. Bardfield Boomer, Am. U.D.T., W.C., Can. U.D., T.D.X. (Am., Can. Ch. Duckdown's Unpredictable, C.D. ex Sandia's Flaxen Babe, C.D.). A distinguished member of the G.R.C.A. Obedience Dog Hall of Fame and an Outstanding Sire, Boomer is the sire of more Obedience Trial Champions and High in trial winners than any other Golden Retriever. He was owned by Cherie Berger and Joanne Hurd of Romeo, Michigan.

Opposite page: *(Above)* O.T. Ch. Stardust Thunderbolt (Ch. Beaumaris Tangleloft Heath, C.D.X. ex Sunstream Amber Mist of Slade, U.D.). "Amber" is the winner of a number of High in Trial awards at specialties, including the 1982 National Specialty. She has sixteen High in Trial awards, one perfect score and seven scores of 199½. Amber is owned by Alfred Einhorn of Greenwood Lake, New York. *(Below)* Riverview King's Hopi, C.D.X., Highest-Scoring Dog in Trial at the 1971 G.R.C.A. National Specialty Obedience Trial. Owned by James and Sally Venerable of Huntley, Illinois.

In the chapter dealing with young puppies, we have already discussed some of the early basics of training your puppy, but they deserve some repetition here. Informal obedience training really begins on the day you first bring your puppy home and continues throughout his life. The young puppy is much like a blank book, its pages waiting to be filled. If left to his own devices, the puppy will quickly pick up bad habits which may become difficult to eliminate. On the other hand, the young pup is wide open to learning and will do so with surprising ease if patience and common sense are exercised. Begin with the basic commands of "no," "come," "sit," and "down." Always use one-word commands to avoid confusing the puppy. The use of the puppy's name should be reserved for commands that involve movement on his part . . . "Rover, come" . . . rather than "Rover, stay." In the latter case it is better to just say "stay." Never combine two commands until the dog has learned each separately; don't ask the dog to come and sit. First tell him to come, and once he has done so, then give him the "sit" command. A common mistake that many people make is to ask their dog to "sit down." These are really two conflicting commands . . . to "sit" is to sit and "down" means to lie down. Using the two commands together only confuses the puppy.

While informal training begins immediately, formal class training probably should not begin until the puppy is at least six months old. Puppies under six months are not yet sufficiently developed physically to deal with the stress of a class situation. By the time a puppy reaches six months or so, he will not only have reached the level of physical maturity required, but by this age he will be mentally capable of dealing with the rigors of class training. Further, he should have been socialized sufficiently by this time so that he will not be unduly frightened by the strange surroundings and new dogs he will encounter in a class. There is an exception to the six months requirement. In some areas, clubs offer what is called "puppy kindergarten" classes. These are specifically geared for young pups and are as much a socialization class as a training class. If one of these classes is offered in your area, it is strongly recommended that you attend with your pup.

When it comes time for formal training, individual in-home training is specifically not recommended. There are several reasons for this, especially if a career in the obedience ring is a possible future goal for your dog. The dog must become accustomed to working and obeying your commands with many distractions and in any location. The security of your home will not provide this climate. In addition, it is important that you act as the dog's trainer if you intend to handle him yourself at obedience trials. The relationship built between the dog and his handler is an essential part of the learning process, and you want to be certain that the dog will listen to *you*, no matter where you may be. In addition, the competition created by working in a group situation will be a major stimulus for you to do the necessary practicing during the week between class sessions. Finally, class training is considerably less expensive than individualized personal training. Locating obedience classes in your area should not be difficult. Check with your vet, your puppy's breeder, local All Breed or Specialty clubs or others in your neighborhood who own dogs. Many dog clubs offers training classes. Sometimes obedience classes are offered by local adult education schools. In addition, there are a number of commercial obedience schools, many of which are run by experienced obedience competitors.

At most obedience schools four basic classes are offered. The first is called Sub-Novice and consists of basic training done on lead. This would include heeling, sitting, coming on command, staying, etc. The next level, called Novice, prepares you and the dog for all the exercises necessary to earn a C.D. degree. Next comes the Open Class where the exercises required for a C.D.X. degree are learned, and finally the Utility Class where really advanced dogs learn the requirements for the U.D. degree.

Some basic rules to remember: Remain calm and confident in your attitude. Your feelings are telegraphed down the lead to your dog and he will react to them. If you are angry or frustrated, he will sense this and react to your feelings. Do not frighten your dog or punish him unjustly because of your own frustration. Losing your temper will accomplish nothing. Be certain that the dog knows and understands what it is you want of him. Be quick and lavish with your praise whenever a command is correctly followed. If you make the experience fun for your dog, he will respond well and will be eager to please you. If you are frequently angry with him, it is unlikely that he will do well. Repetition is most important, but should not be carried to the point of boredom for either yourself or the dog.

Many people who start out training their dog so that he becomes easier and more pleasant to live with find themselves more and more involved in the training process and "graduate" to formal obedience competition. As with conformation showing, this starts with match shows and progresses to licensed obedience trials. The American Ken-

(Foreground:) Ch. Goldenloe's Tawny Tiger, U.D., W.C. *(Background:)* O.T. Ch. Goldenloe's Just Ducky, W.C. A lovely mother and son photo. "Tawny" is shown at the age of thirteen. She is a G.R.C.A. Outstanding Dam who, in one litter sired by Ch. Golden Pine's Courvoisier, C.D.X., W.C.X. produced five bench champions and one O.T. Champion who is pictured with her. Both these dogs are owned by Anne Couttet Shannon of Evergreen, Colorado. Photo: Liz Watford.

Opposite page: *(Above)* Ch. Pepperhill's Bonni Valentine, C.D.X. (Am., Can. Ch. Pepperhill's Basically Bear ex Am., Can. Ch. Russo's Pepperhill Poppy) is shown flying across the broad jump. She is owned by the author and Diane Dorry of Staten Island, New York. *(Below)* An eight-month-old puppy owned by Dave and Leola Flockner practices tracking.

nel Club licenses more than 1000 obedience trials each year in all areas of the country. Most All-Breed Shows offer obedience trials as a part of the day's activities, and almost every Golden Specialty has obedience competition as well as conformation showing. G.R.C.A. has offered a National Specialty Obedience Trial annually since 1950 and this event draws a large entry every year. Special trophies are offered to winning obedience dogs at this show. Dogs who are being shown in other areas of competition are often shown in obedience as well and a number do quite well. There are many conformation champions and field trial dogs who hold obedience degrees.

Three basic obedience titles are offered by the A.K.C. They are:
    Companion Dog (C.D.)
    Companion Dog Excellent (C.D.X.)
    Utility Dog (U.D.)

These degrees are earned by receiving three "legs," or qualifying scores, at each level of competition. A score of 170 or better out of a possible maximum of 200 points is necessary to qualify. Further, the dog must earn at least half of the points available in each individual exercise in order to qualify, even if his total score is over 170. The degrees are successive which means that a dog must have earned a C.D. before it can earn a C.D.X., a C.D.X. before a U.D. To earn the title of Obedience Trial Champion (O.T. Ch.), the ultimate obedience title, a dog must first earn a U.D. He then must earn a total of 100 points by placing first or second in Open or Utility competition, defeating a required number of other dogs to earn the points. Points are granted on the basis of dogs defeated according to a point scale, as in conformation competition.

The exercises a dog must successfully complete become increasingly difficult as the titles progress. Most Goldens can successfully learn the exercises necessary to earn a C.D. title, and many have the ability to continue in more advanced training if their owners wish. Normally, it takes a considerable period of time for a dog to earn the first three titles, time measured in years. However, some Goldens learn so quickly that this time can be greatly compressed. Age is not a major deterrent either. Dogs over the age of eight or nine years have earned advanced titles. The youngest and quickest Golden to earn all three degrees was O.T., Ch. Moreland's Golden Tonka, owned and trained by Russ Klipple. This remarkable bitch started out in Novice (C.D.)

at eleven months of age and had completed all three titles five and a half months later, before she was seventeen months old. This would be accomplishment enough, but she managed this feat having never failed and never placing lower than first in her class. She averaged better than 197 in the sixteen classes she competed in to attain all the titles!

The exercises required in the Novice Class in order to earn a C.D. title are: heeling on lead, standing for examination, heeling off lead, and the recall (coming when called, sitting in front of the handler and then on command moving to a heel position), and a one-minute sit and a three-minute down off lead with the handler in the ring. To earn a C.D.X. title in the Open Class, the dog must complete the same exercises as in Novice-all off lead, must drop (lie down) then, on command, continue on the recall, retrieve a wooden dumbbell both on the flat and over a high jump, complete the broad jump, and do a three-minute sit and a five-minute down with the handler out of the ring and out of sight. In Utility, the dog must complete the heeling exercises with only hand signals given by the handler (no vocal commands are allowed), and pass two separate tests in scent discrimination (retrieve only the article with the handler's scent on it from among a number of similar articles), directed retrieve (retrieve only one of three gloves and the one indicated by the handler), and directed jumping (jumping over a bar jump and a high jump as directed by the handler and then returning directly to the handler), and a group examination.

The sport of obedience competition can be a tremendously satisfying one for both dog and handler. The relationship developed between the team members is a close one and provides a real sense of accomplishment. It is a type of competition in which winning is determined solely by how well you do with your dog.

Dual Ch. A.F.C. Ronakers Novato Cain, C.D. (Ch. Golden Duke of Trey-C, W.C. ex Ch. J's Kate). Bred by Ronald Akers and owned by Desmond MacTavish, Jr. of Newport, Pennsylvania, this dog was one of only three Goldens to become Dual Champions since 1970. He is a G.R.C.A. Field Dog Hall of Fame member and also an Outstanding Sire. Photo: Cary.

Chapter 12

Field Trials and Golden Retrievers

by Sandra Akers

One of my earliest childhood memories is of sitting on my father's shoulders in a group of trees on a river bank watching dogs swim out into the water and retrieve a duck. My mother was particularly impressed by a dark red bitch which she mistakenly thought was an Irish Setter. She made some inquiries and found out the bitch was a Golden Retriever, Judy of Tuckluck, owned and handled by Charles Snell of Hillsboro, Oregon, the owner of Oakcreek Kennels. The event was the first licensed trial put on by the Northwest Retriever Trial Club and was held near Seattle, Washington on June 2-3, 1945. Our family acquired their first Golden shortly thereafter. My father went on to judge both the Open National and Amateur National Championship Stakes in addition to many other trials including several Golden Specialty trials. My mother has also judged a Specialty trial and is a five point judge at this point.

The first official Retriever Field Trial in history was held near Havant, England on October 12-13, 1900. This was an All-Age Stake for Flat-Coated and Curly-Coated Retrievers only. Goldens and Labradors weren't recognized by the (English) Kennel Club at that time. The Golden Retriever Club of England was formed in 1911 and the breed was then recognized by the Kennel Club. Mrs. W. M. Charlesworth was the founder of the Golden Retriever Club and a great contributor to the breed. The first Golden to complete a Field Championship was Dual Champion Balcombe Boy (Culham Tip ex Culham Amber II) in 1921. He was owned by R.O. Herman and attained his bench championship in the same year.

The Retriever Championship Stake of the International Gundog League Retriever Society is held annually in Great Britain in early December. This prestigious event has been won four times by

A.F.C., Ch. Riverview's Chickasaw Thistle, U.D.T. (Ch. High Farms Band's Clarion ex Ch. Tansy of High Farms). Possibly the only Golden bitch to hold both a field and bench championship as well as a U.D.T. degree. She was owned by James and Sally Venerable of Huntley, Illinois.

Eagerly awaiting the command to go to work is Ch. Honor's Kickback, U.D.T., W.C.X.

Awaiting her chance to retrieve is A.F.C., Ch. Riverview's Chickasaw Thistle, U.D.T. (Ch. High Farms Band's Clarion ex Ch. Tansy of High Farms, W.C.). One of very few Goldens to hold all three of her titles, she was a unique bitch, owned by James and Sally Venerable of Huntley, Illinois.

Fresh out of the water, this is Holway Gillie*** owned by Ronakers Kennels of Sonoma, California.

Goldens. The first winner was F.C. Haulstone Larry (Haulstone Lark ex Haulstone Gipsy) in 1937 owned by Mr. J. Eccles. It wasn't won again by a Golden until 1952 or 1953 when Mrs. Jean Lumsden's F.C. Treunair Cala (Treunair Ciabbach ex Gay Vandra) was the winner. He was owner-bred and handled. We must pause here and remember that all canine activity in Great Britain was suspended during the war years. In 1954, the winner was F.C. Mazurka of Wynford (F.C. Westhyde Stubblesdown Major ex F.C. Musicmaker of Yeo), owned, bred, and handled by June Atkinson. The next twenty years were dry ones as far as the Retriever Championship went, but in 1982 the spell was broken. That year the winner was F.C. Little Marston Chorus of Holway, bred by Mr. M.H. Dare and owned and handled by Robert Atkinson. "Chorus" is the first Golden bitch ever to win the Championship.

The first Field Trial in the United States was held on Marshall Field's estate at Lloyd Neck on Long Island, New York in 1928 or 1929. The A.K.C. would not give its approval for that event because the trial was invitational. About twelve dogs were entered. The first A.K.C. licensed trial was held on December 21, 1931 at the Goelet estate, "Glenmere," in Chester, New York. The trial was held on a Monday to discourage attracting a gallery of spectators. These trials were confined to Labrador Retrievers only, and run very much along the lines of British trials.

The first Golden Retriever to place in a licensed trial in America was Haulstone Bell, owned by D.F. Scobie. She won third place in a Non-Winners Stake at the Brookhaven Game Protective Association's trial in East Islip, New York on December 7-8, 1935. The first American Golden Field Champion was F.C. Rip, bred by J.K. Wallace and owned and handled by Paul Bakewell III. Rip was whelped on November 23, 1935 and finished his Field Championship in 1939. He won the Field and Stream Challenge Cup in 1939 and 1940, the major national field event at that time. Rip died on August 24, 1941, just short of six years old. His untimely death was most unfortunate as he was a very consistent competitor. The first National Championship Stake was held on December 7, 1941 and was won by the Golden F.C. King Midas of Woodend owned by N.E. Dodge of Wayzata, Minnesota. Another National Championship Stake winner was F.C. Shelter Cove Beauty in 1944, owned by Dr. L.M. Evans of St. Cloud, Minnesota. Incidentally, this bitch was also the 1942 Derby Champion. Dr. Evans also owned the 1950 National winner, F.C. Beautywood's

Tamarack. The last time the National was won by a Golden Retriever was in 1951 when the winner was F.C. Ready Always of Marianhill, owned by Mahlon B. Wallace, Jr. The National Amateur Championship Stake had its inception in 1957; to date it has not been won by a Golden, a situation which needs rectifying. There are no places awarded in the American Nationals, only a winner.

Hunting in America and Britain is quite different and so are their respective field trials. The British have their trials between October and January, during their hunting season. These trials are modeled very closely on actual hunting situations and are oriented toward upland game hunting. A one-day trial will have twelve dogs and a two-day trial will have twenty-four. Many dogs may be entered but those who will actually compete are determined by a lottery system. There are three judges and each judge has two dogs to observe at a time. Each dog in contention is seen by all three judges. The trial has two parts, the walk-up and the drive. In a walk-up, the judges, handlers, dogs, gunners, beaters and number carriers are in a line, with the gallery at a distance behind. The game is flushed close to the line and shot. The length of the falls is about fifty yards. One of the problems the dogs can have is cover. It can be thick and high as in the case of a kale field, or may be thickly wooded. The judge will pick a dog to make that specific retrieve and all the other dogs must honor. If the dog fails to find the bird or hare, he will be called in and another dog will be given the opportunity to pick up the mark. In a situation where two birds may be flushed and shot at the same time, the judge will ask a handler to have his dog pick up a certain one. The dog must go where he is sent despite the fact that the other bird might be closer. In the drive, the handlers and dogs are again in a line, but this line is crescent-shaped. At the judge's signal, the beaters go through the field and drive the game toward the gunners and the shooting begins. After the drive is over, a signal is sounded to stop shooting and the dogs are requested to make various retrieves. Some of the retrieves may be made over water. The dog is expected to retrieve from the water, although it seems as though not much emphasis is placed on water work. The British have three stakes. They are: the Puppy or Novice, which is open to dogs over six months of age but under two years; the Non-Winners is usually open to dogs which have not won a place in an Open All-Age Stake; the Open Stake is open to all dogs over the age of six months, carries championship points and also qualifies the dogs to enter the Retriever Championship Stake. The requirements for each

The High Point living Field Trial bitch in the United States sits by the water eager to get to work. This is F.C., A.F.C. Topbrass Mandy (A.F.C. Holway Barty ex Ch. Sunstream Gypsy of Topbrass) owned by Joe and Jackie Mertens of Elgin, Illinois.

stake may vary slightly with the Society giving the trial. The British judge their dogs on steadiness, soft mouth and good marking ability, with much emphasis placed on natural game-finding ability.

The American field trials gradually changed from the British methods due to the fact that our hunting situations differ so greatly. We have much more waterfowl hunting here, so much more of our trial emphasis is on water work. Present day American field trials have four stakes: The Open All-Age is open to dogs over six months of age and carries Championship points; the Amateur All-Age is also open to dogs over six months old and also carries Amateur Championship points. However, in this stake the dog must be handled by an amateur handler. The Qualifying is again open to all dogs over six months but carries no Championship points. It is generally regarded as a transition between the Derby and the Open and Amateur, which are also referred to as the "major stakes." Finally, we have the Derby Stake. It is open to dogs between six months of age and two years. There are always two judges for each Stake, with the exception of National Championship Stakes, which have three. Each Stake should be equally

Two Goldens preparing to work at a Field Trial. At line (on the left) is Ch. Honor's Kickback, U.D.T., W.C.X. Honoring is Ch. Pekay's Deliverance, U.D.T., W.C.X. Photo courtesy of Pekay Goldens, Alpharetta, Georgia.

Riverview's Bart Star*** (F.C., A.F.C. Holway Barty ex Riverview King's Hopi, C.D.X.). A Chuck Morgan Trophy winner and a Derby Dog of the Year owned by James Venerable of Huntley, Illinois.

tested on land and water; therefore usually four or more series are run. Judging is done by the elimination process. At the finish of each series, the numbers of those dogs still in contention are called out by the Field Marshal for the next series. At the conclusion of the last series in the Stake, the judges will make their decision of four places. If a couple of other dogs finished the Stake but weren't quite up to placement level, then, at the discretion of the judges, these dogs might receive a JAM (Judge's Award of Merit) for their efforts. The breeds eligible to compete at Retriever Field Trials are Goldens, Labradors, Chesapeakes, Flat Coats, Curly Coats and Irish Water Spaniels. Needless to say, most trials see only the first three breeds listed.

Most licensed trials run three days and there is no limit to the number of dogs which may enter, with the following exceptions: if an Open All-Age has an entry of over sixty-five, then the following year that particular trial-giving club will have to have a Limited All-Age Stake in lieu of an Open. Limited All-Age dogs must be qualified by winning or placing second in a Qualifying Stake, or an Amateur All-Age place, or an Open All-Age placement or JAM in order to compete. If the Limited exceeds the same quota, then the following year that club will have to have a Special All-Age Stake. The requirements for the Special are the same as for the Limited except that each dog must qualify within the calendar year between the Limited and the Special. Dogs who have attained their Field Championships and/or Amateur Field Championships are, of course, qualified. The Derby dogs are judged solely on marks and the other three stakes have blind retrieves in addition to marks. Field trial tests have become very demanding in the last decade and the resemblance to actual hunting conditions is almost nil. What the dogs are required to do, and the fact that they can do it, gives great credibility to their intelligence. We place great emphasis on marking ability and control.

In order for a dog to become a Field Champion, the dog must have one All-Breed Trial Open, Limited or Special All-Age Stake win plus five additional points. Amateur Field Championship status is achieved by an Amateur All-Age Stake win plus ten additional points which may be accomplished by placements in either the Open stakes or the Amateur Stake. Qualifying for the Open National or Amateur National Championship Stakes requires a win plus two points in each calendar year. These are very prestigious events which last for five to six days and are run in different areas of the country each year. The Amateur National is held in June and the Open National is held in

November. The entry fees are approximately $250.00 per dog as of this writing.

There have always been outstanding field trial Goldens, but for a while there were some rather mediocre Goldens in trials. They had slow returns, were poor bird handlers, were slow in the water and just generally made a bad showing. Many people referred to them as "swamp collies" or "rugs" or worse, and rightly so. Fortunately, in the last fifteen years or so the field trial Golden has improved tremendously. There are a great many talented Labradors in field trials and the competition is very keen. But Goldens are holding their own better now.

Breeding field trial quality Goldens is an enigma because you are looking for many intangible qualities. Inheritable qualities such as birdiness, marking ability, love of water, intelligence, trainability, ability to accept correction and intense retrieving desire. All these qualities are paramount for a good field trial Golden. The Breed Standard is vital and should be adhered to for preservation of the breed. However, when breeding for a good field trial or hunting dog, you must also think as much about what is inside the head as what the head looks like. Training never stops during a field trial dog's career because every location is different and every judge has a different concept of what to do with those locations. Because breeding for this purpose can be so elusive, let us look at a few of the "magic combinations" which have produced two or more Field Champions or Amateur Field Champions within the past fifteen years or so.

Jolly Again of Ouillemette, C.D. bred to Nancy's Golden Dawn produced F.C. Bonnie Brooks Tuff And A Half; F.C., A.F.C. and C.F.C. Bonnie Brooks Elmer; and F.C. and A.F.C. Bonnie Brooks Red. Poika of Handjem bred to Shenandoah of Stilrovin produced F.C. and A.F.C. Kinike Chancellor; F.C. and A.F.C. Kinike Coquette; C.D., F.C. and A.F.C. Kinike Oro de Rojo; and F.C. and A.F.C. Northbreak Kinike Sir Jim. When F.C., A.F.C. and C.F.C. Bonnie Brooks Elmer was bred to Tigathoe's Chickasaw****, they produced F.C. and A.F.C. Tigathoe's Magic Marker; F.C. and A.F.C. Tigathoe's Tonga; F.C. and A.F.C. Tigathoe's Kiowa II; and Dual Champion and A.F.C. Tigathoe's Funky Farquar. F.C. and A.F.C. Bonnie Brooks Red bred to Holway Joyful produced F.C. and A.F.C. Firebird of Rocky-Vue and F.C. and A.F.C. Son of Red. A.F.C. Holway Barty ex Champion Sunstream Gypsy of Topbrass produced F.C. and A.F.C. Topbrass Mandy and F.C. and A.F.C. Topbrass Cotton. All of these combinations have also produced Qualified All-Age dogs and many others with field trial placements. You can see a pattern in these breedings of consistency as evidenced by F.C. and A.F.C. Bonnie Brooks Elmer and F.C. and A.F.C. Bonnie Brooks Red. There are a great many more outstanding field sires and dams; we are using these few to illustrate consistent field quality breeding. A.F.C. Holway Barty is considered by many to be the top producer of field Goldens during his lifetime. In addition to Cotton and Mandy, he produced F.C. and A.F.C. Cherryhill's Rowdy Rascal and many Qualified All-Age dogs thus far. He also produced several obedience champions. He was a consistent and dominant sire in almost every breeding.

The High Point field trial Golden of all time is F.C. and A.F.C. Misty's Sungold Lad, C.D.X. owned by Jay and Val Walker. Lad was considered by many people, and not just Golden people, as a canine genius. He had a total of 212½ combined Open and Amateur points at his retirement. He won two double headers (an Open win and an Amateur win at the same trial). The only other Golden to win a double header is A.F.C. Wildfire of Riverview. Lad was an excellent marker and a superb water dog.

Unfortunately, the breed has not had too many Dual Champions. Only three dogs have achieved this coveted status since 1970. They are: Dual Champion, A.F.C. Clickety-Click, Dual Champion, A.F.C. Ronakers Novato Cain, C.D., and Dual Champion, A.F.C. Tigathoe's Funky Farquar. Of the three, only one, Funky Farquar, is still living.

The *average* Golden Field Trial Champion is slightly smaller than his conformation counterpart. These smaller dogs are usually very athletic, sound and well balanced which makes for a physically capable, well coordinated animal. It is truly unfortunate that the rift between the conformation dogs and the field dogs seems to be ever widening.

Choosing a puppy for future field trial competition is about as difficult as breeding for trials. The first thing to consider is the sire and dam. Are they from proven field trial lines? Do they have trial placings and show ability as individuals? The Golden Retriever Club of America has a "star system" of denoting field trial achievements. One star (*) after a dog's name indicates that the dog has a G.R.C.A. Working Certificate or has placed in a sanctioned field trial. Two stars (**) indicate placement or JAM's in a licensed Derby or Qualifying Stake other than a first or second Qualifying placement. Three stars (***) are indicative of a licensed Qualifying first or second place, or a major stake placement or JAM. These stars on a pedigree give you an idea of what the dogs in a pup's background have done. Ideally, you should look for Qualified All-Age (***) dogs and any F.C. or A.F.C. titles in the first three generations of the pedigree when selecting a puppy. There have been many capable field trial dogs from somewhat mediocre backgrounds who have done well as individuals; however , most of these dogs do not reproduce their own good qualities when bred. Unfortunatley, many people mistakenly believe you only have to develop a dog's natural instinct to have a good field dog, and this is totally erroneous.

There have been many excellent volumes written on the subject of training, so we will only look briefly at one aspect. (For more information the reader is referred to those books written specifically on the subject of field training.) The more exposure your potential field trial dog has to birds and new situations as a young dog (and a puppy!) the greater advantage you will have. The old adage that says don't do anything with your dog until he is six months old is outdated. Any good Golden should be able to do at least G.R.C.A. Working Certificate work at six months of age. A Working Certificate is, briefly, a land double and two singles in the water. Puppies can learn a great deal and have a lot of fun in their first six months of life while they are working on these basics.

Retriever Field Trials are expensive, time consuming, fiercely competitive and practically a way of life. Obviously, it is not the sport for everyone. For those who choose this sport and dedicate their time and effort, the rewards can be marvelous. Field trialers have great relationships with their animals and their competitors. They are a very clannish group. You cannot train your dogs alone. You need other people to help you, and who is better than someone you can help in return? And by working with others, you develop an interest in their dogs and are supportive of them. Sometimes you would rather be dropped from a trial than see your training-buddy dropped.

Whatever your interests are, field trials or hunting, Golden Retrievers are suitable. Good field quality dogs are intelligent, challenging and fun to work with. They give their all for our pleasures and we are better individuals for it.

A Golden Guide Dog trained by Guiding Eyes for the Blind, Inc. of Yorktown Heights, New York prepares to take its master aboard a train. Goldens are used extensively in this type of work. Photo: Courtesy of Guiding Eyes for the Blind.

Chapter 13

The Golden Retriever— Training as a Guide Dog

by Guiding Eyes for the Blind, Yorktown Heights, New York

Independence through mobility is the cornerstone of Guiding Eyes for the Blind. The proper utilization of a high quality guide dog means dignity, self-reliance and is an important factor in helping the visually handicapped person become a responsible, contributing member of society.

There are three pure-bred breeds of dogs that dominate the guide dog field. They are the Golden Retriever, the Labrador Retriever and the German Shepherd.

With this in mind I will begin this chapter by discussing what is expected of the Golden Retriever in our program. If we stop to consider the Retriever as a Gun Dog and its development over the years by responsible reputable breeders, the following characteristics are immediately evident. The breed has a friendly disposition toward people and although it obeys the hunter, it accepts all others. The dog's job as a retriever is to wait patiently and quietly until the birds are dropped, to mark them well and upon command, to retrieve them as quickly and efficiently as possible—once the job is done to wait patiently for the process to be repeated again and again. Because of the reports from the guns, the dog must also possess an acceptable level of ear sensitivity.

Body sensitivity or, to a good degree lack of it, is also an important quality in a Gun Dog, for the dog must go through thick brush, cold marshes, ice chunks and floating debris regardless of temporary physical discomfort.

The coat itself must have the ability to provide protection from the elements as well as be relatively maintenance free.

A rare photograph of Ch. Lorelei's Golden Rip** hitting the water. A son of Dual Ch. Stilrovin' Rip's Pride, Rip was a G.R.C.A. Outstanding Sire of ten champions and was owned by Reinhard M. Bischoff who was the owner of the Lorelei Kennels. Photograph courtesy of Mrs. George H. Flinn, Jr.

A big lumbering dog would create a problem especially in a blind or boat where space is limited. Size is a consideration and of course trainability, willingness to learn and most important to fit into the present day family life style and be an acceptable member of society.

So, from the beginning the Retriever possesses a majority of the necessary basic ingredients in the making of a guide dog. Now let us utilize these traits to their best advantage. Since a guide dog is very often placed in the position of being unexpectedly hugged by children or petted by the general public who can't seem to prevent themselves from petting these trustworthy guides, it must be friendly and still try to maintain its responsibility to its blind owner. Thus, temperament and disposition are important. As part of a daily routine, the guide dog must guide his owner through crowds, traffic, barriers, etc., and to sit patiently while the owner is shopping, working, attending classes or enjoying the theatre. Since guide dogs work under all weather conditions—snow, rain, heat of summer or cold of winter—the coat must be easily managed. This daily grooming is performed by the owner and keeps the dog clean and acceptable.

Because of the very size of the dog and the congested city areas in which a blind person may travel puts the dog in a position of being stepped on or squeezed, especially in crowds of pedestrians or rush hour buses and subways, a dog with high body sensitivity would begin to refuse to work in areas that created discomfort to himself. In this day and age of miniaturization with smaller cars and more and more crowded conditions, the dog must be of moderate size to get the job done. Anything excessive could easily become a disadvantage to fitting the dog into tight quarters. As a guide dog is working, there could easily be a number of harsh or loud noises such as truck backfire, jack hammer, thunder storms, etc., so an acceptable level of ear sensitivity is a must. Trainability and sociability, the ability to be aware of its surroundings, to put into practice what it was taught is a necessity—its willingness to perform the same task repeatedly as well as intelligent disobedience; to disobey a command regardless of physical correction if that command was to put them in physical danger. And, when out of harness and not working, to be a well behaved member of the family.

Having made some comparison of the adaptability of the Golden Retriever to our program let me stress one more very important factor; above all, a guide dog must possess a sound mind in a sound body. One without the other would be an impossibility.

Now, let's start at the beginning. In order to achieve a uniform type of dog we began a Breeding Program with the help of established Golden Retriever fanciers. The probationary breeding stock was placed in training and once their stability as potential guide dogs was established, they were added to the breeding colony. As the litters come, the pups once separated from their mothers are placed in foster homes until training age. While in the foster homes the pups are checked periodically and evaluated by a qualified puppy breeding farm staff member who not only checks for physical growth, innoculations, health and temperament but also for mental development. The goal was to show steady progress in all areas. Exposure to the environment is paramount to a guide dog, and the foster families with their involvement in raising future guide dogs take their voluntary job very seriously. Everything a guide dog will encounter later in life should not surprise or startle him unduly and the foster families are indeed happy as the pups mature and become solid in their exposure. During this time from eight weeks to one year of age, all pups that show negative tendencies are watched closely and if they do not meet the high standard of acceptance are dropped from the program. The foster family has the option and usually does adopt the dog with the agreement that the animal be spayed or altered. It should be noted that we use both male and female dogs and find little difference in their working ability.

At one year of age the dogs are returned to the Training Center where they will begin their intensive education. Once through a quarantine period where the dogs are given a complete physical, they are ready to be assigned to an instructor.

The training at the start consists of simple basic obedience. However, it differs from competition obedience exercises. From this moment on the handling will be such as it applies to a blind individual. The dog is first shown, then taught by the instructor the various commands of "come," "sit," "down," and "stay." The dog must obey on the first command; if not, immediate correction is made to reinforce the first command; there is no second or third time. Of course, praise is lavish for a job well done. On all obedience commands the dog should be comfortable so he need not sit straight or lie down in a regal manner, for in applying obedience to the dog's daily work routine, he may have to lie down for long periods of time while the owner is busy. So he may just as well be comfortable. All commands are given with normal conversation volume. No shouting is necessary and would only draw unwanted attention. Guide dogs are trained to work on the left side as most people are right-handed and it frees their most frequently used arm. Unlike all obedience dogs who respond to commands or cues, the guide dog must always be encouraged to take the lead and show initiative. Because of this, and so as not to confuse the dog in these initial stages of training, "heel" is taught at the very end of training as it relieves the dog of all responsibility of guiding.

The working commands are given verbally, as well as with hand signals. These commands are used only when the dog is in harness and is responsible for safe travel. "Forward" means to start or proceed ahead from a stop. Right turn and left turn are 90° turns and are used to maintain direction and orientation. The command "straight" is used in crossing a street. It tells the dog to go from down curb to directly opposite upcurb; regardless of what is blocking the way, the dog must go around it and recover original direction. Example: car blocking intersection. "Hup-Hup" varies with meaning as to when it is used and the degree of voice intonation, but mostly it gets the dog's attention back to the job at hand. The voice command "no" is used for anything negative the dog is doing. Again, if voice will not suffice it is followed by a physical leash correction and immediate praise as soon as the dog responds favorably. There must always be a correct balance of praise and correction to insure a good performance.

As the training progresses, the dog in harness must learn to make adjustments for width and height of the team as a working unit. The team with instructor starts on quiet streets in town under normal conditions. First lessons taught are to stop for all curbs up and down, to cross a street in a straight line to avoid obstacles in the team's path. As the dog becomes more and more confident, the work becomes increasingly more complex and demanding. It is at this point that dogs begin to exhibit their potential as future guide dogs and working patterns begin to form either positive or negative.

Since records are kept on the progress of all dogs it is easy to see the dogs that will continue to improve and the ones that have reached a plateau of accomplishment and either regress or go no further. The latter dogs would then be dropped from the program and offered to the raiser. All others would then be spayed or altered or retained for breeding. They then continue in training, handling traffic, subways, elevators, escalators, crowds, stores, etc. Since we all are familiar with the influence a handler could have on a dog, the instructors work each other's dogs under blindfold to see the strengths and deficiencies in their dogs' work. We are looking for the dog to assume responsibility for the safe travel of its instructor and, at a later stage, its blind owner. Now that the Golden has reached this level of training, which consists of a minimum of three months of intensive training, the dog is ready to begin still another phase; this is being assigned to a blind student. Student and dog will spend 26 days in residence working and getting to know each other and working safely and efficiently as a team. The dogs are matched very closely to the needs of the individual blind student to insure success. The training sessions will cover many eventualities that they may later experience in their own home towns. The student in training must get to know the area they will be working as the master is always in command. And it is the dog's responsibility to get them there safely.

Since the dog has already had his education, the student can progress at a more rapid rate in training with his dog. At this point both dog and owner are achieving a team effort of confidence and the freedom of accomplishment in each other's ability to travel safely and effectively.

Toward the end of class, the foster families are invited to the campus to meet with the blind student who now is using the dog they raised for one year, and all share a very happy reunion.

At the conclusion of the course, the graduates and their dogs embark to put into practice all they have learned. Guiding Eyes for the Blind does provide a follow-up service to its graduates if the need arises, as there are times when a little assistance, especially early in the new environment, helps make the difference between a growing problem or a quick solution.

Earlier in the chapter it was described that most important is a sound mind in a sound body. Once again, let us look back at how many pressure areas the dog has gone through in changes of environment and people in the dog's young life.

Separation from its mother and litter mates.
Living a relatively carefree life with the foster family.
The incarceration of being returned to a kennel.
The training in town with its instructor.
The training with the blind student.
Meeting once again the foster family.
And finally going to the new home with the blind person.

The other pressures and stress are created by the work the dog is asked to perform throughout its life—that of being responsible for the safe travel of both himself and his master, whether it be rural setting or the complexities of city living.

Here once again, we are first looking for the overall breed of dog that can cope with these responsibilities and individuals within the breed that excel in their accomplishment. As we all know only too well, not all dogs are obedience, breed or field champions. But all have a place in society, and fulfill a need.

Guiding Eyes for the Blind is also noted for its work with the multihandicapped blind individuals—people who have secondary handicaps

Am., Can. Ch., O.T. Ch. Sunstreak of Culynwood, T.D., W.C.X. eagerly flies over the high jump. This outstanding dog was owned by David and Susan Bluford of Carmel, California.

along with their blindness. This too requires a very special individual dog to meet the specific needs and responsibilities of the added handicaps. These responsibilities would test the mettle of any dog. The Retrievers seem to have an aptitude conducive to handling these responsibilities.

So one comes full circle. Nothing has been changed in the original characteristics of the Golden Retriever—just the application of a most different, difficult, and satisfying working career and its assistance to humanity.

Guiding Eyes for the Blind has been using Golden Retrievers in its breeding program since 1966.

Can. O.T. Ch. Shadywell Mister Rip, W.C., the Number One obedience dog in Canada in 1979 is shown with his owner and handler, Clint McEvoy of Ottawa, Canada. Photo: Ron Poling.

Chapter 14

Goldens in Canada and Australia

GOLDEN RETRIEVERS IN CANADA

by Judy Taylor

Over the years, Goldens in Canada have changed considerably. Perhaps their recognition as one of the most popular house pets has brought into focus the responsibility of breeders to produce a dog that is not only good in their chosen interests, whether it be show, field, or obedience, but also, of utmost importance, that the animal be sound both in mind and body. We have seen the breed rise from relatively few numbers at shows to one of the largest entries, and being strong contenders in Group and Best in Show competition. In obedience, not only have we seen larger entries in our chosen breed because of their trainability, but also they are consistent contenders for top scores by obedience enthusiasts. In the field there is still the stigma placed on Goldens by the competitors of more excitable breeds, but in spite of the fewer numbers in competition we do maintain a certain respect for the enthusiasm displayed and the natural hunting ability.

There are a certain few individual dogs that have indeed been of considerable influence on the development of the Golden in Canada; however, I will mention them specifically later on. Generally it can be noticed that in conformation there has been an earlier acceptance of the blonder shades, mainly due to the importation of certain English dogs that were used in breeding programs that in turn produced top winning dogs. These dogs have also made breed history with their laurels by regularly placing in the top ten Sporting dogs, calculated annually according to the "Phillips System," that is, one dog defeated equals one point. Just as Goldens have realized success in conformation, they have been as successful in gaining recognition in annual obedience awards. Every year we see more and more Goldens that have made the top ten all-breed awards.

The Golden Retriever Club of Canada has made giant strides in growth and has taken positive action in promoting Golden Retrievers in all areas of endeavors. By adopting a Code of Ethics and endorsing only reputable, conscientious breeders, the club has had tremendous influence on maintaining a certain standard of conduct. The club sponsors one Specialty show a year, plus two licensed trials, with at least two all-breed sanction shows and numerous supported shows. Two licensed obedience trials are held in conjunction with our Specialty show, as well as working certificates the day prior to the show. It is with pride that Canada can boast of official recognition of the W.C. and W.C.X. degrees by the Canadian Kennel Club.

Fortunately, because of public concern, breeders in Canada are finding it mandatory to take the necessary precautions before deciding to breed. All reputable breeders are having their dogs checked annually for any eye problems, and are insuring that their chosen breeding stock are clear of hip dysplasia. Furthermore, it is now more prevalent than ever before that breeders take a concerned look at prospective buyers, and all pets are sold with a non-breeding contract, endorsed by the Canadian Kennel Club, and included in the Golden Retriever Club of Canada's Code of Ethics. It is only with these practices that we will be able to protect our breed in its ever growing popularity and all that entails.

In order for a dog to become a Champion in Canada, a total of ten points must be accumulated, with these points having been awarded by at least three different judges. Where we differ from the United States is that if a dog goes Best of Winners, he is also awarded the points won by the class dog defeated. In other words, if there are two points in bitches and one in dogs, and the dog goes Best of Winners, he is awarded three points. "Majors" are not required in Canada in order to complete a Championship. There is also another twist to our point system; if the Best of Winners dog goes Best of Breed over specials, these specials are counted with the class dogs to calculate the number of dogs defeated. Conversely, if a class bitch goes Best of Opposite Sex over specials, the number of bitch specials is added to the class bitches. Finally, if the class winning Best of Breed dog also places in the Group, additional points may be earned depending on the number of breeds competing at Group level. It must be remembered that no more than five points can be awarded at any one show. A dog winning the breed must compete in the group or all wins for the day will be cancelled.

206

Finally, a new stipulation for a championship in Canada: before the certificate is issued, in any breed where there is a disqualification for size or weight, according to the breed standard, the dog must be officially measured after he reaches one year of age. This is, of course, to avoid penalizing any puppies that may obtain the ten championship points but, due to age, fail to meet the necessary size. I might add that there is serious consideration at this time to introduce the inclusion of one major (three-point win) before a championship is obtained.

Although there are slight differences in our rule book regarding licensed obedience and field trials, the basic qualifications for titles are the same.

INTRODUCTION OF GOLDENS IN CANADA

The Golden Retriever was first recognized by the Canadian Kennel Club in 1927; however information reveals the first Golden to arrive was in 1881, brought over by the Hon. Archie Marjoriebanks.

It wasn't until 1928 that Mr. B.M. Armstrong of Winnipeg took a real interest in the breed and his "Gilnockie" kennel was started. At his death, Col. Samuel Magoffin transferred Gilnockie to his kennel in Denver, Colorado as he had already established Rockhaven Kennels in North Vancouver. Christopher Burton played a significant role in influencing his friend Col. Magoffin in the breeding of Golden Retrievers, and his first import, Speedwell Pluto, was destined to become one of the greatest sires of the breed on the North American continent. Many of the Goldens of today owe their heritage to this very dog.

Over the years there have been significant contributions from a number of established kennels. Shadywell, owned by Cliff MacDonald has produced bench, field and obedience champions. The major stud dog in this kennel was Beckwith's Flintlock and, later, two English imports, Champion Ambassador of Davern and Champion Symbol of Yeo, both of whom are in the Stud Dog Hall of Fame. Shadywell Hi-Speed, owned by Gordon G. Rolph (by Shadywell Golden Rip out of Golden Knoll's Ginger Bug) became a Field Champion in 1958. The Brat of Shadywell, owned by James Taylor, was a top winning Golden and was one of the first bitches to win the National Specialty in 1962. Mention should also be made in this chapter of O.T. Champion Shadywell Mister Rip, W.C.; O.T. Champion Shadywell MacRory, W.C.; O.T. Champion Shadywell Kaylon Kimberlin, Bermudian

C.D.; and Shadywell Pride of Dan, C.D.X., Bermudian C.D., owned and trained by Clint and Vera McEvoy.

Another breeder who has made his influence on Goldens in Canada is Dr. Tom Dales of Goldendale Kennels. His F.C. Goldendale's Rufus is the result of his enthusiasm and perseverance in producing Goldens in Field Trials. Champion Goldendale's Belle, C.D. owned by Shirley Goodman further illustrates his success in producing dual purpose Goldens. This bitch is also a member of the Brood Bitch Hall of Fame.

Finally, a quick look at Jack Reid of Goldrange. Champion Goldrange Fine Fella of Yeo and his son Champion Curranhall's Karo of Goldrange have made a tremendous impact on Goldens on the West Coast. Both are top winners and Karo is in both the Show Dog and Stud Dog Hall of Fame.

A BRIEF HISTORY OF THE GOLDEN RETRIEVER CLUB OF CANADA

by Shirley Goodman

The first club of Golden Retriever fanciers in Canada was formed in 1958 and registered with the Canadian Kennel Club as the Golden Retriever Club of Ontario. The founding meeting was held at the home of Harold Sherlock and John McNicol was the young club's first President. Unfortunately, records of this first meeting are incomplete.

The first function of this newly organized club was to hold a Golden Retriever match at the home of Cliff McDonald. There were 35 Goldens present, including a Specials class. There was keen interest in field work and training sessions were routinely held, as time went on. The following year, in November 1959, the Golden Retriever Club of Ontario held its first licensed Specialty at Major Crawford's home in King, Ontario, with Mrs. Alben E. (Nancy) Sturdee judging. There was an entry of 26 Goldens, with Best of Breed going to Northland's Castor, owned by Dr. T. De Geer.

The first Annual Meeting was held on December 6, 1959, and the records show that the first Officers were as follows: President, John McNicol; Secretary, Roger Drysdale; Treasurer, Mel Angove; and Directors Cliff MacDonald, Dr. T. De Geer, Jutta Baker, Fred Coombs, and Harold Sherlock.

Can. Ch. Carolee's Cafe Au Lait, Am., Can. C.D., W.C. The Top Puppy in 1972 for the Golden Retriever Club of Canada and Top Bitch in 1972 and 1973 was Best of Opposite Sex at the 1973 G.R.C.C. National Specialty. She has produced five show champions, including Can. Dual Ch. A.F.C. Carolee's Something Special II, Am., Can. C.D., W.C.X., owned by George Stewart. Cafe Au Lait was owned by Shirley Goodman of Streetsville, Ontario.

Can., Bda. Ch. Skylon Lancelot (Skylon Figaro ex Can. Ch. Chrys-Haefen Spring Entity). Winner of six All-Breed Bests in Show, "Skye" was a top Canadian winner. He was owned by Peter and Greta Nixon of Canada.

The club grew slowly, and in November, 1960 it became the Golden Retriever Club of Canada with directors from coast to coast. These were: British Columbia, Col. Samuel Magoffin; Manitoba, Dr. Croll; Quebec, Mr. P.A. Quiment; New Brunswick, Mr. A. Wilson; Ontario, Mr. G. Davey, Mr. J. Taylor, Mr. N.C. MacDonald, Mr. R. Drysdale; and from the Ottawa area, Col. Beardmore.

The first Golden Retriever Club of Canada National Specialty was held on November 27, 1960 north of Toronto, with an entry of twenty-six. The G.R.C.C. held National Specialties up to and including 1963 when the tendencies of the members became more field-oriented. However, the show interest amongst members was sufficient to organize another National Specialty in 1970. During the later years of the '60s, the G.R.C.C. continued to hold annual boosters (supported entries) in conjunction with the Canadian National Sportsmen's Dog Show in Toronto, and annual licensed field trials have been organized every year since the first licensed trial in May 1960.

This First Trial was held at Fullerton, Ontario on May 7th and 8th, 1960 with judges Dr. E.E. Pearce from New York, and Mr. M.M. Stevenson of Toronto. There was an entry of 25 Juniors, 18 Qualifying, and 27 in Open. Certificates of Merit were awarded at this trial to Karl of Felsberg, owned by Mark Sequin, and Loch Alvie, owned by Paul Quimet.

In 1961, new officers for the club were: Mr. W.D. Brown, President; Mr. L. Barks, Vice President; Mr. N. Angove, Treasurer; and Mrs. Jutta Baker, Secretary. The Provincial Directors remained unchanged.

In support of the National Specialty Shows and Licensed Field Trials, several challenge and perpetual trophies were donated to the club. Early field trophies included: The Hist Canada Challenge Trophy, donated by Mark Seguin for Open Stake at Licensed trials; The Kerrdail Trophy, donated by Roger Drysdale; the Master Dog Food Challenge Trophy donated by Master Pet Foods; and the John Labatt Trophy, donated by Labatt Breweries.

Early conformation trophies included: The Master Food Challenge for Best Puppy at the National Specialty; the De Navilly Challenge for Best Canadian Bred at the National Specialty, donated by Fred Coombs; and, donated in 1965 by Virginia and Walter Tetlak, a trophy for Best of Winners at the National Specialty. This trophy, the Tetlak Ginwal Perpetual Trophy, was given to promote friendship and good will between the United States and Canada.

The Golden Retriever Club of Canada has continued to grow and prosper, with an ever increasing membership from coast to coast. Along with this growth came a greater desire to make the club truly National. The club constitution has now been revised, and members across Canada can currently vote by ballot, thus allowing all members to participate in their club. Since 1979, G.R.C.C. Specialities have included Licensed Obedience Trials, and in 1983 the club will be holding its first Tracking Test.

As one can readily recognize, Goldens in Canada are in a relatively good position. Because of the accessibility of English and American dogs, and the sincerity of breeders over the years, Golden breeders today can take full advantage of the future to produce top dogs that look like the breed and have the eagerness to please that makes the Golden such a perfect pet. One must never lose the overall picture of our breed and get so involved with a specific area of competition that we lose sight of the true purpose and intention of the breed—the best house dog ever.

GOLDEN RETRIEVERS IN AUSTRALIA

Goldens enjoy a goodly share of popularity in Australia, and a kennel of whose dogs we have heard enthusiastic praise is that belonging to F.T. and Mrs. B. J. Hessian. They are the owners of well-known Australian Champion Goldtreve Cameron, a highly successful dog, big winner at Royal shows.

Cameron was born in June 1979, and is a son of English Champion Camrose Cabus Christopher from Australian Champion Gaewynd Tapestry. The latter is also owned by the Hessians, and is a famed winner in her own right. She is a daughter of Australian Champion Montego Mesqual from Australian Champion Inpack Brandy and was born in 1975.

In the "young hopeful" division there is a lovely puppy, Goldtreve Tosca, already in the winning at the Royals at nine months old, a daughter of Australian Champion Noravon Otto Goldtreve (United Kingdom importation) ex the aforementioned Tapestry.

One notes with interest that at the 1983 Royal Agricultural Society's Spring Fair, the Hessians had a "clean sweep" of the top Golden awards with Cameron taking the dog C.C. and Best of Breed while his dam, Tapestry, gained the bitch C.C. and Reserve Best in Show.

Reserve Challenge Certificates at this Royal Spring Fair were awarded to R.E. and Mrs. R.M. Brown's Goldtreve Camrossie, a full

Aust. Ch. Karrell Happy Union, born 1981, by Ch. Wildheart Caviare, C.D.X. ex Ch. Balandra Deerflight (litter sister to Darius). A champion at 12 months, "Frosty" has had many fine "in Show" and "in Group" wins, and with litter sister, Ch. Harmony Girl, has an unbeaten record in Brace in Show awards. "Frosty" is owned by Jane Trout, Karrell Golden Retrievers, New South Wales, Australia.

Aust. Ch. Balandra Delta Darius, C.D.X., born December 1978. This is the top royal winning Golden in Australia, and has been for the past 3 years. Has won top awards in most Australian states, including Best Exhibit of All Breeds at the 1981 Sydney Royal Easter Show from entry of 5500. Also obedience trial winner, and proving a great sire. Son of U.K. import Stolford Sheriff ex Ch. Cambronze Melody. Owned by Jane Trout, Karrell Golden Retrievers, New South Wales.

Aust. Ch. Ruspervale April Lass with her Australian Champion sash. Owned by M.P. and M.T. Frost. Sydney, New South Wales.

brother to Cameron; and to M.P. and Mrs. M.T. Frost's Australian Champion Ruspervale April Lass, a daughter of Australian Champion Balandra Delta Darius C.D.X. ex Australian Champion Goldholm Lady Rebecca.

Other breeders of Goldens in Australia include J.R.E. and Mrs. J.L. Trout who are the owners of Australian Champion Karrell Happy Union (Australian Champion Wildheart Caviare, C.D.X. – Australian Champion Balandra Deerflight), Australian Champion Karrell Harmony Girl (litter sister to Happy Union), and Australian Champion Balandra Delta Darius, C.D.X., (Stolford Sheriff, imported from U.K. – Australian Champion Cambronze Melody).

Also Mrs. D.M. Hutcheson has Briden Te Amie C.D. (Australian Champion Santamaria Te Amo – Australian Champion Goldtreve Waterwisp, U.D.) and, in co-ownership with Miss E.A. Smith, Australian Champion Glennessa Post Haste, imported from U.K. – Glenessa Escapade), and Australian Champion Beckenglad Khan (Australian Champion Santamaria Te Amo – Briden Peseta).

AUSTRALIAN STANDARD FOR GOLDEN RETRIEVERS

The Australian Standard is virtually identical to the English Standard, except for the precise conversion of the English units to metric units in the section on Weight and Size.

Irish Ch. Mandingo Beau Geste of Yeo. Father of Eng. Ch. Deerflite Endeavour of Yeo, this dog has a typically English head. He is owned by Lucille Sawtell of the well-known Yeo kennels in England.

214

Chapter 15

Dog Shows in England

by Sandra J.B. McDowell

As in any country, judging of dogs in England is based on the approved Breed Standard. The Golden Retriever Standard in England is somewhat different than the American Kennel Club Standard discussed in a previous chapter. The most distinct differences between the English and American Standards are in color and size. The American Standard calls for "color lustrous golden of various shades," as opposed to the English "Cream or Gold"; and, the American size standard (for which there are disqualifications for above and below) are larger than the English counterparts. The American Standard has provisions for gait and temperament that do not appear at all in the English Standard. Overall, the American Standard is much more specific in what is wanted in a dog when compared to the English Standard.

The complete English Standard for Golden Retrievers, approved by the Kennel Club, is as follows:

GENERAL APPEARANCE: Should be a symmetrical active powerful dog, a good level mover, sound and well put together, with kindly expression, not clumsy, nor long in leg.

HEAD AND SKULL: Broad skull, well set on and a clean muscular neck, muzzle, powerful and wide, not weak jawed, good stop.

EYES: Dark and well set apart, very kindly expression, with dark rims.

EARS: Well proportioned, of moderate size, and well set on.

MOUTH: Teeth should be sound and strong. Neither overshot nor undershot, the lower teeth just behind but touching the upper.

NECK: The neck should be clean and muscular.

FOREQUARTERS: The forelegs should be straight with good bone. Shoulders should be well laid back and long in the blade.

BODY: Well-balanced, short coupled, and deep through the heart. Ribs deep and well sprung.

HINDQUARTERS: The loins and legs should be strong and muscular, with good second thighs and well bent stifles. Hocks well let down, not cow-hocked.

FEET: Round and cat-like, not open or splayed.

TAIL: Should not be carried too gay nor curled at the tip.

COAT: Should be flat or wavy with good feathering, and dense water repellent undercoat.

COLOUR: Any shade of gold or cream but neither red nor mahogany. The presence of a few white hairs on the chest permissible. White collar, feet, toes, or blaze should be penalised. Nose should be black.

WEIGHT AND SIZE: The average weight in good hard condition should be: Dogs 32-37 kg (70-80 lbs); bitches 27-32 kg (60-70 lbs); Height at the shoulder: Dogs 56-61 cm (22"-24"); bitches 51-56 cm (20"-22").

English Ch. Deerflite Endeavour of Yeo. Owned by Lucille Sawtell, this bitch is the dam of three English Champions.

An important field dog and G.R.C.A. Outstanding Sire, this is A.F.C. Holway Barty (Eng. F.C. Holway Westhyde Zues ex Eng. F.C. Holway Flush of Yeo) owned and imported from England by Barbara Howard of Longmont, Colorado.

English Ch. Moorquest Mugwump is typical of the English type of Golden Retriever today. This dog is the sire of the 1982 Best of Breed Winner at the Golden Retriever Club of England. The winner of three All-Breed Best in Show awards, "Mr. Mugs" won the Progeny Class at the 1981 Golden Retriever Club Championship show, where his son was Best Puppy in Show. Another son is a Best in Show winner. Mugwump is owned by Mrs. Shirley Crick of Devon.

English Show Ch. Muskan Miss Dior (Ch. Moorquest Mugwump ex Show Ch. Hingstondown Notoriety of Muskan). This lovely bitch was the Best of Breed winner at the 1982 Golden Retriever Club of England Specialty over an entry of 806 Goldens. She is owned by Mrs. H. Lambshead.

English Show Ch. Hingstondown Notoriety of Muskan (Show Ch. Brackengold Max ex Hingstondown Lady Capulet). This mother of the 1982 Best of Breed winner at the Golden Retriever Club of England Specialty is owned by Hilary Lambshead.

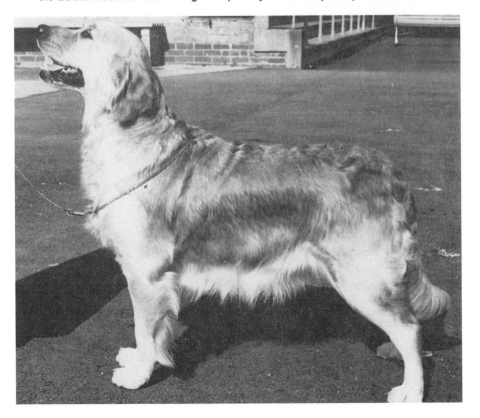

THE ENGLISH SHOWS

The British Kennel Club scheme by which one may show his Golden Retriever is based on five different types of shows. As in the United States, certain types of shows must be pre-entered in order to compete. The information for these dog shows may be obtained in the weekly publication, *Our Dogs* and *Dog World*.

The simplest show in England is the Exemption Show which is usually held in conjunction with a local fair or market. It consists of classes such as "the happiest dog" or "the dog with the longest tail," etc. It may be compared to our Fun Matches.

The second type of show is the Sanctioned Show. These are the smallest shows for which one must be registered with the Kennel Club. These shows do exclude all Challenge Certificate winners. Sanctioned shows cater to classes called "Any Variety," which means that dogs of all breeds compete in the same ring. Sanctioned shows are open only to dogs who have not won five or more first prizes in the post-graduate or higher classes.

The third type of show is the Limited Show. While some of these shows will separate classes for several breeds, they also hold classes for "Any Variety."

The fourth type of show is the Open Show. These shows often contain any number of classes; smaller events are not benched, but the Kennel Club requires that Open shows must be benched. Open shows often offer prizes of money, and owners are encouraged to enter young dogs. It is at these shows that points may be won for a Junior Warrant title.

The fifth and last type of show is the Championship Show. It is at these events that the Kennel Club offers Challenge Certificates. There are approximately twenty-five All-Breed Championship Shows held in England each year. In addition, the Golden Retriever Club holds four Specialist Club Shows (Specialties) where Challenge Certificates are offered. Goldens are usually allotted at least twelve different classes, and sometimes as many as twenty. These classes are divided by sex, age, and previous wins.

The Kennel Club awards and titles differ significantly from those awarded by the American Kennel Club. The equivalent to the awarding of points at American shows is a coveted Challenge Certificate which is won by the best of each sex at Championship shows. In order to receive this award, the dog must have won his or her individual class and then compete and win a class in which all others who have won their respective classes are shown. The competition in these classes will often contain many Champions and it is very difficult to obtain a Challenge Certificate unless the dog is of outstanding merit.

Once a Golden Retriever has accumulated three Challenge Certificates from three different judges, he has earned the title of Show Champion. This is solely a title for Gundogs (the equivalent of our Sporting Dogs). Goldens in England do not become full champions until they have earned a "Qualifying Certificate" (similar to the G.R.C.A. Working Certificate), or have won an award at a recognized Field Trial. No dog is allowed to run for a Qualifying Certificate unless he has won at least one Challenge Certificate. A dog may not run for a Qualifying Certificate more than three times a year.

Another coveted title is that of Field Champion. A Golden is given this award if it wins two first prizes at two different Field Trials in the Open or All-Age Stakes for Retrievers, or if he wins the Retriever Championship Stake. As in this country, a dog that has earned both the titles of Champion and Field Champion is awarded the title of Dual Champion.

The Junior Warrant title is given after winning twenty-five points in breed classes at Open and Championship shows before reaching the age of eighteen months.

All of these awards and titles are given to dogs of significant merit. Exhibitors work diligently at conditioning, training and grooming their dogs for competition at Kennel Club shows. Interestingly, there is no such thing as a professional handler in England. Almost all dogs are shown by their owners. Actual exhibiting also tends to be much less formal than in the United States, with very little stacking, or posing, done by the exhibitors.

As with every endeavor, there are always those individuals who have made their mark of distinction in their chosen field. Some of the more influential kennels that have distinguished themselves in the English Golden Club include: Anbria, Camrose, Deerflite, Stolford, Synspur, Westley, and Yeo. Dogs from these kennels have been imported to North America and figure in some American dogs' pedigrees. These are but a few of the many truly fine kennels that have been the foundation and mainstay of breeding stock in England today.

Am., Can. Ch. Golden Pine's Courvoisier, Am., Can. C.D.X., W.C. (Ch. Misty Morn's Sunset, C.D., T.D., W.C. ex Ch. Golden Pine's Punkin Pi, C.D.). "Cognac" is a G.R.C.A. Outstanding Sire and has produced some exceptional dogs. Bred by Marilu Seamans of Golden Pine Kennels, he is owned by Nancy K. Belsaas of San Mateo, California.

Chapter 16

Important Golden Kennels of Today

Over the years, a number of kennels have made especially significant contributions to improving and refining the quality of the Golden Retriever. Many of the important kennels of the past are no longer active today, though their bloodlines have been carried on by others. Some of the important kennels of the '40s and '50s produced the dogs that are behind many big winners of today. For example, the Cragmount Kennels of Mrs. C.W. Englehard is no longer in existence, but a number of dogs and bitches carrying the Cragmount prefix continue to have tremendous influence on the Goldens of today through their offspring. Both Champion Misty Morn's Sunset and Champion Cummings Gold-Rush Charlie have Cragmount dogs in the second generation of their pedigrees, and these two dogs' influence on the breed today is unquestioned. Numerous other now dormant kennels have been important factors in today's Goldens, including Lorelei, Nerrissida, Finderne, Des Lacs, Sprucewood, High Farms, Featherquest, and Golden Knoll, to name but a few.

Many of those who develop an interest in breeding Goldens do not, unfortunately, maintain that interest over a long period of time. A number do well with one or two dogs, but are unable or unwilling to carry out a well planned breeding program over a period of years. The art and science of breeding pure-bred dogs that are consistently superior is one that takes an intense interest in the breed, knowledge, money and, above all, time, to do well. It takes dedication and time, along with a measure of luck, to breed consistently good dogs from generation to generation. Breeding involves a thorough knowledge and understanding of the Standard and what it is that makes a good dog, as well as the willingness to honestly evaluate one's own dogs and their faults. Unfortunately, ego enters into this evaluation process and often gets in the way of sound, critical judgment. The breeding or

223

ownership of one outstanding dog does not necessarily lead to the automatic establishment of an important breeding kennel. Not every winner has the capability of being a good producer, and one must be extremely careful not to confuse a winning record with a producing record. The former does not always mean the latter.

With a number of notable exceptions, many of the better Golden kennels of today are less than fifteen years old, though almost all have been actively involved in breeding for over ten years. Very few of the important kennels of the late 40s and 50s are still around today. Each of these kennels has experienced many successes and all have suffered some failures. Each has strived to achieve the ultimate goal of producing the perfect dog, and each continues to do so despite their occasional failures. Many new kennels are established each year as the popularity of Goldens continues to increase, but few kennels have been able to maintain consistently superior breeding programs that stand the test of time.

The kennels mentioned in this chapter are those which, in the author's estimation, have withstood the challenges and who have produced top quality dogs over a number of generations. They have established a bloodline and type of their own and have produced superior winning and producing dogs over the years. My thanks to the owners of each of these kennels for taking the time to send me photographs of some of their dogs and information on their kennels. Due to a lack of space, there are a few other kennels that I would have liked to include but could not. Finally, there are a number of newer kennels who show a great deal of promise and in a few years might well be included in a listing such as the one here.

AMBERAC KENNELS

Amberac Kennels, owned by Ellen and Leon Manke, is located in Hartland, Wisconsin. Probably the best known dog bred by the Mankes is Champion Amberac's Austerling Aruba, one of those extremely rare Best in Show Golden bitches who is also a member of the Show Dog Hall of Fame. Since 1972, the Mankes have bred 17 champions, one O.T. Champion and three U.D. title holders. At least two Outstanding Dams were also bred in their kennel.

After five years of searching for a sound, well bred, show quality bitch, the Mankes obtained Amberac's Reeva Rustelle, who was to become a G.R.C.A. Outstanding Dam. Her litter sister, Amberac's Sungria de Ora, C.D. was also bred, producing an Outstanding Dam,

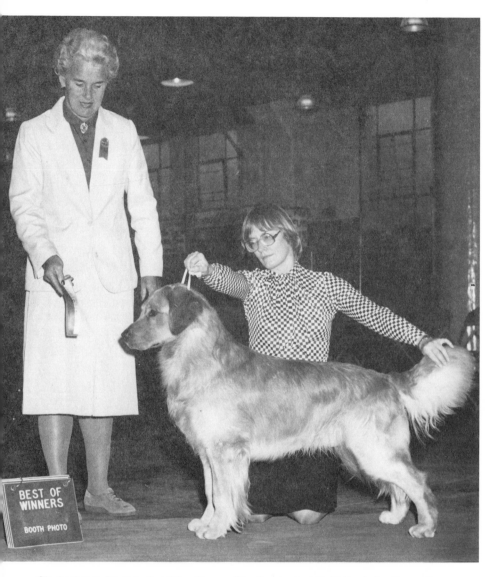

Ch. Amberac Ramala Rambling Rouge (Ch. Copper Lee Gold Rush Apollo ex Ch. Amberac's Sweet 'n Sassy). Sire of Ch. Amberac Sheza Q.T., this young dog is shown going Best of Winners under judge Jane Forsyth, handled by Lisa Schultz. Owned by Ellen Manke of Amberac Goldens. Photo: Martin Booth.

Amberac's Sunburst Sunbrave, W.C. A third foundation bitch was Champion Krishna's Klassic Fantasy.

Ellen Manke writes, "In our limited breeding program over the past 10 years, I have sought and strived for the best possible in overall structure, working ability and true loving disposition. We totally believe that unless a male or bitch can produce the soundness and quality to ideally represent the Golden Retriever, that animal is not worthy of being bred." With a relatively young kennel, the Mankes have already produced a number of fine Goldens.

BECKWITH GOLDEN RETRIEVERS

For the past twenty-six years, the names of Richard and Ludell Beckwith have been associated with the finest in Golden Retrievers. Over the years, they have bred more than 108 American and Canadian Champions of Record and numerous dogs with obedience titles. Both Mr. and Mrs. Beckwith are currently A.K.C. licensed judges, but they continue their breeding program on a limited scale. Their fifteen-year-old daughter Lynn is an avid competitor in the Junior Showmanship ring and has finished her own Goldens to championships.

The record of the Beckwith kennels over the years is an impressive one. Eight of their Goldens have been awarded All-Breed Best in Show awards, including American, Canadian, Mexican, Bermudian, and Colombian Champion Beckwiths Copper Coin who was a Group winner in all five countries as well as a Best in Show winner in three. His career record includes 16 All-Breed Best in Show wins plus 98 Group placements, including 42 Group wins. He was breeder/owner-handled to all these wins. This dog became the cornerstone of the breeding program and went on to become a G.R.C.A. Outstanding Sire with fifteen champions to his credit.

The Beckwith foundation bitch was an English import, American and Canadian Champion Beckwith's Frolic of Yeo, C.D.X., who is a G.R.C.A. Outstanding Dam with twelve American champions to her credit. Together with American, Canadian, and Mexican Champion Beckwith's Copper Ingot, a son of Copper Coin, who produced 27 Champions of Record, these dogs became an important part of a tremendously successful breeding program.

The tremendous contribution to the breed made by the Beckwiths over the years is reflected in the lists of Hall of Fame dogs. Fourteen Outstanding Dams carry the Beckwith prefix as well as seven Outstanding Sires. In addition, three Beckwith dogs are members of the

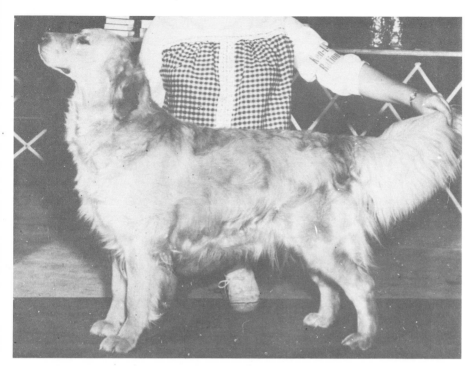

Am., Can. Ch. Beckwith's Frolic of Yeo, C.D.X., Can. C.D. (Ch. Orlando of Yeo ex Jessica of Yeo). Frolic, an English import was owned by Mr. and Mrs. Richard Beckwith and bred by Lucille Sawtell.

Am., Can., Bda., Mex., Col. Ch. Beckwith's Copper Coin (Beckwith's Golden Blaze, C.D. ex Venos Vixen, C.D.). Winner of Best of Breed at the 1964 G.R.C.A. National Specialty, sixteen Bests in Show and Group Firsts in all five countries.

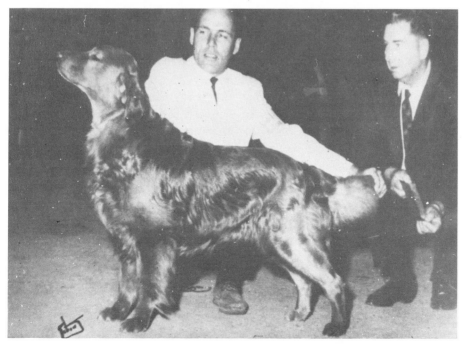

Returning over the high jump with her retrieved dumbbell is O.T. Ch. Beckwith's Eta of Spindrift, T.D., W.C.X. (Ch. Beckwith's Tally-Ho, C.D.X. ex Ch. Beckwith's Malagold Omega, W.C.). Owned by Pat Klausman of Alpharetta, Georgia, this Obedience Hall of Fame member has more than 20 High in Trial awards.

Obedience Hall of Fame and five are listed in the Show Dog Hall of Fame. A sixth dog was added to the latter list in 1982, when American and Canadian Champion Beckwith's Chianti, American and Canadian C.D., became the sixth bitch in Breed history to enter the Show Dog Hall of Fame. The Beckwith family currently resides in Snohomish, Washington.

BRANDYWINE GOLDENS

The Brandywine kennels of Ben and Bonnie Gikis, located in Los Altos Hills, California, began in 1970 with their first bitch, Ch. Brandywine Tansu D'Oro. As a youngster, Brandywine earned thirteen points as a puppy and gained the last two needed to complete her championship shortly thereafter. As the Gikis' foundation bitch, Brandywine produced five Champions of Record from four different sires. One of these was the Gikis' first homebred champion, Champion Brandywine's Dusty Dandy, C.D.X. who went on to produce four champions himself, all out of Aurora's Sunshine Sadie from two litters. One of these pups, Champion Sadie's Sundance Kidd, C.D.X. is a G.R.C.A. Show Dog Hall of Fame member.

Still quite active in the breed ring and occasionally in the obedience ring, Ben and Bonnie Gikis continue to show and breed. For a time, they co-owned Champion Gold-Rush Lightin' and showed him to a number of good wins on the West Coast.

Ch. Brandywine's Dusty Dandy, C.D.X. (Ch. Aubrey's Golden Sundance, C.D. ex Ch. Brandywine's Tansu D'oro). Sire of Ch. Sadie's Sundance Kidd, C.D.X. shown going Winners Dog. The sire of four champions to date, he was the first homebred champion for his owners Ben and Bonnie Gikis.

Can. Ch. Carolee's Bran Muffin (Can. Ch. HGL's Golden Pine Gibson Solo ex Can. Ch. Carolee's Cafe Au Lait, Am., Can. C.D., W.C.), litter sister to Can. Dual Ch. A.F.C. Carolee's Something Special, Am., Can. C.D., W.C.X., winning Best of Opposite Sex for the second year at the 1981 National Specialty Show of the Golden Retriever Club of Canada under judge William Hammond. Breeder-owned by Shirley Goodman.

CAROLEE

Carolee Goldens is the kennel name of Shirley M. Goodman of Don Mills, Ontario, Canada, a name derived by combining the first names of Mrs. Goodman's daughter and herself. Beginning with Goldens in 1966, a bitch was purchased who later became Canadian Champion Goldendale Belle, C.D., the dam of five champions. Belle was bred on American lines, including Stilrovin, Golden Knolls and Des Lacs, and English lines including International Dual Champion David of Westley and Irish Dual Champion Stubblesdown Golden Lass.

Breeding to Canadian and American dogs, the Goodmans produced a number of top winners, including Canadian Champion Carolee's Cafe Au Lait, American and Canadian C.D., W.C., who produced five champions herself and was a daughter of Belle, and Canadian Champion Carolee's Bran Muffin, two-time winner of Best of Opposite Sex at the Canadian Golden Retriever Club's National Specialty.

Carolee made breed history in Canada with their Dual Champion and A.F.C. Carolee's Something Special II, the first Canadian Golden Dual Champion in twenty years. He is only the fifth Golden Dual Champion in Canadian breed history. He has proved to be an important sire as well, already having four champions to his credit and a number of offspring doing well in field trials. This outstanding dog has a number of Best of Breed awards to his credit as well as Group placements. He has also won a five point major in the United States and was Best Canadian Bred at the 1980 G.R.C.C. National Specialty.

Carolee has not been involved in a heavy breeding program, having, on average, only one litter a year. Mrs. Goodman writes, "I had always admired the beauty and placidness of the Golden, combined with its natural field abilities, and I was determined, when I started to breed this versatile animal, to better every generation." So far, she has succeeded in reaching this goal.

CLOVERDALE GOLDENS

The Cloverdale Goldens of Richard and Jane Zimmerman is a good example of how, with perseverance and good luck, a young kennel can develop an enviable record. Begun in 1971, the Zimmermans' foundation bitch was purchased from Ruth Worrest Soule, owner of the well established High Farms Kennels. This bitch, High Farms Beau Brittany, was bred to the outstanding sire Champion Misty Morn's Sunset, C.D., T.D., W.C. This litter produced Champion Cloverdale's Sweet Sadie and Champion Cloverdale's Ringold Tobey owned by Nancy Fenn. Sadie was Winners Bitch at the 1975 National Specialty and went on to become one of the first bitches in many years to earn multiple Best of Breed awards, winning a total of eight. Tobey was a Best in Show winner at age three and is a member of the G.R.C.A. Show Dog Hall of Fame.

Sadie was bred to Champion Wochica's Okeechobee Jake and produced three champions, one a multiple group winner. Later, she was bred to Champion Cloverdale Bunker Hill Seth, producing one champion and a bitch who was named Cloverdale Sabrina. Sabrina, bred to

Ch. Cloverdale's Ringold Tobey (Ch. Misty Morn's Sunset, C.D., T.D., W.C. ex High Farms Beau Brittany). Shown here going Best in Show under Mrs. Doris Wear, handled by Bob Stebbins. Tobey was bred by Richard and Jane Zimmerman. Photo: John Ashbey.

Champion Sutter Creek Goldrush Flyboy, produced Champion Cloverdale Twin-Beau-D Joy, owned by Nancy and Robert Dallaire. Joy became the first Golden bitch in 27 years to win an All Breed Best in Show, doing so from the Open Bitch class to complete her championship. She later earned enough points to enter the G.R.C.A. Show Dog Hall of Fame.

Another bitch sired by Seth is American and Canadian Champion Sutter Creek Cloverdale Erin, co-owned by the Zimmermans and Susan Breakell. Erin won a number of Best of Breed awards and three Group Firsts. Another winning Cloverdale dog was American and Canadian Champion October Cloverdale Frost, who was bred by Sharon Smith and is co-owned by the Zimmermans and Mrs. R.V. Clark, Jr. The Cloverdale kennel is located in Tolland, Connecticut.

AMBERCROFT KENNELS

Carole A. Lee of Ambercroft in Mississauga, Ontario, Canada began working with Goldens in 1969, starting with a foundation dam that represented a combination of American and English lines. She was Canadian Champion Elizabeth of Aspen, whose pedigree was based on American and Canadian Champion Golden Band of High Farms and Champion Star Spray Maria's Gloria on one side and Canadian Champion Ambassador of Davern (an English import) and English Show Champion Camrose Nicholas of Westley and Sutton Rudy on the other side. Breeding programs at Ambercroft have been based on this bitch, who is now in the fifth generation of some of the most recent dogs' pedigrees.

One of the top dogs bred at Ambercroft is Canadian Champion Ambercroft's Bimbo, American and Canadian C.D. and Canadian W.C. sire of multi Best in Show winner, American and Canadian Champion Main Topic of Ambercroft, American and Canadian C.D., who was awarded the trophy for Top Producing Stud Dog in the Golden Retriever Club of Canada in 1980.

In 1976, the Lees imported an American Champion from Nancy K. Belsaas. He was Champion HGL's Golden Pine Gibson Solo, American and Canadian C.D., W.C. This dog sired many Canadian Champions and obedience title holders, including a Canadian Obedience Trial Champion and the first Canadian Dual Champion in twenty years, Dual Champion and A.F.C. Carolee's Something Special II, American and Canadian C.D., W.C.X. Liking the lines that Gibson represented, the Lees purchased a dog sired by Champion Misty Morn's Sunset, C.D., T.D., W.C. and another dog sired by a Misty Morn son, Champion Sir Duncan of Woodbury. Both are Canadian Champions. Writes Carole, "A special part of our breeding and showing has been the striving to produce better Goldens capable of multipurpose work and the comradeship of breeders and friends on both sides of the border."

GAYHAVEN KENNELS

Gayhaven Kennels started inauspiciously in 1951 when Sam and Betty Gay bought their first hunting Golden Retriever from Shelter Cove Kennels in Minnesota. In 1957 their first home-bred Champion was born. Champion Gayhaven Harmony C.D.X. (co-owned with Marcia Schlehr) became an Outstanding Dam of six champions including American and Canadian Gayhaven Lidiel, C.D.X., W.C. (sire

In a photo taken in 1971, at the age of seven and a half years, this is Gayhaven Timidiquis, a G.R.C.A. Outstanding Sire, with his owner, Mrs. Betty Gay, Rockwood, Michigan.

of eight champions) and American and Canadian Champion Kyrie Daemon, C.D.X., W.C. (sire of 14 champions).

Another early stud was Gayhaven Timidiquis, sire of four champions and grandsire of American and Canadian Champion Beckwith's Copper Ingot (sire of 27 champions), American and Canadian Champion Ciadar Tintinabulation, U.D.T., W.C. (sire of seven champions), and Champion Braevue's Vixen, W.C. (dam of four champions).

Gayhaven Lldiel was B.W. at the 1960 National Specialty when only eight and a half months old, and his son, American and Canadian Champion Kyrie Loch Cambeauly, C.D.X., W.C., got the Reserve at the 1967 event. Tim's daughter, American and Canadian Champion Gayhaven Fashion Plate was Reserve Winners Bitch in 1966, while Daemon's daughters took two top National awards. American and Canadian Champion Kyrie Daemon's Rebil, C.D.X., W.C. being W.B. in 1965 and Gayhaven Kayla of Norlyn, W.C. going R.W.B. at the 1971 National.

Although seldom maintaining more than six dogs and with most of the family handled by their amateur-owners, we find Gayhaven ancestors in the pedigrees of virtually hundreds of Golden champions with foundation stock in early Beckwith, Kyrie, Ciadar, and Ocoee lines coming from this background.

Having an early agreement not to keep anything Sam could not hunt with and Betty could not show, and with particular care regarding genetic testing, this small kennel has maintained its reputation of producing quality, stable Golden Retrievers for over 25 years.

GOLDEN PINE KENNELS

The Golden Pine Kennels, owned by Mary Luise Semans of Chesapeake, Virginia, has been around since the early 1950s. The first dog owned by the Semans, Champion Duke of Rochester II, C.D., began a tradition of excellence that continues to the present day. This first dog at his third show went Best of Breed and Group third, and not just at any show, but at the Westminster Kennel Club show in New York!

Duke of Rochester sired Champion Wessala Pride of Golden Pine. This bitch was bred to Champion Little Joe of Tigathoe ***, a combination that produced well, including multi-group winners and a Best in Show dog. This became the foundation for a breeding program that has had and continues to have a major effect on our Goldens today. Mrs. Seamans writes "I'm not too good about blowing my own horn." Nevertheless, there have been at least 160 Golden Champions bred at Golden Pine Kennels and many more with obedience titles and Working Certificates.

When asked what she thinks is her greatest accomplishment in Goldens, Mrs. Semans writes, "I feel my greatest accomplishment is that I have kept true to what a Golden should be in size – looks – and temperament. I knew what I liked from the beginning and have tried to stick to it without blowing with the popular wind."

Working with Mrs. Semans on the West Coast and sharing her kennel name are Nancy and Dean Belsaas, who live in San Mateo, California. As a youngster, Nancy became interested in Goldens when she wanted a dog to train and show in Junior Showmanship competition. Her first dog had been a Collie, but when it died her parents would not allow her to purchase another. They did, however, permit the purchase, in 1955, of a Golden puppy. Her visit to see the litter resulted in the purchase of two pups and Nancy eventually completed a championship title on the male. Showing this dog in Junior Showmanship, she won the Champion Junior Showman of the United States title at the 1958 Westminster Kennel Club show. This dog, Champion Brandy's Golden Ghost, also became a Group Winner.

Nancy found a job with Lloyd Case, a well-known professional handler at the time, and in this manner met many of the most important Golden breeders of the time, among them the Semans of Golden Pine Kennels. A strong relationship developed and has continued over the years, even after Nancy married and moved to the West Coast. In 1971, Nancy obtained from Mrs. Semans a dog who would become

Ch. Golden Pine's Down Payment (Ch. Duncan Dell's Drummond, C.D.** ex Ch. Golden Pine's Bambi's Lady). A G.R.C.A. Outstanding Dam who figures in many of today's pedigrees, she was owned by Mary-Luise Semans of Golden Pine Kennels. Photo was taken in October, 1968 with Bob Walgate handling. Photo: E. Shafer.

American and Canadian Champion Golden Pine's Courvoisier, American and Canadian C.D.X, W.C., American W.C.X. With the idea of maintaining the multi-purpose aspect of the Goldens, Mrs. Belsaas kept a daughter of her dog out of Champion Odu's Bianca of Manorloch. This bitch, Chaparrel of Golden Pine, C.D., W.C., was bred to Champion Golden Pine's Shehazarin, U.D.T., W.C. A male was kept, American and Canadian Champion Golden Pine's Remy Martin, American and Canadian C.D., American W.C. A son of Courvoisier (who is called "Cognac") was sold to Jim and Carol Lee of Ambercroft Kennels in Streetsville, Canada. This dog, Canadian Champion HGL's Golden Pine Gibson Solo, American and Canadian C.D., W.C. was an Outstanding Sire in Canada and produced the only current Dual Champion in Canada, Dual Champion Carolee's Something Special II.

236

Recently, a bitch out of Westmont's Diana, C.D., W.C. (a Cognac daughter) was purchased. She became Champion Golden Pine's O'Luv Amaretto, W.C. She was able to produce only one litter before she was spayed due to an infection, so another bitch was purchased from Pepperhill Kennels. She became Champion Pepperhill Golden Pine Irish. Irish was recently bred to Cognac, thus continuing the Belsaas' work towards their goal of producing multi-purpose Goldens who maintain the reputation of the Semans' Golden Pine Kennels.

GOLD-RUSH KENNELS

On rare occasions, a dog purchased as a pet turns out to be of a high enough quality that he is able to complete his championship. Only once in a great while will this dog be of "specials" quality. In the unique case of R. Ann and Larry Johnson, a dog purchased at five weeks of age, to become a family pet, became the top winning Golden Retriever of all time. This great dog was American, Canadian and Bermudian Champion Cummings Gold-Rush Charlie. As detailed in another chapter, Charlie's record as a show dog is unparalleled in the history of the breed.

Ann Johnson's Gold-Rush kennels, located in Princeton, New Jersey, was founded in the early 1970s and its bloodlines are based on Charlie. The Johnsons were faced with a difficult problem in beginning a breeding program, as Charlie was their only dog. They acquired a quality bitch from Mary Luise Seman's Golden Pine kennels, Golden Pines Glorybe's Angel, and, after completing her championship, bred her to Charlie. This combination produced a total of 12 champions, a number of whom qualified for the Show Dog Hall of Fame, including Champion Gold-Rush's Great Teddy Bear, co-owned with Diane Smith, who was Best of Breed at the 1978 National Specialty (where a Charlie daughter, American and Canadian Champion Russo's Pepperhill Poppy was Best of Opposite Sex, and the two won Charlie the Stud Dog Class).

A second foundation bitch was purchased from the Jungold Kennel; she was Jungold's L.C.'s Lady Ambassador. Also an Outstanding Dam from her breeding to Charlie, she produced Champion Stone's Gold-Rush Shiloh, owned by Dr. Gary Stone. Shiloh was the Top Golden in the Country for a year a few years ago.

The Johnsons selected two Charlie daughters bred by other breeders to keep in their kennel. One was Champion Wochica's Gold-Rush Bonanza, a Best of Breed winning bitch and another Outstanding

Dam. Another well known Charlie daughter is O.T. Champion, Champion Russo's Gold-Rush Sensation, the first dog of any breed to hold both the bench and obedience champion titles. She was co-owned with Edward L. Hamm.

Numerous other champions have been bred by or sired by Gold-Rush dogs, including several Best in Show Winners and at least three National Specialty winners. Through a program of linebreeding, the Gold-Rush kennel has achieved notable successes in the breed ring. The effects of their stud dogs, particularly Charlie, have made a lasting impression and impact on the breed as a whole.

Ch. Gold-Rush's Great Teddy Bear (Am., Can., Bda. Ch. Cummings Gold-Rush Charlie ex Ch. Golden Pines Glorybe's Angel). Winner of Best of Breed at the 1978 G.R.C.A. National Specialty as well as other specialty wins, Teddy is here winning one of his many Best of Breed awards, with L.C. Johnson handling. Photo: John Ashbey.

Going Winners Dog at the 1980 Potomac Valley Golden Retriever Club Specialty is Ch. Westben's Dancing Bear, C.D.X. (Ch. Gold-Rush's Great Teddy Bear ex Ch. Goldwing's Tiffany). Owner is Craig Westergaard of Princeton, New Jersey. Photo: Bernard Kernan.

The winner of the Brood Bitch Class at the 1965 G.R.C.A. National Specialty was Ch. Gayhaven Harmony, C.D.X. With two of her sons, Am., Can. Ch. Kyrie Daemon, C.D.X., W.C. (center) and Am., Can. Ch. Gayhaven Lidiel, Am., Can. C.D.X., W.C. Judge is Mrs. R. Gilman Smith.

241

A foundation dam at the Jolly Kennels, this is Ch. Indanda Thembalisha completing her championship. A G.R.C.A. Outstanding Dam, "Dandy" was owned by John Lounsbury and Tina Lewesky. She was sired by Ch. Misty Morn's Sunset, C.D., T.D., W.C. out of Khetha Thembalisha.

JOLLY KENNEL

John and Lynne Lounsbury's Jolly Kennel, located in Billings, New York, began in 1963 with the purchase of a pet Golden. By 1967, the Lounsburys decided to become seriously involved in breeding and showing, but it took five more years before they were able to purchase a quality Golden bitch who could become the foundation bitch for the Jolly Kennel. This bitch, purchased from the Rev. Edward French, became Ch. Indanda Thembalisha, now a G.R.C.A. Outstanding Dam of seven Champions. "Dandy" is a Champion Misty Morn's Sunset, C.D., T.D., W.C. daughter and her pedigree is all Cragmount for three generations. Two of Dandy's offspring are Outstanding Producers and one qualified as a member of the Show Dog Hall of Fame. Three of her grandchildren are Hall of Fame members as well.

242

The best known stud dog at Jolly Kennel is undoubtedly Champion Sir Duncan of Woodbury, who was taken in at the age of six years after family difficulties in his original pet home. Duncan was brought into show condition and finished his championship in just twelve shows. Despite his age, he went on to win a number of Best of Breed awards, including one at the 1979 Westminster show. Duncan's influence on Goldens was impressive. Through 1982, he had sired 24 champions.

Over a relatively short period of time, the Lounsburys have owned or bred at least 23 Champions and a large number of dogs with obedience degrees. Four of their dogs have been named Outstanding Producers, including Champion Indanda Thembalisha, Jolly Victoria of Misty Morn, American and Canadian Champion Jolly Jake Daniels, and, of course Duncan.

KYRIE

The Kyrie Goldens of Marcia Schlehr, who lives in Clinton, Michigan, trace their beginnings back to the late 1950s. Ms. Schlehr's first Golden, Sidram Selectric, U.D.T., W.C., Canadian C.D.X., writes Ms. Schlehr, "showed me what a marvelous dog the Golden can be, should be. He set standards in my mind that have held through more than 27 years."

Kyrie's foundation bitch was Champion Gayhaven Harmony, C.D.X., acquired from Sam and Betty Gay's Gayhaven Kennels in 1959. She quickly earned her titles and is, according to Ms. Schlehr, one of only two Golden bitches to produce champions by four different sires. Subsequent breeding at Kyrie has followed a pattern of linebreeding on Harmony with specific reasons for rare outcrosses. Harmony's offspring include two G.R.C.A. Outstanding Sires and several Outstanding Producers in subsequent generations.

Writes Ms. Schlehr, "With a very limited breeding program, a small kennel, and very restricted showing, we have concentrated on the Golden that is genetically and physically sound, capable of performing any of the Golden Retriever's basic purposes; a balanced and moderate dog of proper breed type, long lived, and with truly Golden personality. I have had so much enjoyment with these dogs—so much more than a recital of wins and titles could indicate."

Two of the most outstanding Kyrie dogs are American and Canadian Champion Gayhaven Lldiel, American and Canadian C.D.X., American W.C., one of the youngest dogs ever to take points at a Na-

Ch. Sun Dance's Bootleg Whiskey, U.D. (Ch. Kyrie Daemon, C.D.X. ex Ch. Sun Dance's Contessa). Owned by Nick Pecora of Elmwood Park, Illinois, this dog is not only a champion, but is a member of the G.R.C.A. Obedience Dog Hall of Fame and is an Outstanding Sire. Photo: Ritter.

tional Specialty, and the sire of eight American and sixteen Canadian Champions. His son, American and Canadian Champion Kyrie Daemon, American C.D.X, W.C., Canadian C.D. owned by Pat and Joan Nazark is also an Outstanding Sire.

Marcia Schlehr is the author of the excellent paperback, *A Study of the Golden Retriever*.

244

LAURELL KENNELS

Laurell Kennels traces its beginnings to a ten year old girl's desire for a trainable dog to take to obedience classes. Her original dog, of another breed, turned vicious and had to be put down. With the help of Edie Munneke of Rusticana Goldens, a replacement Golden Retriever was purchased, but she developed a bad bite. This dog was replaced with a free puppy who became Champion Rusticana's Princess Teena, C.D., the foundation bitch for the Laurell Kennel, now located in Cincinnati, Ohio and run by this now grown-up girl, Laura Ellis Kling and her husband Tom.

Teena was eventually bred to Champion High Farms Sutters Gold, and the resulting litter produced the first two Laurell Champion home-breds, Champion Laurell's Allspice, C.D. and Champion Laurell's Amiable Caboose, this while Laura was in high school.

Winning Best of Breed at a Fort Detroit Golden Retriever Club Specialty is Am., Can. Ch. Duckdown's Unpredictable, C.D., W.C. (Ch. Sun Dance's Moonlight Gambler, C.D.X., W.C. ex Ch. Sprucewood's Harvest Sugar, C.D.). A G.R.C.A. Show Dog Hall of Fame member and an Outstanding Sire of 22 champions, he was owned by Laura Ellis Kling.

Winning Best of Breed at the 1982 G.R.C.A. National Specialty under judge Mrs. Judith Fellton is Am., Can. Ch. Laurell's York (Ch. Gold-Rush Lightnin' ex Ch. Laurell's Kilimanjaro). "Denver" is a G.R.C.A. Show Dog Hall of Fame member owned by Thomas and Laura Ellis Kling. Photo: Tom Morrissette.

Ch. Little Bit of Laurel (Am., Can. Ch. Laurell's Allspice ex Hulls Bay Beauty). A G.R.C.A. Outstanding Dam from the Laurell Kennels.

One of Laura's dogs, Champion Duckdown's Unpredictable, attended Laura's wedding. That same year, Champion Laurell's Amiable Caboose was bred to Champion Major Gregory of High Farms, and the resulting litter produced three dogs who later became champions, the most famous of which was Champion Laurell's Especial Jason, U.D.T., owned by Cherie Berger.

There were three stud dogs at Laurell that the Klings especially liked: Champion Duckdown's Unpredictable, C.D.; Champion Laurell's Allspice, C.D.; and Champion Vagabond's Cougar Bill, C.D. Laura set a goal of combining all three in one pedigree. This was accomplished by breeding an Unpredictable daughter to Allspice, which produced Champion Little Bit of Laurell, who was in turn bred to Cougar, which produced Champion Laurell's Kilimanjaro. "Killer" presently has ten champions to her credit with several others nearing their titles. One of Killer's breedings was to Champion Gold-Rush Lightnin', a breeding which produced six champions, including Champion Laurell's York, a Best in Show and Hall of Fame dog who won Best of Breed at the 1982 National Specialty.

The Klings continue to breed and show their dogs and have several youngsters who are doing quite well in the ring.

Am., Can., Mex. Ch. Cal-Vo's Happy Ambassador, C.D. (Ch. Footprint of Yeo, C.D. ex Ch. Beckwith's Malagold Starfarm). "Adolph" is a member of the G.R.C.A. Show Dog Hall of Fame and is an Outstanding Sire. He produced a number of top-quality bitches who became important breeding stock at several important kennels. He is shown winning the Stud Dog Class at a G.R.C.A. Western Regional Specialty. Behind him are Ch. Lark Mill Genevieve, C.D. and Ch. Karmiloch Starquest, W.C. Adolph was owned by Bill and Joan Young.

HAPPY-GO-LUCKY KENNELS

Happy-Go-Lucky Kennels was established in 1965, beginning at first with German Shepherd Dogs and English Springer Spaniels. At one dog show, owner Joan Young of Concord, California, met a new Golden who had just arrived from the East Coast. Tremendously impressed with this dog, Champion Footprint of Yeo owned by Carol Vogel, Joan was able to purchase a puppy of his, quickly named "Adolph" and registered as Cal-Vo's Happy Ambassador. At the tender age of ten months Adolph won his first Best of Breed award and a Sporting Group fourth. Shortly thereafter he was Winners Dog and Best of Winners at the 1971 G.R.C.A. National Specialty. Quickly

completing his title, he was specialed for a number of years, achieving Top Ten status each year.

Adolph proved to be an important producer and became the foundation of a Golden breeding program at HGL. He was a G.R.C.A. Outstanding Sire and Show Dog Hall of Fame member. Some of his better known offspring include: Champion Lark Mill Genevieve, C.D., Champion HGL's Golden West Coquette; and Champion Valhalla Trowsnest Folly, U.D.T., W.C.X.

Other champions from HGL include Champion HGL's Happy Charisma of Cal-Vo, Champion Krishna Klassic Melody of HGL, Champion Krishna HGL Ragtime Rhythm, and Champion Krishna HGL Fascinatin' Rhythm.

MALAGOLD KENNELS

Malagold Kennels was begun in the mid 1960s by Ken and Connie Gerstner and is located in DeForest, Wisconsin. At the time, the Gerstners raised both Goldens and Malamutes, hence their kennel name. First working primarily in the obedience ring, the Gerstners soon started showing in conformation at some local shows.

In establishing a breeding line, Connie and Ken worked closely with Dick and Ludell Beckwith of Beckwith Goldens, who then lived in Wisconsin. The two families co-bred several litters. Out of a litter sired by Champion Beckwith's Copper Coin, came Champion Malagold Beckwith Big Buff, C.D., the foundation sire of Malagold. Buff won three Best in Show awards as well as numerous Group firsts and was a Top Ten Golden for several years.

From Buff and Beckwith's Chickasaw Jingle came the kennel's foundation dam, Malagold Beckwith Bootes, a G.R.C.A. Outstanding Dam of ten champions. She was bred to Champion Appollo of Yeo, an English import, on two occasions and produced six champions from these two litters. Several of these champions went on to become Outstanding Producers themselves. One of these was Champion Malagold's Svea, the dam of two top winning dogs, Champion Malagold Summer Chant and Champion Malagold Summer Encore.

Future plans for Malagold lie with Bootes' grandchildren. The Gerstners write, "We always try to produce the soundest Goldens possible with the showiness, intelligence and structure to improve the breed."

MEADOWPOND GOLDEN RETRIEVERS

When it comes to dual purpose Goldens who excel in the obedience ring, the Meadowpond Goldens of Cherie Berger in Romeo, Michigan is a kennel to remember. Since 1968, Cherie has been raising Goldens. She writes, "We are striving for sound all-around dogs that can excel in both conformation and obedience, as well as retaining the desire to do field work." A look at the current list of top obedience dogs confirms that Cherie is reaching her goal.

Foundation sires used at Meadowpond include American and Canadian Champion Bardfield Boomer, American U.D.T., W.C., Canadian U.D., T.D.X. Boomer was Best of Winners at the 1970 G.R.C.A. National Specialty and is the sire of at least eleven Obedience Trial Champions as well as other High in Trial winners and bench champions. A second sire used at Meadowpond was American and Cana-

Ch. Malagold Beckwith Big Buff, C.D. (Am., Can., Bda., Mex., Col. Ch. Beckwith's Copper Coin ex Beckwith's Chrys-Haefen Belinda). Winner of Best of Breed at the 1970 G.R.C.A. National Specialty, he is shown winning a Group First at Land O Lakes Kennel Club in 1971. Owned by Connie Gerstner.

Outstanding Meadowpond Goldens, (left to right): Am., Can. Ch. Bardfield Boomer, Am. U.D.T., W.C., Can. U.D., T.D.X. (Outstanding Sire and Obedience Dog Hall of Fame); Am., Can. Ch. Laurell's Especial Jason, Am. U.D.T., W.C., Can., U.D.T. (G.R.C.A. Show Dog Hall of Fame and Outstanding Sire); Laurell's Jaunty Jinn-Jinn, C.D.X. (Outstanding Dam); Am., Can. Ch. Cimaron's Dazzle Dust, Am. C.D.X., T.D., W.C.X., Can. C.D., T.D. (Outstanding Dam); Am., Can. Ch. Chafa Honeybun of Jungold, C.D.X., T.D., W.C. (Outstanding Dam); Am., Can. Ch. Meadowpond Dazzle's Sparkle, C.D. (Outstanding Dam); Huntrail's Meadowpond Solo, C.D., W.C., O.T.; Ch. Meadowpond Tackle, Can. C.D.X.; and Am., Can. Ch. Jagersbo Meadowpond Melody, Am., Can. C.D.

dian Laurell's Especial Jason, W.C., American, Canadian U.D.T., a Show Dog Hall of Fame member, and a third, Champion Cimaron's Dusty Dawn U.D.T. ***, one of very few dogs to hold all these titles.

Meadowpond's foundation bitches include four G.R.C.A. Outstanding Dams: American and Canadian Champion Cimaron's Dazzle Dust, C.D.X., T.D., W.C.; American and Canadian Champion Chafa Honeybun of Jungold, C.D.X., T.D., W.C.; Laurell's Jaunty Jinn-Jinn, C.D.X.; and American and Canadian Champion Meadowpond's Dazzle's Sparkle, C.D.

Among the many Meadowpond dogs who have done especially well are: Champion and O.T. Champion Meadowpond Dust Commander, who was the top obedience dog in the country in 1979, 1980 and 1981 and is the number one dog, all breeds, in lifetime obedience trial points; O.T. Champion Meadowpond Fem de Fortune, W.C., winner of the Super Dog Award at the 1981 Gaines Obedience Classic; and American and Canadian Champion Meadowpond David the Bold, American and Canadian C.D., a member of the Show Dog Hall of Fame.

A look at the 1982 Obedience statistics gives a picture of the quality of Meadowpond Goldens in the obedience ring. Of the top 25 dogs, all breeds, four carry the Meadowpond prefix.

PEPPERHILL KENNELS

The author's Pepperhill Kennels, located in Putnam Valley, New York, traces its beginnings back to the late 1960s when a Golden was purchased as a pet. This dog was first shown in the obedience ring and, following a good deal of encouragement from breed people, started his show career at the age of more than four years. He became Champion Sir Richard of Fleetwood, C.D. and was responsible for involving my wife Barbara and me in the world of show dogs.

A bitch puppy was later purchased, but did not work out as a producer. Our foundation bitch, Champion Cummings Dame Pepperhill, was purchased as an eight-week-old pup from Lynn and Mary Cummings, breeders of American, Canadian and Bermudian Champion Cummings Gold-Rush Charlie, who was a full brother to this bitch. Bred to a Charlie son, Champion Gold-Rush's Great Teddy Bear, De De produced five champions, two of whom, like their mother, are Outstanding Producers. They are Champion Pepperhill's Return Ticket and American and Canadian Champion Pepperhill's Basically Bear, sire of seven champions to date. Each of these dogs produced a

Ch. Cummings Dame Pepperhill (Ch. Sunset's Happy Duke ex Am., Can. Ch. Cummings Golden Princess). The foundation dam at Pepperhill Kennels, "DeDe" is shown completing her championship at the age of six years. She was already a G.R.C.A. Outstanding Dam at the time and now has five champions to her credit. Judge is the late James Trullinger. Photo: William Gilbert.

Specialty Best of Breed winner, and Return Ticket is the mother of Champion Pepperhill East Point Airily, who recently qualified for the Show Dog Hall of Fame, only the eighth bitch ever to accomplish this.

In 1975 an eight-week-old puppy bitch was purchased from Mercer Russo. This bitch went on to become our second foundation bitch, after De De, and also accomplished a feat that had not happened for more than 25 years and by only two other bitches—qualification for the Show Dog Hall of Fame. She is, of course, American and Canadian Champion Russo's Pepperhill Poppy. Poppy is also an Outstanding Dam and the mother of six champions as of this writing.

Ch. Pepperhill's Return Ticket (Ch. Gold-Rush's Great Teddy Bear ex Ch. Cummings Dame Pepperhill). "Ginny" is shown completing her championship in 1979. A G.R.C.A. Outstanding Dam, she is the mother of two Specials bitches, Am., Can. Ch. Pepperhill Lady Ruston, a Multiple Breed winner with several Group placements and a Specialty Best of Breed to her credit, and Ch. Pepperhill East Point Airily, a Hall of Fame bitch. Ginny presently has three champions to her credit. Photo: Earl Graham.

Through a careful process of linebreeding with only rare outcrosses, we have worked to hold on to the typical Golden temperament in producing dogs that can win in the breed ring and work well in obedience. Special emphasis has also been placed on maintaining good shoulders and correct reach and drive when moving. More than 25 championships and numerous obedience titles have been won by Pepperhill dogs.

254

RIVERVIEW KENNELS

One of the difficulties in setting a goal for a breeding program is that initial attempts may not be successful, and it sometimes is necessary to stand back, look at what you have, and realize that you must start over again from the beginning. Such a problem occurred with Jim and Sally Venerable of Riverview Kennels in Huntley, Illinois.

Beginning in 1952, the Venerables decided that Golden Retrievers would be the breed for them. They were able to purchase a bitch who was to become Lucky Tuck's Cindy, C.D.X. She was bred to Field Champion Tri Stada Upset and produced several nice pups, including Champion Riverview's Golden Shot, C.D.X. Concerned about soundness, Jim and Sally became interested in hip dysplasia, a relatively newly discovered problem at that time, and embarked on a program of breeding designed to produce dogs with clear hips. This continued for four generations with successful results. However, at about the time of the fourth generation, the Venerables purchased some pups from the Kinike Kennel. Not only did these pups have clear hips, but they had, writes Jim "Much better style and working abilities than those from

Four early Riverview dogs sit with their mistress Sally Venerable. They are Riverview King's Handyman***, Riverview's Kinike Rocket***, F.C., A.F.C., Kinike Coquette, C.D., and A.F.C. Ch. Riverview's Chickasaw Thistle, U.D.T., all owned by James and Sally Venerable.

King Kinike of Handjem*** (Poika of Handjem ex Shenandoah of Stilrovin, C.D.***), one of James and Sally Venerable's Kinike dogs that caused them to drop their previous breeding program.

our own breeding program. So, we abandoned the upgraded (original) line in spite of the great effort we had put into it."

At about the same time, Sally purchased a bitch puppy out of very typy High Farms stock. She was to become A.F.C., Champion Riverview's Chickasaw Thistle, U.D.T. This bitch had great empathy and was an ideal companion and family dog as well as being an exceptional shooting dog. As her titles indicate, she was competitive in all areas of competition.

The Kinike dogs did quite well. One became F.C., A.F.C. Kinike Coquette, C.D. who Jim considers to be their greatest trial dog. She qualified for several National Amateurs and National Opens.

Breeding programs at Riverview have produced some of the best field trial Goldens in the country. Dogs owned or bred by the Venerables continue to appear in the pedigrees of many of the best field dogs today.

RONAKERS KENNELS

The Ronakers Kennels, owned by Dixie, Ron and Sandy Akers of Sonoma, California, has been working with Golden Retrievers since 1961. Beginning with a dog who was never to be bred because he was dysplastic, Champion Ron's Golden Sabre, C.D., the Akers purchased what was to become their foundation bitch. She was Champion J's Kate, out of F.C. and A.F.C. Nicholas of Logan's End and Champion J's Teeko of Tigathoe ***. Kate was eventually bred to Champion Duck's Ripple of Golden Harp, producing Champion Ronaker's Novato Flash, and then bred to Champion Golden Duke of Trey-C which produced seven champions in two litters, six from the first. One of these champions was a rare Dual Champion. These dogs were: Dual Champion and A.F.C. Ronakers Novato Cain, C.D.; Champion Ronaker's Golden Orion, U.D. ***; Champion Ronakers Darling Diana, U.D.T., W.C.; Champion Ronakers Novato Gunner; Champion Ronakers Shadow of Duke, W.C.; and Champion Ronakers Fearless Leader, U.D. As one can easily tell from the titles, these dogs were all truly triple purpose dogs.

From that point on, the Akers have strived to produce dogs who are enthusiastic, intelligent workers. Efforts have concentrated on producing field trial dogs and obedience dogs, and the kennel has produced a number of obedience titled dogs as well as quite a few field qualified dogs with two and three stars.

Sandy Akers has written the chapter on Field Goldens for this book.

Ch. J's Kate, the Foundation bitch at Ronakers Kennels (F.C., A.F.C. Nicholas of Logan's End ex Ch. J's Teeko of Tigathoe***). A G.R.C.A. Outstanding Dam, Kate is the dam of a rare Dual Champion, Dual Ch. Ronaker's Novato Cain, C.D. as well as seven Bench Champions, most with obedience degrees. Photo: Roberts.

SENECA KENNELS

As with so many others, John and Sandra Kelly became interested in Goldens by purchasing a pet for their children. This first dog eventually led to the establishment of the Seneca Kennels in Germantown, Maryland.

A son of their first dog really began the Kellys' showing career. He was American and Canadian Champion Seneca's Riparian Chief, C.D., T.D., W.C. "Rip" went on to become a Show Dog Hall of Fame member. Among his wins was a Best of Breed and Group Second at the 1969 Westminster Kennel Club show. He is also an Outstanding Sire.

A son of Rip's, Champion Seneca's Tuckernuck Gold, C.D., W.C., followed in his father's footsteps and won an owner-handled Best in Show. Like his father, Tuck is a Hall of Fame dog and Outstanding Sire. He also placed in Sanctioned Field Trials. Tuck's mother was

Am., Can. Ch. Seneca's Riparian Chief, C.D., T.D., W.C. is shown in the foreground with his son, Ch. Seneca's Tuckernuck Gold, C.D., W.C. "Tuck" placed in licensed field trials and was a Best in Show winner. His mother, Ch. Candy of Sleepy Hollow was a granddaughter of Ch. Chee Chee of Sprucewood, the top-winning Golden bitch of all time.

Am., Can. Ch. Seneca's Riparian Chief, C.D., T.D., W.C. (Ch. Betaberk's Rockcrest Apache*** ex Prudant Penelope). "Rip" was a Best in Show winner owned by John and Sandra Kelly. He was Best of Breed and won Group Second at the 1969 Westminster Kennel Club show in New York City. Rip is shown at the age of five years.

Champion Candy of Sleepy Hollow, a grandaughter of the breed's top winning bitch, Champion Chee Chee of Sprucewood.

Sandy Kelly writes: Without succumbing to the desire to become owners of multitudes of Goldens, we have tried to do the best possible job with a breeding and training program with no more than six dogs at one time in our kennel and only one litter per year. Our breeding program has been based on our foundation bitch, Penny, mother of Rip.

We feel strongly that Goldens are an extremely versatile dog and, though they undoubtedly make excellent companions, they really are in their element when working—either in the field, obedience ring, or as tracking, scenting or seeing-eye dogs. Consequently, we have tried to produce versatile Goldens and breed for this purpose: a good looking Golden that can work.

SKYLON AND CHRYS-HAEFEN GOLDENS

These two top Canadian kennels began as one in 1965, run by twin sisters Judy Taylor and Jennifer McAuley under the "Chrys-Haefen" prefix. Beginning at first with American bloodlines, the sisters soon decided that they preferred the English type and in 1968 imported a bitch from England who became Canadian Champion Drexholme Ling, who became the foundation of their breeding program. In her first litter, she produced Champion Chrys-Haefen Spring Entity who Judy and Jennifer feel is their most influential dam.

That same year Judy and her husband Brian had the opportunity to purchase the Skylon kennel from John McNicol along with his breeding stock. Jennifer continued the original breeding program at Chrys-Haefen and thus the two kennels began to work side-by-side.

Breeding programs at Skylon and Chrys-Haefen have produced many of the top winning dogs in Canada since 1973. These include Canadian and Bermudian Champion Skylon Lancelot, the top Sporting dog in Canada in 1973, '74, '75, and his son Canadian and Bermudian Champion Nanno Chrys-Haefen Son of Skye, bred by Nancy

Shown winning the Stud Dog Class at a Canadian Golden Retriever Specialty is Can., Bda. Ch. Nanno Chrys-Haefen Son of Skye, C.D. and his children: (right to left) Can. Ch. Chrys-Haefen Thor's Fury; Can. Ch. Chrys-Haefen Foolish Pride; Am., Can. Ch. Chrys-Haefen Fox Fire, C.D.; Can., Bda. Ch. Saddleback Goodness Gracious Me; Can. Ch. Chrys-Haefen Chorus O'The Dawn, C.D.; and Can. Ch. Saddleback Christmas Crinkle. "Junior" is owned by Ian and Jennifer McAuley.

261

Freeman, who was top Sporting dog in 1978. A number of Canadian Best in Show winners have either been bred at one of these kennels or were sired by Skylon or Chrys-Haefen dogs.

Dogs who were imported from England and played an important role in these kennels' breeding programs include Canadian Champion Tugwood Cavalier, Canadian Champion Glennessa Uppity and Westley Lisbeth.

Working mainly with linebreedings, these kennels have a consistent record of producing top winning dogs. Writes Judy, "Linebreeding is certainly the main ingredient in our success, and when it becomes necessary to introduce new 'blood' we always try to choose a dog similar in type, that further back in the pedigree has similar lines. We have always been criticized for our 'light' Goldens and wish people would get past the colour prejudice and appreciate the pigmentation and eye colour as well as the conformation. Colour can be changed in one generation, but we have always considered too many other qualities to be concerned with the shade of gold."

SUN DANCE KENNELS

Few kennels have had as much influence on the Golden Retriever as the Sun Dance Kennels of Shirley and William Worley and Shirley's daughter, Lisa Schultz. Bill Worley's interest in dogs goes back to his childhood. In 1936 he began working with dogs, continued this work in the Army K-9 Corps during the Second World War, and has maintained this interest since then. In 1955, Bill became interested in Golden Retrievers, and by 1957 had bred his first litter, one which produced four champions. In 1962, Bill married Shirley who, with her daughter Lisa, brought a strong interest in dogs to complement Bill's.

The accomplishments of the Sun Dance Kennels are too great to list here. A look at the lists of Hall of Fame Dogs, Outstanding Sires and Dams and Obedience Hall of Fame dogs provide the reader with an idea of this kennel's influence on the breed. There are over 160 champions with the Sun Dance prefix, as well as literally hundreds of Sun Dance dogs with obedience titles. Top winning Sun Dance dogs include Champion Sun Dance Rarue, the top winning Golden in the country in 1976 and a National Specialty Best of Breed winner, as well as, to name a few: Champion Sun Dance's Esquire, C.D.; Champion Sun Dance's Vagabond Lover, C.D.X.; and Champion Sun Dance's Bronze, C.D., a two-time National Specialty winner.

First concentrating on the obedience ring, more recently the

Ch. Sun Dance's Contessa (Ch. Sun Dance's Esquire, C.D. ex Ch. Sun Dance's Taffeta Doll, C.D.X.). Like her mother, Contessa is a G.R.C.A. Outstanding Dam. Not only does she have twelve champions to her credit, but she also is one of the few Golden bitches who have won Best of Breed awards. Shown with her breeder/owner Bill Worley.

Worleys have been concentrating on the show ring. Writes Lisa Schultz, "I don't know how many generations of Outstanding Producers we have, but it's a long way. That, to me, says more than anything, considering that our bitches are never bred more than three times and produce small litters. Bill always said that to have a great producing kennel you must have great bitches, not just good ones, then breed great to great." Certainly, the Worleys have reached this goal.

263

Mrs. George H. Flinn, Jr. of Tigathoe Kennels in Greenwich, Connecticut is pictured with her F.C., A.F.C., Can. F.C. Bonnie Brooks Elmer. A G.R.C.A. Outstanding Sire and Field Dog Hall of Fame member, Elmer has probably sired more Field Champions than any other Golden Retriever, with six to his credit. Photo: Maryanne Gjersvik.

TIGATHOE

Perhaps no Golden Kennel in the country has remained active and important as long as Mrs. George Flinn, Jr.'s Tigathoe kennel of Greenwich, Connecticut. Certainly, the influence of Tigathoe dogs on the breed as a whole is unquestioned. Beginning in the 1940s, Torch Flinn's dogs established a pattern of Field and Bench wins that is perhaps unparalleled in the breed.

When I asked Mrs. Flinn to send me a resume of her kennel, she sent me the following:

My older sister, who saved her allowance, bought a puppy from the pound for $1.00. My life from five to eighteen years was closely supervised and totally dominated by this animal who looked and acted like a Golden Retriever. Her breeding was quite aptly described by my baby sister, who, when asked what this lovely dog was, replied, "part Collie, part Airedale, part female, part perfect." Upon meeting my first Golden Retriever sixteen years later, I was positively programmed to say "This is it."

How right I was!

Being a do-it-yourselfer, I have deliberately kept my kennel small. There are never more than eight here and that includes old dogs who live in the house and younger dogs and pups who are either in training or being looked over.

But there is more to the story than this. A list of Tigathoe dogs reads like a list of Who's Who in Goldens. Tigathoe Goldens that won Bench titles and are behind many of the top winning Goldens of today include (to name but a few): Champion Gold Button of Catawba **, Champion Little Joe of Tigathoe ***, Champion Tigathoe's Brass Tacks **, and Champion Rozzy Duchess.

Perhaps the greatest influence of the Tigathoe dogs, however, is in the area of Field Trials. At least thirteen Field Champions were owned or bred at Tigathoe kennels, and two of these were Dual Champions, a real rarity in the breed. Included in this list are: Canadian Dual Champion F.C. and A.F.C. Rockhaven Raynard of Fo-Go-Ta; A.F.C. Sunshine Cake; Dual Champion and A.F.C. Tigathoe's Funky Farquar; F.C. and A.F.C. Tigathoe's Magic Marker; F.C. and A.F.C. Tigathoe's Tonga; F.C., A.F.C. and Canadian F.C. Bonnie Brooks Elmer; F.C. and A.F.C. Chips of Sands; and A.F.C. Tigathoe's Choptank Child.

When asked to name her most important producers, Mrs. Flinn listed: Champion Little Joe of Tigathoe***. Bred 36 times in his sixteen years, Joe produced eighteen Champions, eight of whom were Sporting Group winners and three, Best in Show winners. And this at a time when Goldens were relatively unknown in Sporting Group competition. The second sire she listed was F.C., A.F.C. and Canadian F.C. Bonnie Brooks Elmer, a dog that has probably produced more Field Champions than any other Golden, with six to his credit.

Three bitches were listed by Mrs. Flinn as important producers to Tigathoe. They are: Champion Gold Button of Catawba** who, in two litters, produced four Champions, three of whom became qualified Open All-Age dogs; F.C., A.F.C. and Canadian F.C. Stilrovin Tuppee Tee who was for many years the high point Amateur bitch; and Tigathoe's Chickasaw*** who in two litters produced one Dual Champion, three Field Champions and a National Derby Champion.

Overall, Tigathoe kennels has produced generation after generation of outstanding dogs in a limited breeding program of linebreeding. It is a record that will be difficult to equal.

TOPBRASS GOLDENS

Topbrass Goldens, located in Elgin, Illinois, is owned by Joe and Jackie Mertens. Beginning in 1967, the Mertens have built a bloodline of dogs who have done well in all areas of competition, with special emphasis on the obedience ring and the Field. Their first dog, purchased in 1967 was shown to his championship, Working Certificate and C.D.X. degree.

Deciding to breed, Joe and Jackie purchased a bitch, Champion Goldenloe's Bronze Lustre. She was bred to Champion Rockgold Chug's Ric O Shay and produced a bitch that was to become the foundation of the Topbrass breeding program. This was Valentine Torch of Topbrass, W.C. At one year of age, "Torch" was caught in a fox trap and as a result had to have her left front leg amputated, precluding any real competitive career. In 1970 running on three legs she earned her W.C.

Torch was bred four times to four different field trial sires. She produced winning dogs in all three phases of competition, including O.T. Champion Topbrass Cisco Kidd, the second dog of any breed to be awarded the O.T. Champion title; Champion Topbrass Ad-Lib's Bangor, C.D.***, one of the few champion Open All-Age bitches in the country; and her sister, Champion Topbrass San Francisco Flame, who is a G.R.C.A. Outstanding Dam.

266

Ch. Topbrass San Francisco Flame (Dual Ch. A.F.C. Ronaker's Novato Cain ex Valentine Torch of Topbrass, W.C.). Owned and bred by Joe and Jackie Mertens of Topbrass Goldens. Flame is a G.R.C.A. Outstanding Dam.

All the present Topbrass dogs are descendants of Torch. F.C. and A.F.C. Topbrass Mandy, the high point living field trial bitch in the country, is a Torch great granddaughter. 1982's top obedience dog, all breeds, O.T. Champion Topbrass Ric O Shay Barty, owned by Sharon Long, is a littermate to Mandy.

Topbrass is the breeder of record for fifteen bench champions, five Obedience Trial champions and two Field champions. Certainly, the Mertens have produced true triple purpose Goldens.

268

Chapter 17

Eight Outstanding Recent Show Goldens

On the pages that follow are pictured eight Golden Retrievers whose accomplishments as winners or producers merit special attention. During the past ten to fifteen years, these dogs have had careers that place them at the apex of all Goldens in this country. Brief notes regarding each dog's accomplishments accompany each photograph. There are a number of dogs not included here who have attained significant wins, but the few dogs included have gone beyond even this point. The dogs' records are likely to have a significant impact on the breed as a whole for years to come.

AMERICAN AND CANADIAN CHAMPION AND O.T. CHAMPION SUNSTREAK OF CULYNWOOD, T.D., W.C.X., CANADIAN C.D.

"Streaker" was an outstanding combination breed and obedience dog owned by Dave and Susie Bluford of Carmel, California and bred by Lynn Fletcher. Streaker was born April 6, 1974 and died March 2, 1982. He was sired by Champion Sabahka's Alexander of Cal-Vo, C.D. and is out of Champion Tanfelo's End of the Rainbow, C.D. Streaker was a top obedience dog, being the first male of any breed to hold both bench and obedience Championships (the first of either sex being Champion, O.T. Champion Russo's Gold-Rush Sensation). He was the nation's top Obedience Dog for all breeds in 1978. Streaker also did quite well in the show ring. In 1979 he was able to go High in Trial and Sporting Group First at the same show, this after winning the Western Regional Specialty of G.R.C.A. which was held at the same show. Quite an accomplishment for any dog.

Opposite page: Am., Can. Ch. O.T. Ch. Sunstreak of Culynwood, T.D., W.C.X. (Ch. Sabahkas Alexander of Cal-Vo, C.D. ex Ch. Tangelos End Of The Rainbow, C.D., W.C.).

CHAMPION THISTLEDUE'S SHINING STAR

"Star," owned by Carter Foss of Liberty, Missouri, was bred by Mr. Foss and is sired by Champion Wochica's Okeechobee Jake and is out of Champion Goldenquest's Thistledue. He was whelped October 7, 1976. For five years, 1978 through 1982, Star was the top-winning breeder/owner/amateur-handled Golden in the United States, always handled by Mr. Foss. He was one of the top ten Goldens each of these years as well. In his career, Star has, so far, won three Best in Show awards, 25 Group Firsts and 48 other placements. In addition, he was Best of Breed at two Specialties. Still being shown occasionally at the time of this writing, he continues to add to his outstanding show record.

Ch. Thistledue's Shining Star (Ch. Wochica's Okeechobee Jake ex Ch. Goldenquest's Thistledue). This top-winning breeder/owner/amateur-handled Golden is owned by Carter Foss. Photo: Wayne Cott.

Ch. Asterling's Tahiti Sweetie (Ch. Goldrush's Judgement Day ex Am., Can. Ch. Amberac's Asterling Aruba) is shown winning Best of Breed under judge William Geisenhaffer. Photo: Alverson.

CHAMPION ASTERLING'S TAHITI SWEETIE

"Brooke," as she is called, is owned by Sylvia Donahey of Willis, Michigan and Mary Wuestenberg of Waukesha, Wisconsin and is handled by Sylvia. Brooke was whelped April 27, 1981 and is sired by Champion Goldrush's Judgement Day and is out of Champion Amberac's Austerling Aruba, another Best in Show winning bitch. Brooke was bred by Mary Wuestenberg. According to G.R.C.A. records, Brooke is the youngest Golden Retriever of either sex ever to win a Sporting Group, an especially significant honor considering that she is a bitch. She completed her championship at the ripe "old" age of ten months, entirely from the puppy classes. She is the youngest Golden to achieve the requirements for the Show Dog Hall of Fame and the seventh bitch ever to achieve this honor. With her show career just beginning, Brooke has a Best in Show award to her credit along with four Group wins and several placements.

271

Ch. Wochica's Okeechobee Jake (Ch. Misty Morn's Sunset, C.D., T.D., W.C. ex Little Dawn of Chickasaw) winning Best of Breed at the 1977 National Specialty from the Veterans Class at the age of eight and a half. This was Jake's third National Specialty win, a record for the breed. Photo: Dorothy Carter.

CHAMPION WOCHICA'S OKEECHOBEE JAKE

"Jake," a son of Sammy's, was owned by Susan Taylor of Asbury Park, N.J. and co-owned for a time by Rose Lewesky. He was bred by Janet Bunce and was whelped April 3, 1969. Jake died on February 10, 1980. He was sired by Champion Misty Morn's Sunset, C.D., T.D., W.C. and out of Little Dawn of Chickasaw. As a special, Jake was handled by Robert Stebbins and attained an outstanding record, with seven Best in Shows, 21 Group firsts and 56 other placements. Jake is the only Golden in breed history to win the National Specialty three times, doing so in 1972, 1975, and again in 1977 from the Veterans Dog class. Jake has also made a strong mark on the breed as a sire. Through 1981, he was the breed's second highest producer with 62 champions and U.D. dogs to his credit, a record second only to his father's.

CHAMPION CLOVERDALE TWIN-BEAU-D JOY

"Joy," owned by Nancy and Robert Dallaire of Warren, Rhode Island, and bred by Richard and Jane Zimmerman, was the first Golden Retriever Bitch to win an All-Breed Best in Show in twenty-seven years, doing so in 1981. Joy did it the hard way, achieving this honor from the Open Bitch Class to finish her title. She has been handled by her owner, Nancy Dallaire. Joy was sired by Champion Sutter Creek Goldrush Flyboy and is out of Cloverdale Sabrina. She was whelped July 7, 1979. Since her Best in Show win, Joy has completed the requirements for admission to the Show Dog Hall of Fame. Joy recently whelped her first litter during the winter of 1983.

The first Golden bitch to win Best in Show in over twenty-seven years, this is Ch. Cloverdale Twin-Beau-D Joy (Ch. Sutter Creek Goldrush Flyboy ex Cloverdale Sabrina). Photo: Stephen Klein.

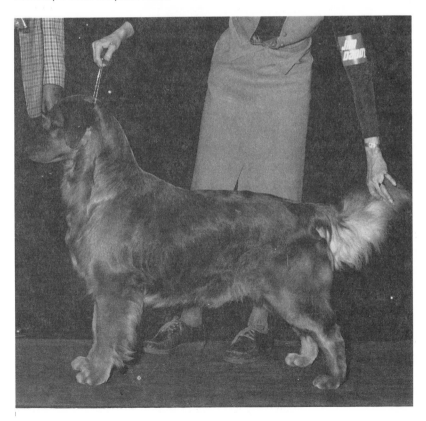

Winning the Veteran Dog Class at the 1980 Long Island Golden Retriever Club Specialty is Ch. Sir Duncan of Woodbury (Ch. Misty Morn's Sunset, C.D., T.D., W.C. ex Autumn Lodge's L'il Indian). A G.R.C.A. Outstanding Sire, Duncan was owned by Lynne Lounsbury of Jolly Kennels. He is handled here by Patricia McCoy. Photo: Bushman.

CHAMPION MISTY MORN'S SUNSET, C.D., T.D., W.C.

The top producing Golden Retriever sire of all time, and one of the top producing sires of any breed in the United States, "Sammy" as he was called, was owned by Peter Lewesky who now lives in Ohio. This great dog was bred by Virginia Hunter. He was whelped on September 25, 1967 and died December 1, 1977. Sam was sired by Ch. Sunset's Happy Duke and is out of Amber Lady of Tercor Farm. As a show dog, Sammy had a good record, with fifteen Group wins and 37 other placements for a total of 138½ Hall of Fame points. His versatility is shown by his other titles. However, it was as a sire that Sam had his greatest impact on the breed. Available records only go through the end of 1981, but Sam's record as a producer is unparalleled in the breed with a total of at least 127 dogs to his credit who hold the title of Champion, O.T. Champion or Utility Dog. There are still some Sam-sired puppies who are active in the rings, so this number may be expected to increase. Among the outstanding dogs produced by Sam are Champion Wochica's Okeechobee Jake, the only dog ever to win Best of Breed at the G.R.C.A. National Specialty three times, and O.T. Champion Moreland's Golden Tonka, the first dog of any breed to earn the Obedience Trial Champion title. In addition, Sam is the sire of numerous other dogs who, in turn, are Outstanding Producers themselves. The impact of Champion Misty Morn's Sunset, C.D., T.D., W.C. on the Golden Retriever breed is incalculable. His record as a producer will probably remain untouched for many years to come.

AMERICAN, CANADIAN AND BERMUDIAN CHAMPION CUMMINGS GOLD-RUSH CHARLIE

Without question the top winning show Golden of all time, "Charlie" was owned by R. Ann and L.C. Johnson of Princeton, New Jersey and co-owned, for a time, by Mrs. R.V. Clark, Jr. of Virginia. During most of his special's career, he was handled by William Trainor. Charlie was bred by Lynn Cummings and was sired by Champion Sunset's Happy Duke and was out of American and Canadian Champion Cummings Golden Princess. He was whelped October 10, 1970 and died November 12, 1982. Charlie's record far surpasses that of any other Golden, with 43 Best in Show awards, 96

Shown winning one of his 38 American Best in Show awards is Am., Can. Ch. Cummings Gold-Rush Charlie, the top-winning show Golden of all time. He was handled by William Trainor for owners Mrs. R.V. Clark, Jr. and L.C. Johnson. Photo: William Gilbert.

Group wins and 75 group placements. He was the winner of eight specialties including the 1974 National Specialty. During his career, Charlie was the number one Sporting Dog in the country in 1974 and before his retirement in 1976 he had defeated over 100,000 dogs while earning 1004½ Hall of Fame points. Charlie was also an outstanding producer, having sired 54 champions and U.D. dogs through 1981 with numerous others nearing their titles. Among his best known progeny are Champion Gold-Rush's Great Teddy Bear, Winner of the 1978 National Specialty and an Outstanding Sire, American and Canadian Champion Russo's Pepperhill Poppy, winner of the 1979 national Specialty, and O.T. Champion and Champion Russo's Gold-Rush Sensation, the first dog of any breed to hold both Champion and Obedience Trial Champion titles. "Sadie" and "Poppy" are full sisters. It is interesting to note that Charlie and Sammy were ¾ brothers, having the same father and mothers that were half-sisters.

AMERICAN AND CANADIAN CHAMPION RUSSO'S PEPPERHILL POPPY

Poppy, a daughter of American, Canadian and Bermudian Champion Cummings Gold-Rush Charlie, was bred by Mercer Russo and is owned by the author and his wife. She became only the third bitch in breed history and the first in twenty-six years to qualify for the Show Champions Hall of Fame in 1979. She was handled by Barbara Pepper and professional handler Elliot More. In Goldens, as is true with most coated breeds, the males have traditionally won the vast majority of Best of Breed awards. After the long hiatus, Poppy was able to break this tradition, and several other bitches followed her into the Hall of Fame in 1982. Poppy's dam, Russo's Wildwood Flower, was a daughter of Champion Misty Morn's Sunset and had fourteen points, four majors to her credit before her untimely death of cancer. Poppy was whelped on January 13, 1975 and was purchased as an eight-week-old pup. At the time of this writing, she had defeated more dogs, all breeds, than any other bitch in breed history. With a lifetime record of six Group Firsts and nineteen other placements, she has 59 Hall of Fame points to her credit, the second highest total of any bitch. Poppy has two Best of Breed Specialty wins to her credit, including the 1979 G.R.C.A. National Specialty, and seven Specialty Best of Opposite Sex wins, including the 1978 National Specialty, making her the only bitch ever to win both awards at a National Specialty. Poppy is also an Outstanding Dam, having produced six champions through 1982.

Am., Can. Ch. Russo's Pepperhill Poppy (Am., Can., Bda. Ch. Cummings Gold-Rush Charlie ex Russo's Wildwood Flower) is shown winning another Best of Breed award under breeder/judge Edward Syder. Her handler is Elliot More. Photo: John Ashbey.

Appendices

TITLE ABBREVIATIONS USED IN THIS BOOK

Ch.	—Conformation Champion
F.C.	—Field Trial Champion
A.F.C.	—Amateur Field Champion
O.T. Ch.	—Obedience Trial Champion
W.C.	—Dog has earned G.R.C.A. Working Certificate
W.C.X.	—Dog has earned G.R.C.A. Working Certificate Excellent
*	—Dog has earned W.C.
**	—Placement in Licensed Field Trial
***	—Placement in Championship Stake; Qualified All-Age
C.D.	—Companion Dog. First obedience degree
C.D.X.	—Companion Dog Excellent. Second obedience degree
U.D.	—Utility Dog. Third obedience degree
T.D.	—Tracking Dog
T.D.X.	—Tracking Dog Excellent
U.D.T.	—Dog with both Utility Degree and Tracking Degree

GLOSSARY

AMERICAN KENNEL CLUB: The official registry for most pure-bred dogs in the United States. Publishes and maintains the Stud Book, handles all litter and individual registrations, transfers of ownership, etc. Keeps all United States dog show award records, issues championships and other titles as earned, approves and licenses dog show, obedience and field trial judges, licenses or issues approval to all point shows or recognized match shows. Creates and enforces the rules and regulations by which the breeding, raising, exhibiting, handling and judging of pure-bred dogs in this country is governed. Clubs, not individuals, are members of the American Kennel Club, represented by a delegate chosen from their own membership for the purpose of attending the quarterly A.K.C. Delegate's Meetings.

ANGULATION: The angles formed by the meeting of the bones, generally referring to the shoulder and upper arm in the forequarters and the stifle and hock in the hindquarters.

BAD BITE: One in which the teeth do not meet correctly according to the specifications of the Breed Standard.

BAD MOUTH: Can refer to a malformation of the jaw or to incorrect dentition.

BALANCE: Symmetry and proportion. A well-balanced dog is one in which all parts appear in correct ratio to one another: height to length, head to body, neck to head and body, and skull to foreface.

BEST IN SHOW: The dog or bitch chosen as the most representative of any dog in any breed from among the seven Group winners at an all-breed dog show.

BEST OF BREED: The dog or bitch that has been judged the best of its breed in competition at a dog show. The only dog of its breed to enter Group competition.

BEST OF OPPOSITE SEX: The dog or bitch judged Best of Opposite Sex to the one judged Best of Breed. If the Best of Breed is a dog, then the Best of Opposite Sex is a bitch judged to be the best of her sex over the Winners Bitch and any other bitches entered for Best of Breed competition, or vice versa.

BEST OF WINNERS: The dog or bitch selected as the better of the two between Winners Dog and Winners Bitch.

BITCH: The correct term for a female dog.

BITE: The manner in which the dog's upper and lower teeth meet.

BLUE RIBBON WINNER: A Golden who has won a first prize in a class at an A.K.C. Point show.

BRACE: Two dogs, or a dog and a bitch, closely similar in appearance and moving together in unison. Also, a class offered at some shows, where two dogs of identical ownership are shown together at the same time by one handler.

BREED: Pure-bred dogs descended from mutual ancestors refined and developed by man.

BREEDER: A person who breeds dogs.

BRISKET: The forepart of the body between the forelegs and beneath the chest.

BROOD BITCH: A bitch used primarily for breeding.

CANINE TEETH: The four sharp pointed teeth at the front of the jaws, two upper and two lower, flanking the incisors; often referred to as fangs.

CASTRATE: Neuter a dog by removal of the testicles.

CAT-FOOT: A short toed, round, tight foot similar to that of a cat. The desired shape of a Golden's feet.

CHAMPION (Ch.): A dog or bitch who has won a total of fifteen points including two "majors" the total under not less than three judges, two of whom must have awarded the "majors" at A.K.C. point shows.

CHARACTER: Appearance, behavior, and temperament considered correct in a Golden.

CHEST: The part of the body enclosed by the ribs.

CHOKE COLLAR: A chain or leather collar that gives maximum control over the dog. It is tightened or relaxed by the pressure on the lead caused either by the pulling of the dog or the tautness with which it is held by the handler.

CLOSE-COUPLED: Compact in appearance. Short in loin.

CONDITION: A dog said to be in good condition is one carrying exactly the right amount of weight, whose coat looks alive and glossy, who has muscles that are properly hardened by exercise, and who exhibits a general appearance and demeanor of well-being.

CONFIRMATION: The confirming of a dog's title by A.K.C.

CONFORMATION: The framework of the dog, its form and structure.

COUPLING: The section of the body known as the loin. A short coupled dog is one in which the loin is short.

COARSE: Lacking in refinement and elegance. A dog who is over-done, having too much bone.

COW-HOCKED: When the hocks turn inward at the joint, causing the hock joints to approach one another with the result that the feet toe outward instead of straight ahead.

CROSSING ACTION: A movement fault where the legs cross each other in front as the dog moves.

CROUP: The portion of the back directly above the hind legs.

CRYPTORCHID: An adult dog with testicles not normally descended. A disqualification; a dog with this condition cannot be shown.

DAM: Female parent of a dog or bitch.

DENTITION: Arrangement of the teeth.

DEW CLAWS: Extra claws on the inside of the legs. Removal of the dew claws is permitted but not recommended by the Golden Breed Standard.

DISQUALIFICATION: A fault or condition so designated by the breed Standard or by the A.K.C. Judges must withhold awards at dog shows from dogs having disqualifying faults, noting the reason in the Judges' Book. The owner may appeal this decision, but if disqualified three times, a dog cannot again be shown.

DOG: A male of the species. Also used to collectively describe male and female canines.

DOG SHOW: A competition in which dogs have been entered for the purpose of receiving the opinion of a judge.

DOG SHOW, ALL-BREED: A dog show in which classification may be provided, and usually is, for every breed of dog recognized by the American Kennel Club.

DOG SHOW, SPECIALTY: A dog show featuring one breed only. Specialty shows are generally considered to be the showcases of a breed, and to win at one is an especially coveted honor and achievement, competition at them being particularly keen.

DOMED: A condition of the top-skull in which it is rounded.

DOUBLE COAT: A coat that consists of a harsh, weather-resistant protective outer coat, with a short soft undercoat providing warmth. Goldens are a double coated breed.

DOWN IN PASTERN: A softness or weakness of the pastern causing a pronounced variation from the vertical.

DRIVE: The powerful action of the hindquarters which should equal the degree of reach of the forequarters.

DUDLEY NOSE: Flesh colored nose. Mentioned in the old Breed Standard.

ELBOW: The joint of the forearm and upper arm.

ELBOW, OUT AT: The condition by which the elbow points out from the body rather than being close and parallel to the ribs.

EVEN BITE: Exact meeting of the front teeth, tip to tip with no overlap of the uppers or lowers.

EXPRESSION: The typical expression of the breed as one studies the head. Determined largely by the shape, color and placement of the eyes. Should be friendly and intelligent in a Golden Retriever.

FANCIER: A person actively involved in the sport of pure-bred dogs.

FANCY: Dog breeders, exhibitors, judges, and others actively involved with pure-bred dogs comprise the Dog Fancy.

FANGS: The canine teeth.

FEET EAST AND WEST: An expression describing toes on the forefeet that turn outward rather than pointing ahead.

FINISHING A DOG: Refers to completing a dog's A.K.C. title, *i.e.* Championship, Field Championship, C.D., etc.

FIELD CHAMPION (F.C.) OR AMATEUR FIELD CHAMPION (A.F.C.): A title given by A.K.C to dogs who have met the requirements at licensed or member field trials.

FLANK: The side of the body through the loin area.

FOREARM: The front leg from elbow to pastern.

FRONT: The forepart of the body viewed head-on, including the head, forelegs, shoulders and feet.

GAIT: The manner in which a dog moves.

GAY TAIL: Tail carried too high.

G.R.C.A.: The Golden Retriever Club of America.

GROOM: To bathe, brush, comb, and trim a dog.

HANDLER: A person who shows dogs in competition, either as an amateur (without pay) or as a professional (receiving payment for the service).

HARE FOOT: An elongated paw, like the foot of a hare. Not desirable in a Golden.

HAW: A third eyelid.

HEAT: The period during which a bitch can be bred. Also referred to as "season".

HINDQUARTERS: Rear assembly of the leg.

HOCK: The joint between the second thigh and the foot.

HOCKS WELL LET DOWN: Expression denoting that the hock joint should be placed low toward the ground.

INCISORS: The front teeth between the canines.

JUDGE: The person making the decisions at a dog show, obedience trial or field trial. Must be approved by A.K.C.

KENNEL: The building in which dogs are housed. Also used to denote a person's collective dogs.

KNEE JOINT: Stifle joint.

LAYBACK: Description of correctly angulated shoulders.

LEATHER: The ear flap.

LEVEL BITE: Another way of saying even bite, as teeth of both jaws meet.

LEVEL GAIT: A dog moving smoothly, topline carried level as he does so.

LOADED SHOULDERS: Those overburdened with excessive muscular development or excess skin and hair.

LOIN: Area of sides between lower ribs and hindquarters.

MAJOR: A dog show at which there are three or more points awarded the Winner's Dog and/or Winners Bitch.

MATCH SHOW: An informal dog show where no championship points are awarded and entries can usually be made upon arrival.

MATE: To breed a dog and a bitch to one another. Litter mates are dogs which were born in the same litter.

MONORCHID: A dog with only one properly descended testicle.

NICK: A successful breeding that results in puppies of excellent quality is said to "nick."

NOSE: Describes the dog's organ of smell, but also refers to his talent at scenting. A dog with "a good nose" is one adept at picking up and following a scent trail.

OBEDIENCE TRIAL: A licensed obedience trial is one held under A.K.C. rules at which it is possible to gain a "leg" (one of three wins necessary to gain an obedience title) towards a dog's title.

OBEDIENCE TRIAL CHAMPION (O.T.Ch.): Indicates that a dog has attained Obedience Trial Championship under A.K.C. rules.

OCCIPUT: Upper back point of skull.

ORTHOPEDIC FOUNDATION FOR ANIMALS (O.F.A.): This organization, an outgrowth of a G.R.C.A. committee, is the central location for the reading of radiographs of dogs and granting of certification of freedom from hip dysplasia. Board Certified radiologists read vast numbers of these films each year.

OUT AT ELBOW: When the elbows point away from the body.

OVERSHOT: Upper incisors overlap the lower incisors leaving a gap between them.

PADS: Thick protective covering of the bottom of each foot. Serves as a shock absorber.

QUALITY: Excellence of type and conformation.

RANGY: Excessive length of body combined with lack of depth through ribs and chest.

REACH: The distance to which the forelegs stretch out while gaiting, which should correspond with the strength and drive of the hindquarters.

REGISTER: To record your dog with the American Kennel Club.

REGISTRATION CERTIFICATE: The paper you receive from A.K.C. denoting your dog's registration has been recorded with A.K.C. and giving the breed, assigned name, names of sire and dam, date of birth, breeder and owner along with the assigned Stud Book number of the dog.

RESERVE WINNERS DOG OR RESERVE WINNERS BITCH: After the judging of Winners Dog or Winners Bitch, the remaining first place winners remain in the ring where they are joined by the dog or bitch that placed second in the class from which the Winners Dog or Bitch came, provided he or she was defeated only by that one dog on that day. From these the Reserve Winner is selected. Should the Winners Dog or Winners Bitch award subsequently be disallowed due to any error or technicality, the Reserve Winner is then moved up automatically to Winners in the A.K.C. records and the points awarded to the Winners are then transferred to the dog or bitch that was Reserve Winners.

ROACH BACK: A convex curvature of the topline of the dog.

SADDLE BACK: Of excessive length with a dip behind the shoulders.

SCISSORS BITE: The correct bite for a Golden Retriever in which the outer sides of the lower incisors touch the inner side of the upper incisors.

SEASON: See Heat.

SET UP: To pose your dog in position for examination by the judge. Sometimes referred to as stacking.

SIRE: The male parent.

SLAB SIDES: Flat sides with little spring of rib.

SPAY: To neuter a bitch by surgery.

SPECIAL: A dog or bitch entered only for best of breed competition at a dog show. A dog or bitch that has completed its championship.

STACKING: See Set Up.

STANCE: The natural position a dog assumes in standing.

STANDARD: The official description of the ideal specimen of a breed. The Standard of Perfection is drawn up by the Parent Specialty Club, approved by its membership and by the American Kennel Club, and serves as a guide to breeders and to judges in decisions regarding the merit or lack of merit in individual dogs.

STIFLE: The joint of the hind leg corresponding to a person's knee.

STOP: The step-up from nose to skull. An indentation at the juncture of the skull and the foreface.

STRAIGHT BEHIND: Lacking angulation of hindquarters.

STRAIGHT SHOULDERS: Lacking angulation of the shoulder blades.

STUD: A male dog that is a proven sire.

SUBSTANCE: Degree of bone size.

SWAYBACK: Weakness in the topline between the withers and the hip bones.

TAIL SET: Placement of the tail at its base.

THIGH: Hindquarters from the stifle to the hip.

THROATINESS: Excessive loose skin at the throat.

TOPLINE: The dog's back from withers to tail set or croup.

TRACKING DOG (T.D.): A title awarded dogs that have filled the A.K.C. requirements at licensed tracking tests.

T.D.X.: An advanced tracking degree. See Tracking Dog.

TRAIL: Hunting by following a ground scent.

TUCK-UP: A noticeable shallowness of the body at the loin, creating a small-waisted appearance.

TYPE: The combination of features which makes a breed unique, distinguishing it from all others.

UNDERSHOT: The front teeth of the lower jaw overlap or reach beyond the front teeth of the upper jaw.

UPPER ARM: The foreleg between the forearm and the shoulder blade.

UTILITY DOG (U.D.): The highest level of Obedience Degrees.

UTILITY DOG TRACKING (U.D.T.): A dog having both a U.D. and a T.D.

WEEDY: Lacking in sufficient bone and substance.

WELL LET DOWN: Short hocks, hock joint placed low to the ground.

WHELPED: When a puppy is born. A pregnant bitch is said to be in whelp.

WINNERS DOG OR WINNERS BITCH: The awards which are accompanied by the awarding of championship points, based on the number of dogs defeated, at A.K.C. member or licensed dog shows.

WITHERS: The highest point of the shoulders.

G.R.C.A. SHOW DOG HALL OF FAME MEMBERS (Through 1981)

"Any Golden Retriever which accumulates 25 points or more based on his performance in Sporting Groups and Best in Show wins will automatically be honored in the Hall of Fame" (G.R.C.A. requirements). Points assigned as follows: B.I.S. 10 points; Group 1st, 5 points; 2nd, 3 points; 3rd, 1 point; 4th, ½ point.

NAME OF DOG	AKC NO.	SEX	POINTS	OWNER(S)
Ch. Ashlyn's AJ Golden Boy	SB952703	Dog	45½	Donna Kitchel
Am. Can. Ch. Auric of Wildwood	S97283	Dog	37	Frank L. Root
Am.Can.Mex.Bda.Ch.Beckwith's Copper Coin	SA76391	Dog	148	R.E. & L.L. Beckwith
Ch. Beckwith's Duke of York	SA79473216	Dog	44	D.Murry,G.Hershberger & C.Gerstner
Am.Can.Ch.Beckwith's Malagold Flash, CDX	TD SA6297	Dog	50	Marvin & Carol Kvamme
Am.Can.Ch.Beckwith's North Wind,CD	SB141783	Dog	53	Lynda G. Reddington
Ch. Braevick's King's Choice	S811009	Dog	34½	Mr. & Mrs. R. E. Hayes
Ch. Bundock's Bowman of Eldomac	SA664124	Dog	231	Dr. Alan & Kathleen McDowell
Ch. Buster Ballyhoo of Inverness	SA259124	Dog	43	Katharine G. Weed
Am.Can.Ch.Cal-Vo's Happy Ambassador,CD	SA837152	Dog	52	Bill & Joan Young
Ch. Camelot's Noble Fella, CDX	SB975282	Dog	314½	Kay Bickford & Margo Zonghetti
Am.Can.Ch.Chee-Chee of Sprucewood	S448601	Bitch	122½	Mr. & Mrs. M.C. Zwang
Ch. Cheyenne Golden's King	S721806	Dog	239½	Cheyenne Golden Kennels
Ch. Cheyenne Golden's King John	SA116119	Dog	818	Cheyenne Golden Kennels
Ch. Cheyenne Golden's Long Shot,CD	S845850	Dog	77	Craig M. Rowley & Cheyenne Golden Knls.
Ch. Cheyenne Golden's Son of James	SA652275	Dog	927	Cheyenne Golden Kennels
Ch. Cloverdale's Ringold Tobey	SB585769	Dog	63	Nancy R. Fenn
Ch. Copper Kettles Apple Of My Eye	SB258062	Dog	38½	Thelma H. Cahoon
Ch. Copper's Czar Again	S386334	Dog	95½	H. Paul Warwick
Ch. Cragmount's Hi-Lo	SA160236	Dog	277	Mrs. C. W. Engelhard
Ch. Cragmount's Peter	SA31166	Dog	234½	Jane Engelhard
Am.Can.Bda.CH.Cummings Gold-Rush Charlie	SA871725	Dog	1004½	L.C. Johnson & Mrs. R.V.Clark,Jr.

NAME OF DOG	AKC NO.	SEX	POINTS	OWNER(S)
Ch. Cupid's Beau of Lady Kirk, CD	SC136347	Dog	50	R. Steve Andrews
Ch. Czar of Wildwood	A889104	Dog	196½	Eric S. Johnson
Am.Can.Mex.Ch.Czarbella's Copper Prince	S788977	Dog	26½	C.S. & F.G. Fox
Ch. Czargold's Storm King	S595581	Dog	100½	H. Paul Warwick
Am.Can.Ch.Deirdre's Bonn Or of Baliff	SB067892	Dog	55	David & Deirdre Reynolds
AM.Can.Ch.Deirdre's Fionn Or Of Bran CD*	SA787927	Dog	33½	David R. Reynolds
Ch. Deirdre's Molega Mac, CD	SB610327	Dog	36	Margaret & William J. Freeburg
Am. Can.Ch. Des Lacs Lassie	A994369	Bitch	58½	Des Lacs Kennels
Ch. Duckdown's Spannew, CD	SA374268	Dog	89	Jack & Jacquelyn Waggoner
Am.Can.Ch.Duckdown's Unpredictable	SA483975	Dog	28½	Laura Ellis Kling
Am.Can.Ch.Duck Pass Shore Breaker	SA488229	Dog	34	Doris E. Deschene
Ch. Eastgate's Golden Blazer	SA633916	Dog	52	Joan Emery & Wm. E. Bedingfield,Jr.
Ch. Eastgate's Golden Charger	SA469410	Dog	25½	Wm. E. Bedingfield, Jr.
Ch. Faera's Sun Dance Risen Shine	SB730439	Dog	68½	Louise Connally Haley
Eng. Am. Ch. Figaro of Yeo	SA171898	Dog	53	Mrs. C.W. Engelhard
Ch. Finderne Gold Cloud of Kent	S872044	Dog	34	Jane Engelhard
Ch. Finderne Gold Rascal, CD	S993097	Dog	26½	Mrs. Eric Peterson
Ch. Frantelle's Fiddler	A927544	Dog	27½	Michael A. Clemens
Ch. Furore Harvest Gold	S887633	Dog	38	Mr. & Mrs. M.C. Zwang
Ch. Ginwal's Hi-Flyer	S917912	Dog	32	Marcia Rosenberger
Ch. Gold Coast Here Comes The Sun,CD	SB981196	Dog	68½	Louise Connally
Ch. Gold-Rush Copper Lee	SC572167	Dog	50	Wm. M. Wingard & R. Ann Johnson
Ch. Gold-Rush's Great Teddy Bear	SB555537	Dog	43	Diane J. Smith & R. Ann Johnson
Ch. Golden Knoll's Copper Prince,CDX	S346280	Dog	27	Mary Ellen Hogewoning
Am.Can.Ch.Golden Knoll's Duke of Hammett,CD	SA55923	Dog	48½	Pat & Ollie Click
Am.Can.Ch. Golden Knoll's King Alphonzo	S346285	Dog	632½	N. Bruce Ashbey
Ch. Golden Knoll's Shur Shot	S230864	Dog	395	Mrs. R. S. Peterson

SHOW DOG HALL OF FAME

NAME OF DOG	AKC NO.	SEX	POINTS	OWNER(S)
Ch. Golden Knoll's Town Talk, CD ***	S693266	Dog	56	D. A. Smith, Jr.
Ch. Goldenloe's Tanfastic, CDX	SA338313	Dog	74½	James C. Enloe
Ch. Goldenloe's Tawny Sam Son, UD	SB21103	Dog	101	Eliesa W. Enloe & John W. Girton, Jr.
Ch. Golden Pine's Brown Bear	S786269	Dog	145½	Golden Pine Kennels
Am.Can.Ch.Golden Pine's Easy Ace	S908646	Dog	67½	Golden Pine Kennels
Ch. Golden Pine's Full House,CD	SB4530	Dog	29	Susan Slade & Warren J. Cox
Am.Can.Ch.Goldrush's Contender,UD	SB483011	Dog	30	Clark & Colleen Williams & D. Jean Baird
Am.Can.Ch.Goldrush's Galligaskins	SC164341	Dog	49½	James Marcus & Janine Stephenson
Ch. Goldwing True Bear	SC407652	Dog	114½	Leslie Dove
Ch. High Farms Sutter's Gold	SA338973	Dog	57½	Lester A. Browne
Ch. Hilane Sirocco, WC	S873650	Dog	41	Mr. & Mrs. S. B. Bowles
Ch. Honor's Grandeur,CDX WC	SA770080	Dog	38½	Cleo & Bob Friederichsen
Ch. Hunt's Copperfield Daemon,CD WC	SA734306	Dog	25½	A. Robert Dismukes,Jr.
Ch. Hunt's Daniel Boone	SA919257	Dog	31½	A. Robert Dismukes, Jr.
Ch. Hunt's Finnegan	SB179371	Dog	35½	A. Robert Dismukes,Jr.
Ch. Joel of Claymyr	S610937	Dog	35	Hertha Sponer-Franck
Ch. Jolly October's Chevalier	SC071534	Dog	29	Sharon C. Smith & Lynne Lounsbury
Ch. Kachina's Kamiakin O'Darnley	SC667899	Dog	97	Robert A. & Barbara Fell
Ch. King of Braewick's Falcon	S738729	Dog	47½	N. Bruce Ashbey
Ch. Kinnikinnik's Jamboree	SB463902	Dog	32½	B. Jean Kistle & Betty Ann Story
Ch. Kinnikinnik's Talee of Gaylen	SB432903	Dog	29½	Gayle L. Nash
Ch. Krishna's E. Z. Goin',CD	SB623191	Dog	43½	Betty Villella & Gloria Kerr
Ch. Krishna's Ja-Jam Extra Special	SC313170	Dog	100	Jerome Oxenberg
Am.Can.Ch.Krishna's Klassic Kachina	SB895018	Dog	25½	Lyn & Buzz Splittgerber
Am.Can.Ch.Laurell's Especial Jason, WC Am.Can.UDT	SA934760	Dog	25	Cherie & Alan Berger
Ch. Laurell's York	SC025275	Dog	222	Thomas C. & Laura E. Kling

NAME OF DOG	AKC NO.	SEX	POINTS	OWNER(S)
Am.Can.Ch. Little Big Man	SA906339	Dog	32	Joanne A. Lastoka
Am.Can.Ch.Lochvier's Hey U Sun Bear	SB422952	Dog	30	Virginia V. Rutter
Ch.-AFC Lorelei's Golden Rockbottom,UD	S270654	Dog	92	Reinhard M. Bischoff
Ch. Lorelei's Zajac Archer	SA350933	Dog	38½	Reinhard M. Bischoff
Ch. Malagold Beckwith Big Buff, CD	SA456646	Dog	225	Gary Mankowsky & Connie Gerstner
Ch. Malagold Summer Chant	SC082369	Dog	37½	Connie D. Gerstner
Ch. Malagold Summer Encore	SC653174	Dog	54½	Sandy Bator & Connie Gerstner
Am.Can.Ch.Meadowpond's David The Bold,CD	SC406692	Dog	45½	Auldeen L. Hall
Ch. Megary's Sunmark Aquarius,CD	SA756236	Dog	31½	Jocelyn A. Siegenthaler
Ch. Missy's Eager Beaver	S999825	Dog	44½	Herbert F. Feldman
Ch. Misty Morn's Sunset,CD TD WC	SA464440	Dog	140	Peter Lewesky
Ch. Moreland's Major Sam, CD	SA881282	Dog	128½	William C. Prentiss
Ch. Nerrissida's Finderne Folly II	S664722	Dog	34	Richard N. Hargrave
Ch. Prince Alexander	S297503	Dog	222½	Elizabeth Tuttle
Ch. Prince Copper of Malibu	S211485	Dog	75½	Dr. N. K. Forster
Ch. Prince Royal of Los Altos	S892844	Dog	91½	Oliver & Jane Wilhelm
Am.Can.Ch. Reddigold's Dignitary	SC328797	Dog	56	Jackie Ann Cole
Ch. Rockhaven Rory	905893	Dog	26	Henry B. Christian
Ch. Ruanme Blockbuster	S761816	Dog	110	Giralda Farms
Am.Can.Ch.Russo's Pepperhill Poppy	SB666153	Bitch	58	Barbara & Jeffrey Pepper
Am.Can.Ch.Sadie's Sundance Kidd,CDX WC	SB211403	Dog	26	Jamie & Jack Warren
Am.Can.Ch.Sailor's Copper King,CD	SA419028	Dog	129½	Mrs. Philip & James Kulig
Am.Can.Ch.Seneca's Riparian Chief,CD WC	SA336799	Dog	39½	John I. & Sandra Kelly
Ch. Seneca's Tuckernuck Gold,CD WC	SA750316	Dog	25	John & Sandra Kelly
Ch. Sham-O-Jets Luvamike	SB211403	Dog	301½	John A. & Joan Kipping
Ch. Sir Dindiago of Woodside	SC347809	Dog	28	R. & S. Humphreys & J. & L. Lounsbury
Am.Can.Ch.Southern's Gold-Rush Traveler	SC74688	Dog	51½	Colleen & Clark Williams

NAME OF DOG	AKC NO	SEX	POINTS	OWNER(S)
Ch. Spannen's Pat Hand	SB996797	Dog	27	Jack & Theresa Waggoner
Ch. Spannen's Rainmaker	SB17209	Dog	243	Jack & Jacquelyne Waggoner
Am.Can.Ch. Speedwell Pluto (Honorary)	839660	Dog	23	Samuel S. Magoffin
Am.Can.Ch.Sprucewood's Chocki	S665061	Dog	411½	Mr. & Mrs. M.C. Zwang
Am.Can.Ch.Sprucewood's Chore Boy ***	S665062	Dog	219	Mrs. Henry D. Barbour
Ch. Star Spray's Maria's Reyo del Sol,*	SA165405	Dog	72½	Pauline T. Ring
Ch. Stone's Gold-Rush Shiloh	SB872238	Dog	143	Gary D. Stone, M.D.
Ch. Sun Dance's Esquire,CD	SA441192	Dog	51	Shirley & William Worley
Ch. Sun Dance's Moonlight Gambler,CDX *	SA194110	Dog	27½	H.G. & M.R. Henderson
Ch. Sun Dance's Rarue	SB434862	Dog	179	Shirley & William Worley
Am.Can.Ch.Sun Dance's Vagabond Lover,CDX	SA171198	Dog	60	Violet F. Topmiller
Ch. Sun Dance's Vegas Dealer, CDX WC	SA173922	Dog	29½	James & Viva Jean Watson
Ch. Sundance's Rainmaker	SB721460	Dog	104½	Anthony & Penelope D'Alessandro
Ch. Sunshine's Golden Tomorrows,CD WC	SB264414	Dog	28	Sharon & Steve Ferrario
Ch. Sutter Creek Goldrush Flyboy	SC142905	Dog	45½	Susan G. Breakell
Ch. Tawny Toro of Los Altos, CDX	S892849	Dog	53	Oliver & Jane Wilhelm
Ch. Tempo's Frontier Bronco	SC190521	Dog	163½	Vivian Wright & Hank Arszman
Ch. Thistledue's Shining Star	SC061147	Dog	182½	Carter F. Foss
Ch. Tonkahof Bang (Honorary)	A489313	Dog	23½	Joseph MacGaheran & Henry W. Norton
Ch. Tumbleweed of Sprucewood	SA173486	Dog	36	Donna Kay Gatlin
Ch. Vagabond's Cougar Bill, CD	SA426354	Dog	39	William Zimmer & Laura Ellis Kling
Ch. Valhalla's Dogo Dancer,TD	SB753356	Dog	34	Arthur & Caroline Baihly
Ch. Veno's Tidal Wave	SA25611	Dog	51	Doris Deschene & M.M. Hubenette
Ch. Virgil of Nerrissida	S827751	Dog	27½	D.L. & S.B. Hopkins
Ch. Wochica's Okeechobee Jake	SA679062	Dog	286½	Susan Taylor
Ch. Yorkhill's Circus Clown	S533264	Dog	240½	Giralda Kennels

G.R.C.A. OBEDIENCE CHAMPIONS HALL OF FAME MEMBERS (Through 1981)

"All Golden Retriever Utility Dog that accumulates a total of 5 highest scores in trial (or ties for highest score) will automatically be honored in the Hall of Fame" (G.R.C.A. requirements)

NAME OF DOG	AKC NO.	SEX	NO. H.I.T.	NO. PERFECT	OWNER(S)
Ch. Alstone Sutter Creek Charade,UD WC	SA716328	dog	6	0	Mrs. Susan Breakell
Amberac's Boisterous Brett, UD	SB801224	dog	12	0	Rick L. Garvin
Ch.-OT Ch. Amber of Fairlawn Acres	SB478780	bitch	11	0	L. Gerard & Lillian Hart
OT Ch. Amberac's Sunrise Duke	SC343310	dog	6	0	Mitchell R. Schneider
OT Ch. Andrew	SB131985	dog	40	1	Joanne Johnson
Art-Line's Gideon of Eldomac,UD	SB74120	dog	71	0	Patricia N. & Michael Goldhamer,MD
Avidstal's Big Red, UD	SB149857	dog	10	0	Crystal Holcomb
Am.Can.Ch.Bardfield Boomer,AM.Can.UDT *	SA614915	dog	14	0	Cherie Berger & Joanne Hurd
Beckwith's Commanche,UD	SA923787	dog	8	0	Mrs. Catherine W. Sullivan
Beckwith's Eta of Spindrift,UDT WCX	SA884492	bitch	24	0	Mrs. Henry M. Klausman
OT Ch Beckwith's Indian Summer,TD	SB92555	bitch	5	0	Elizabeth O. Taylor
Ch. Ben's Major of Sun Dance,UD	S895008	dog	37	14	Bennie Lakes
Bluebell's Golden Knight,UD	S941211	dog	8	2	James R. Mardis
OT Ch. Bonnie Brooks Harvey,WC	SB057443	dog	12	0	Richard F. Guetzloff
Braewick's Pecos Bill, UD	S999614	dog	7	3	Charles A. Frank
OT Ch. Chance By Milo,WC	SB348548	dog	22	0	Bud E. Burge
Clipper of Circle Ridge,UD	S689067	dog	20	7	John W. Henry
Dede's Baskin of Moreland, UD WC	SB523645	bitch	6	0	John & Shelia Loerke
OT Ch. Double J's Buffalo Bill Cody	SB802424	dog	16	0	Richard P. & Sharon L. Wood
Ch. Duckerbird Atomic, UD	S16459	dog	36	12	Duckerbird Kennels
Duckerbird Atomic II,UD	S299038	dog	19	4	Mary L. Frank
Ch. Duckerbird Atomic III, UD	S738257	dog	15	3	Charles A. Frank
OT Ch. Eastgate's Golden Trisha	SC247745	bitch	12	0	Bill & Jeanette Bedingfield & Laurie Snell

OBEDIENCE HALL OF FAME

NAME OF DOG	AKC NO.	SEX	NO. H.I.T.	NO. PERFECT	OWNER(S)
Elder's Ruff And Tuff Buffy, UD	SA498589	dog	7	0	John & Rose Weiss
OT Ch. Enchanted Chaparell's Tug	SB573613	dog	19	0	Kay Bickford
Featherquest Trigger, UDT	S117205	dog	9	1	Mrs. Margorie B. Perry
Am.Can.OT Ch. Galway's Sun Down's Tango *	SB773170	dog	6	0	Addison & Deborah Igleheart
Gigi of Circle Ridge, UD	SA12775	bitch	11	0	William G. Chenez
OT Ch. Goldenloe's Just Ducky, WC	SB526482	dog	54	1	Anne Couttet
OT Ch. Golden Tobiah of Tara	SB611313	dog	8	0	David J & Nikki Berthold Illias
Ch. Gold-Rush Wild Trout, UD WC	SC321147	dog	6	0	Joan & Drew Armentrout
Goldwood Michael, UD	A660362	dog	33	14	Morgan B. Brainard
Goldwood Toby, UD (First Golden UD)	A541514	dog	(Honorary)		Mrs. Mark D. Elliott
OT Ch. Graelyn Red Rooster	SC696010	dog	19	0	Marilyn W. Ford
Gwin-Dell's King Midas, UD WC	SA471769	dog	25	0	Barbara & Florence B. Griffin
Hammerlock's Sunny Side Up, UD	SA519755	dog	38	1	Leslie J. Rowe
High Farms Cinnamon Toast, UD	SA815099	bitch	5	0	Janice O'Sullivan
Hoadleygold Duster, UD WC	SB960374	dog	6	0	Brett Adele Hoadley
Honey's Thrupence Goldkist, UD	SB984937	bitch	9	1	Hubert W. Hinton
Ch. Indian Knoll's Colonel, UD ***	S632660	dog	5	0	Anne W. Christiansen
Ch. Indian Knoll's Roc-Cloud, UD	S751387	dog	25	6	Alice & William Worley
OT Ch. Jack's Golden Joy	SB817325	bitch	7	0	John McManus
Jackpot O'Luck, UD	SA574075	dog	13	0	George W. & Beverly Keener
OT Ch. Jamacs Sunnyday Betyar, TD	SC085952	bitch	8	0	H. M. McConnell
OT Ch. Jason's Golden Shadow	SB285697	dog	13	0	Larry & Charlotte W. Kerr
OT Ch. Jim-Jam of Fairlawn Acres	SC465043	dog	10	0	L. Gerard & Lillian Hart
Jungold's Lucky Lindy of Sue-Ner, UD	SC189573	bitch	6	0	Richard Fyfe
Karagold's Magic Marker, UD	SC523374	dog	8	1	Theodore S. Aranda
Lady Rachel, UD	SA898540	bitch	8	0	Evelyn K. Prouty
OT Ch. Lady Windham	SB985643	bitch	20	0	William S. & Jeanne K. Leedale

OBEDIENCE HALL OF FAME

NAME OF DOG	AKC NO.	SEX	NO. H.I.T.	NO. PERFECT	OWNER(S)
OT Ch. Lucky Days Gretchen	SB898684	bitch	9	0	Thomas Barabowski
Malagold's Fire Dancer, UD	SB16775	dog	16	0	Bernie Brown
Malagold's Red Rouser, UD	SA419728	dog	13	1	Barbara Goodman
Mary's Butterscotch, UD	S580618	dog	8	1	John E. Stafford
OT Ch. Meadowpond Angelic Abbey, TD WCX	SB648592	bitch	22	0	Renee L. Schulte
OT Ch. Meadowpond Christopher	SC266657	dog	37	1	Russell H. & Alda I. Klipple
Ch.-OT Ch. Meadowpond Dust Commander	SB926716	dog	94	2	Bernie & Elaine S. Brown
OT Ch. Meadowpond Fem De Fortune, WC	SC340712	bitch	18	0	Diane L. Bauman
OT Ch. Meadowpond Happy Valentine, WC	SB691140	dog	35	1	Ron Roberts
OT Ch. Meadowpond's Tuf Tiger	SB681532	dog	18	0	Max Parris
Merrimac's Miss Molly, UD	SA237973	bitch	9	2	Max & Mary McCammon
Merry Maxine of Dorado, UD	SB336323	bitch	7	0	Joel Prouty
Milo's Korkay of Double J, UD	SB214765	bitch	8	0	Sharon Long
Milo of Ben's Major, UD WC	SA227305	dog	28	1	Frank E. Holmay
Mr. Chips of Silver Bay, UDT ***	SA33196	dog	14	1	Alvin M. Hall
OT Ch. Moreland's Golden Tonka	SB127707	bitch	204	8	Russel H. Klipple
Ch. Morgens Deerfield Panama Red, UD*	SC112118	dog	5	0	Linda M & Marc A. Lowy
OT Ch. Mr. Bo Jangles XXIII, WC	SB663270	dog	9	0	Mary E. Chaillot
Nashotah Shores Captain Milo, UD	SB140430	dog	6	0	Donald J. Williquette
OT Ch. Pekay's Charm Temptress, TD*	SB778666	bitch	36	1	Jeannie T. Brown
OT Ch. Pekay's Magic Moment	SC514490	bitch	27	0	Kenneth L. Miller
Pekay's Spirit of Atlanta, UD	SC769237	bitch	6	0	Kenneth L. & Karen E. Miller
Proud Phrogg of Jocar, UD	SB136258	dog	8	0	John S. & Amy B. Loewen
OT Ch. Quantock's Rick-Rack, TD	SB836186	dog	18	0	Grace L. Keller
Rengo Rusti, UDT	SA326911	dog	12	0	John H. Goad
OT Ch. Robert De Brus of Cocopal, WC	SB450873	dog	6	0	Mrs. John G. Babbitt
Ch. Roc-Knoll Golden Clipper, UD	SA83409	dog	9	0	Minerva & Walter Peck

OBEDIENCE HALL OF FAME

NAME OF DOG	AKC NO.	SEX	NO. H.I.T.	NO. PERFECT	OWNER(S)
Ch. Ruanme Ball-Hi, UD	S731659	bitch	11	2	Elizabeth W. Strawbridge
Ruanme Gayling's Gaiety, UD	S657883	bitch	22	6	Betty W. Strawbridge
Ch. Ruanme Yankee Tonka, UD	S790563	bitch	15	7	Emily C. Strawbridge
Ruanme Yankee Traveler II UD	S734152	dog	24	4	Elizabeth W. Strawbridge
Ch.-OT Ch. Russo's Gold-Rush Sensation	SB542485	bitch	30	1	Edward L. Hamm & L.C. Johnson
Rusticana Cloud-Nine, UD	SA741680	bitch	10	0	Frances R. Tuck
Rusticana's Sancy, UDT WC	SA667785	bitch	23	0	Jeannie Fox
OT Ch. Rustivus Rustler Pool	SB879255	dog	5	0	Stephen G. Pool
Rustler of Red River, UD	S916884	dog	7	0	Richard Lee Pond
Rusty of Crum Penny, UD	SA918937	dog	7	0	Robert H. & Virginia A. Ball
Sancy's Georgie Girl, UDT WC	SB940970	bitch	12	0	Robert H. & Virginia A. Ball
Sancy's High Seas Treasure, UDT	SB861289	bitch	8	0	Jeannie Fox
OT Ch. Sancy's Miki O Puapualenalena	SB862860	bitch	22	0	Janis Teichman & Charles Egan
Sandy's Galliano Girl, UDT	SB323933	bitch	7	0	Charles E. & Sandra L. Ball
Shannon Shamrock Pfeifer, UD WCX	SB782921	bitch	10	0	Erick B. & Kathleen J. Pfeifer
Sidram Satan, UD	S834415	dog	8	1	Max E. McCammon
Ch. Sidram Sea Power, UD	SA197692	dog	10	0	Shirley & William Worley
Sidram Sharmaine, UD	S525690	bitch	10	0	Max & Mary McCammon
OT Ch. Sir Duke of Benton	SB554005	dog	10	0	Wayne Lystra & Janet Lystra
Sir Mo-Bee-Oh, UD	SA558699	dog	29	0	Barbara Griffin & Charles McKenzie
OT Ch. Stardust Thunderbolt	SC618166	bitch	8	0	Alfred Einhorn
Ch. Sun Dance's Bootleg Whiskey, UD	SB110382	dog	5	0	Nicholas Pecora
Sun Dance's Brass, UD	S854851	dog	5	0	Shirley Klein
Ch. Sun Dance's Copper Drum, UD	SA774993	dog	5	0	Robert J. Hopwood, Jr.
Sun Dance's Hardbottom Xpress, UD WC	SA203253	dog	26	1	Howard & Marcia Henderson
Ch. Sun Dance's Nugget, UD WC	SA57625	dog	55	5	Howard & Marcia Henderson
Am.Can.Ch.Sun Dance's Rusticana,UDT	S885880	dog	135	36	Albert & Edith Munneke

OBEDIENCE HALL OF FAME

NAME OF DOG	AKC NO.	SEX	NO. H.I.T.	NO. PERFECT	OWNER(S)
OT Ch. Sungold Duke of Brookshire, WCX	SB857613	dog	7	0	Ronald & Carolyn Ochylski
Sundowner II, UD	SA924377	dog	9	0	Wayne & Irene Rohweder
Am.Can.Ch. OT Ch. Sunstreak of Culynwood, TD WCX	SB533366	dog	37	3	Susan B & David B. Bluford
Tabaka's Golden Rhapsody, UD	SB146	dog	7	0	Katherine Naomi Tabaka
OT Ch. Tass Of The West	SC199301	dog	8	0	Arthur E. Schmitt
Tomahawk's Cindy Oh Cindy, UD	SA740346	bitch	9	0	Thomas J. Campbell
OT Ch. Topbrass Cisco Kid	SB287386	dog	42	0	Pauline Czarnecki
Topbrass Ric O Shay Barty, UD WCX	SC000913	dog	37	0	Sharon L. Long
OT Ch. Topbrass Rocky Mountain High WC	SB317353	dog	12	0	E.G. & L.F. Schillenkamp,Jr.
OT Ch. Topbrass Stubblefield Pippa	SB849682	bitch	23	0	Kay Thompson Guetzloff
Ttentrah's Golden Frosty, UD	SB311231	bitch	7	0	John J. & Diane F. Hartnett
Am.Can. OT Ch. Tyler of Ripscallion Ways*	SB691924	dog	9	0	Judy Reynolds
OT Ch. Vikay's Ace of Diamonds	SB494458	dog	12	0	Mrs. Max Parris
OT Ch. Vikay's Jiggs	SC214403	dog	18	0	Max Parris
OT Ch. Wessala Naughty Nannette	SA585507	bitch	38	2	Joel W. Prouty
Westmont's Natty Bumppo, UDT WCX **	SC382573	dog	7	0	Margaret English
Whiskey, UD	SA128650	dog	7	0	G.E. & M.L. Blackstock
Wildwood's Autumn Aspenglow, UDT	SC318724	dog	11	0	Richard C. Olshock, MD
Windy's The Forecast, UD	SB91591	dog	25	0	Leslie J. Rowe

G.R.C.A. FIELD DOGS HALL OF FAME MEMBERS (Through 1981)

"Any Golden Retriever that accumulates a total of 25 points or more based on his performance in Licensed Field Trials will automatically be honored in the Hall of Fame. Any Golden Retriever that wins the National Field Trial or National Amateur Field Trial will also be included." (G.R.C.A. Requirements)

NAME OF DOG	AKC NO.	SEX	TOTAL POINTS	OWNER(S)
Nat'l. F.C. Beautywood's Tamarack	S153955	dog	18½	Dr. Leslie M. Evans
AFC Benjamin Rajah Frisbie	SA933226	dog	89	Darrell D. Frisbie
AFC Bonnie Belle of Hunt Trails	SB256566	bitch	45½	Dr. Robert & Sandee Peterson
FC-AFC Can.FC. Bonnie Brook's Elmer	SA297157	dog	2¢	Mrs. George H. Flinn, Jr.
AFC Bonnie Brook's Mike	SA306961	dog	30½	Walter K. Scherer, Jr.
FC-AFC Bonnie Brook's Red	SA776255	dog	47½	Harold J. Bruninga
FC Bonnie Brook's Tuff And A Half	SA297155	dog	52	Mrs. Jane D. Cooney
FC-AFC Brandy Snifter	S683575	dog	91½	Keith M. Barnett
FC-AFC Briggs Lake Mac	S792678	dog	27½	Henri P. Emond
FC-AFC Chief Sands	SA438222	dog	87	Richard L. Sampson
Dual Ch. - AFC Clickety Click	SA263912	dog	32	Mabel Smith & Len Floberg
FC Commanche Cayenne	S477091	dog	53½	Sheldon Coleman
Dual Ch.-AFC Craigmar Dustrack	S459592	dog	30	Dr. F. L. Flashman
FC-AFC Fairhaven Donner	S781503	dog	32½	Mrs. Snowden Rowe
FC-AFC Golden Rocket's Missile	SA175930	dog	65	B.F. Shearer, Jr.
AFC Goldenrod's Thanksgiving	S862443	dog	37	Ann A. Fowler
FC Goldwood Tuck	A205346	dog	31	Harold J. Kaufman
AFC Gunnerman's Coin of Copper	S822112	dog	25½	Vernon Weber
AFC Happy Thanksgiving, CD	S576101	dog	71½	Ann H. Fowler
FC Harbor City Rebel	S405972	dog	26½	Alec D. Thomson
Ch.-AFC Honor's Darado of Spindrift	SA707435	dog	26½	John J. Sprude
FC-AFC Joaquin Nugget	S608926	dog	49½	Hugh Adams
FC-AFC Kate of Rocky-Vue	SA866355	bitch	50½	Carma Futhey

FIELD DOGS HALL OF FAME

NAME OF DOG	AKC NO.	SEX	TOTAL POINTS	OWNER(S)
Nat'l. FC King Midas of Woodend	A207518	dog	17	Edwin N. Dodge
FC-AFC Kinike Chancellor	SA708517	dog	134½	Dr. John A. Barrow III
FC-AFC Kinike Coquette, CD	SA378622	bitch	50	James T. & Sally S. Venerable
FC-AFC Macopin Expectation	S702541	dog	96½	Mrs. George Murnane
FC Macopin Maximum	S836811	dog	86	Mrs. George Murnane
FC-AFC Misty's Sungold Lad, CDX	SA327277	dog	212½	Ken & Valerie Fisher
FC-AFC Moll-Leo Cayenne	SA182290	dog	37	James D. Browning
FC-AFC Nickolas of Logan's End	S918564	dog	176½	Hugh Adams
FC-AFC Northbreak Kinike Sir Jim	SB297944	dog	37½	Joan G. Morter
FC-AFC Oakcreek's Fremont	S466782	dog	101½	Cyril R. Tobin
FC-AFC Oakcreek's Sir Dorchester	S217227	dog	69½	James F. Stilwell
FC-AFC Can.Nat'l FC Oakcreek's Van Cleve	S49753	dog	125	Alfred H. Schmidt
FC-AFC Pajim's Klondyke	SB749927	dog	39½	Pattie E. Harper
FC Pirate of Golden Valley	A507433	dog	33	Carlton Grassle
AFC Pride of Roaring Canyon	S779285	dog	31½	Donald L. Burnett
Nat'l FC-AFC Can.FC Ready Always of Marianhill	S90917	dog	80	Mr. & Mrs. M.B. Wallace
FC-AFC Red Ruff	S466780	dog	92½	Cyril R. Tobin
FC-AFC Right-On Dynamite John	SB465134	dog	76	Elaine Klicker
FC Rip	A86933	dog	63	Paul Bakewell III
FC-AFC Ripp N' Ready	SA81585	dog	67	William D. Connor
FC-AFC Can.Dual Ch. Rockhaven Raynard of Fo-Go-Ta	S469424	dog	76	Mrs. G.H. FLinn, Jr.
FC-AFC Rocky Mack	S655578	dog	45½	Harold Mack, Jr.
Dual Ch.-AFC Ronakers Novato Cain	SA380537	dog	86	Desmond MacTavish, Jr.

297

FIELD DOGS HALL OF FAME

NAME OF DOG	AKC NO.	SEX	TOTAL POINTS	OWNER(S)
FC Royal Peter Golden Boy	A616198	dog	36½	Clifford H. Overvold
FC Sandstorm II	SB97397	dog	45	Vern Weber
Nat'l FC Shelter Cove Beauty	A487805	bitch	29	Dr. Leslie M. Evans
Dual Ch.-AFC Squawkie Hill Dapper Dexter	S187838	dog	40½	Dr. Gerald W. Howe
FC-AFC Stilrovin Luke Adew	S951922	dog	52	Kenneth K. Williams
Dual Ch. Stilrovin Nitro Express	A396107	dog	54½	Ben L. Boalt
FC Stilrovin Super Speed	A396108	dog	34	Paul Bakewell III, then Mrs. Gerald M. Livingston
FC-AFC Stilrovin Savanah Gay	SA44248	bitch	94	Ann A. Fowler
FC-AFC Stilrovin Tuppee Tee	S978112	bitch	83	Mrs. G.H. Flinn, Jr.
FC-AFC Sungold Lad's Talisman	SB49314	dog	59	Valerie F. Walker & Jay Walker
FC-AFC Sungold Sprite, CD	SA382654	bitch	50½	Valerie F. Walker
AFC Sunshine Cake	S699147	dog	46½	Mrs. G.H. Flinn, Jr.
FC The Golden Kidd	S20621	dog	64½	Kingswere Knls., then Mrs.Gerald Livingston
FC-AFC Tigathoe's Funky Farquar	SB170187	dog	52	Dorothy T. Ramsay & Elinor L. Tribon
FC-AFC Tigathoe's Kiowa II	SB045105	dog	68	Mrs. Robert R. Sadler
FC-AFC Tigathoe's Magic Marker	SA916015	bitch	117	Joseph A. Wattleworth
FC-AFC Tigathoe's Tonga	SA928990	dog	90½	Broughton M. & Ray Earnest
AFC Tioga Joe	SA352221	dog	63	Vern Weber
FC-AFC Topbrass Mandy	SC152486	bitch	57	Joseph & Jacquelyn Mertens
FC-AFC Tyson Rowdy	S869708	dog	42	James F. Stilwell
FC Whitebridge Wally	A226373	dog	28	M.B. Wallace, Jr.
FC Zip	S257572	dog	29½	Robert V. Speer

"All dogs which have sired two Field Champions; one Field Champion and one Show Champion; or five Champions of any kind (Show, Field, and/or Obedience) are included. A dog holding a Utility Dog or Utility Dog Tracking title is the same value as a Show Champion." (Official G.R.C.A. Requirements)

NAME OF DOG	AKC NO.	NO. OF CHAMPIONS	OWNER(S)
Ch. Alstone Sutter Creek Charade, UD WC	SA716328	9	Mrs. Susan G. Breakell
Ch. Angerlair's Sherwood Lad, CDX WC	SA706877	5	Harry R. & Alice J. Tripp
Ch. Apollo Of Yeo	SA653928	8	Mrs. Mary Strange
Ch. Autumn Lodge's Mr. Zap, CD **	SA968871	18	Richard M. Patterson
Bainin Of Caernac, CD ***	SA915780	4	Frank J. & Mimi A. Kearny
Am.Can.Ch.Bardfield Boomer,UDT WC Can.UDTX WC	SA614915	21	Cherrie & Alan Berger
Ch. Baron Sunset Hue, CD ***	S887248	5	H.S. & M.C. Buckhan
Beautywood's Buckshot	A916762	2	Dr. Leslie M. Evans
Am.Can.Mex.Bda.Ch. Beckwith's Copper Coin	SA76391	15	R.E. & L.L. Beckwith
Am.Can.Ch. Beckwith's Copper Ingot	SA424388	27	R.E. & L.L. Beckwith
Am.Can.Ch. Beckwith's Malagold Flash, WC Am. Can. UDT	SA629716	23	Marvin & Carol Kvamme
Am. Can. Ch. Beckwith's North Wind, CD	SB143273	5	Lynda G. Reddington
Ch. Beckwith's Tally-Ho, CDX	SA530414	9	Doris E. Deschene
Am.Can.Ch. Beckwith Xciting Fellow	SB570389	6	Mr. & Mrs. R.E. Beckwith
Ch. Beckwith's Xemoki Kachina, CD	SB570386	5	Evelyn & Lauren Splittgerber
FC-AFC Bonnie Brook's Elmer	SA297157	7	Mrs. George H. Flinn, Jr.
FC-AFC Bonnie Brook's Red	SA726255	2	Harold J. Bruninga
Brett of Westley, CDX	S860990	7	James R. Mardis
Ch. Bundock's Bowman Of Eldomac, CD	SA664124	15	Dr.A. & K. McDowell then Douglas Bundock
Am.Can.Ch. Cal-Vo's Happy Ambassador, CD	SA837152	28	Mr. & Mrs. William D. Young
Ch. Celloyd Golden Rory	S707638	7	Celloyd Kennels
FC-AFC Chief Sands	SA438222	4	Richard L. Sampson
Chips Of Gold	S428915	2	Ben L. Boalt
Am.Can.Ch. Ciadar Tintinabulation, UDT WC	SA794411	7	Pamela & Keith Ruddick
Ch. Cloverdale Bunker Hill Seth	SB974642	6	Jane & Richard Zimmerman
Ch. Copper's Czar Again	S386334	6	H. Paul Warwick

NAME OF DOG	AKC NO.	NO. OF CHAMPIONS	OWNER(S)
Dual Ch. AFC Craigmar Dustrack	S459592	5	Dr. F.L. Flashman
Ch. Cragmount's Hi-Lo	SA160236	16	Mrs. Charles W. Engelhard
Ch. Cragmount's Peter	SA31166	10	Mrs. Charles W. Engelhard
Am.Can.Bda.Ch.Cummings Gold-Rush Charlie	SA871725	54	Mrs. R.V. Clark & L.C. Johnson
Czargold's Discovery	S492118	6	Lyle D. Ashburn
Ch. Czar of Wildwood	A889104	8	Eric S. Johnson
Am.Can.Ch.Des Lacs Laddie of Rip's Pride,CDX	S48355	8	Des Lacs Kennels
Digger of Golden Valley ***	A507436	5	Ralph G. Boalt
Ch. Duckdown's Spannew, CD	SA374268	6	Jack & Jacqueline Waggoner
Am.Can.Ch.Duckdown's Unpredictable	SA483975	22	Laura Ellis Kling
Ch.Duck's Ripple of Golden Harp	SA47734	5	Carol Harp
Ch. Eagle's Ace of Tercor Farm	SA264056	8	Catherine C. Welling
Ch. Eastgate's Golden Charger	SA469410	8	Wm. E. Bedingfield, Jr. & Jack Valerius
Am.Can.Ch.Eastgate's Golden Nugget **	SA156100	9	Jack Valerius
Ch. Featherquest Jay's Blond Tom	S780791	14	Lyle R. Ring
Ch. Featherquest Storm Tide	SA164982	6	Rachael W. Elliott
Ch. Finderne Gold Cloud of Kent	S872044	5	Mrs. C.W. Englehard
Ch. Finderne Square Shadow's Fury, CD WC	SA73628	8	Frances Hargrave
Ch.Finderne Star Route, CDX	SA113486	5	Glenn & Phyllis Butler
Ch. Footprint Of Yeo, CD	SA594626	18	Carol T. Vogel
Am.Can.Ch.Gayhaven Lidiel, CDX WC	SA26523	7	Marcia R. Schlehr & Diane M. Lavene
Ch. Gilder of Elsiville	S281348	7	Des Lacs Kennels
Am.Can.Ch. Gilder's Wingra Beau	S462966	7	N. Bruce Ashbey
Ch. Gold Coast Here Comes The Sun, CD	SB981196	8	Louise Connolly
Ch. Golden Band of High Farms,WC	S894074	15	Robert C. Worrest
Ch. Golden Duke of Trey-C, WC	S921174	12	Wm. C. Stanton
Ch. Goldenloe's Tanfastic, CDX	SA337313	8	James E. Enloe
Am.Can.Ch. Golden Knoll's King Alphonzo	S346285	33	N. Bruce Ashbey

OUTSTANDING SIRES

NAME OF DOG	AKC NO.	NO. OF CHAMPIONS	OWNER(S)
Ch. Golden Knoll's Ringmaster	S481686	5	Russell D. Law
Ch. Golden Knoll's Shur Shot, CD	S230864	28	Mrs. R. S. Peterson
Ch. Golden Pines Ace's Hi	SA42245	5	Wellington Powell
Am.Can.Ch. Golden Pines Courvoisier, CDX WC	SA996971	12	Nancy Kelly Belsaas
Am.Can.Ch. Golden Pine's Easy Ace,WC	S908646	26	Golden Pine Kennels
Ch. Golden Pine's Full House, CD	SB004530	7	Susan Slade & Warner J. Cox
Ch. Golden Pine's Gradene's JD, CDX WC	SA958931	7	William J. Dean
Ch. Golden Pine's High Farms Fez	S960754	8	Harry & Dawn Erickson
Golden Pines Tiny Tim	SA589195	9	Golden Pine Kennels
AFC Golden Rocket VI	S976261	2	Donald R. Pryor
Am.Can.Ch. Goldrush's Contender, UD	SB483011	8	Clark & Colleen Williams
Ch. Gold-Rush's Great Teddy Bear	SB555537	36	Diane J. Smith & R. Ann Johnson
Ch. Gold-Rush Lightnin	SC234181	11	R. Ann & L.C. Johnson
FC Goldwood Tuck	A205346	5	Harold J. Kaufman
Harbor City Shadrack ***	S565674	2	Mrs. George Murnane
Ch. High Farms Band's Clarion	S993916	3	Harry & Dawn Erickson
Ch. High Farms Brassy Gold Braid	SA129853	6	Ruth E. Worrest
Am.Can.Ch. High Farms Charlie Brown, CD	SA489308	5	Gay Garrison
Ch. High Farms Golden Liddell, CDX	SA55174	5	Martha & Elmer Palm
AFC Holway Barty	SB147050	4	Barbara Howard
Ch.-AFC Honor's Dorado of Spindrift	SA707435	7	John J. Sprude
Am.Can.Ch. Honor's Grandeur, CDX WC	SA770080	6	Cleo & Bob Friederichsen
Ch. Honor's Let Em' Have It, CD WC	SB143862	7	Robert W. Lund & Avis Swanson Friberg
Ch. Hunt's Copperfield Daemon, CD	SA734306	20	A. Roberts Dismukes
Ch. Hunt's Finnegan	SB179371	10	A. Roberts Dismukes, Jr.
Ch. Imvubu Thembalisha, CD	SA807711	6	Orland & Mary C. Merchant
Ch. Indian Knoll's Roc-Cloud, UD	S751387	23	Alice & Wm. Worley

301

OUTSTANDING SIRES

NAME OF DOG	AKC NO.	NO. OF CHAMPIONS	OWNER(S)
Jolly Again of Ouilmette, CD ***	SA159661	4	Richard & Helen Kerns
Ch. Keeper of Willow Island, CD **	SA241402	5	L.L. Fisk & William Armitage
Ch. Krishna's E Z Goin', CD	SB623121	8	Betty Villela & Gloria Kerr
Am. Can. Ch. Krishna's Klassic Kachina	SB895018	6	Lynn & Buzz Splittgerber
Am. Can. Ch. Kyrie Daemon, CDX WC	SA108897	14	Patricia & Joan Nazark
Am. Can. Ch. Laurell's Allspice, CD	SA551579	5	Laura E. Kling
Am. Can. Ch. Laurell's Especial Jason WC, Am. Can. UDT	SA934760	17	Cherie & Alan Berger
Ch. Little Joe Of Tigathoe, ***	S389961	18	Mr. G. H. Flinn, Jr.
Ch. Lorelei's Golden Rip, **	S34006	10	Reinhard M. Bischoff
Ch.-AFC Lorelei's Golden Rockbottom, UD	S270654	6	R. M. Bischoff
Ch. Lorelei's Marshgrass Rebel, CD **	S253662	16	R. M. Bischoff
Ch. Lorelei's Reza Odu, CD	SA732301	8	Terrance P. & Juliet E. Hubbs
Ch. Lorelei's Star Spray	S580135	7	Lyle R. Ring
Ch. Major Gregory of High Farms	SA381553	22	Ruth E. Worrest
Ch. Malagold Beckwith Big Buff, CD	SA456646	12	Connie Gerstner
Ch. Malagold Beckwith OM K Ivan	SA614317	15	Dr. Bruce & Marilyn Hartman
Ch. Maple Leaf's Shamrock	SA125398	6	Clary & Irene Gingerich
Ch. Maple Leaf's Trace-O-Copper	SA281178	7	Clary & Irene Gingerich
Ch. Marshgrass Rogue, CD	S229167	8	Mr. & Mrs. Malcolm MacNaught
Michael of Woodend	A327770	2	Arthur H. Rand, Jr.
Midas' Timba	A780622	6	Mr. & Mrs. Luther H. Blount.
Ch. Milaur's Baal Benefactor, CD	SA374637	7	Dick & Avis Ekdahl
Milo of Ben's Major, UD	SA227305	5	Jack D. Godsil
Ch. Misty Morn's Sunset, CD TD WC	SA464440	127	Peter Lewesky
FC-AFC Misty's Sungold Lad, CDX	SA327277	3	Valerie F. Walker
Ch. Moreland's Major Sam, CD	SA881282	7	William C. Prentiss
Ch. Nerrissida's Finderne Folly II	S664722	11	Richard N. Hargrave

OUTSTANDING SIRES

NAME OF DOG	AKC NO.	NO. OF CHAMPIONS	OWNER(S)
FC-AFC Oakcreek's Sir Dorchester	S 217227	4	James F. Stilwell
Ch. Oakwin Junior	S570750	5	Dr. & Mrs. D. D. Fischer
Am. Can. Ch. Pepperhill's Basically Bear	SB906387	6	Barbara & Jeffrey Pepper
Peter of Woodend ***	A569148	2	George D. Alt
Polka of Handjem	SA188963	8	Carl Toby Potter
Ch. Ritz of High Farms	S604651	9	Ralph N. Worrest
Ch. Rockgold Chug's Ric O Shay	SA387987	22	Rockgold Kennels
Rockhaven Ben Bolt	A184622	2	Ralph G. Boalt
Rockhaven Plutoboy	Canada	2	Samuel S. Magoffin
Ch. Rockhaven Rory	905893	(Honorary)	Henry B. Christian
Rockhaven Tuck	A20613	4	Woodend Kennels
Dual Ch. AFC Ronakers Novato Cain	SA380533	9	Desmond MacTavish
Ch. Sabahka's Alexander of Cal-Vo	SA823141	5	Gloria Bechini & Diane Washburn
Am.Can.Ch. Seneca's Riparian Chief, CD TD WC	SA336799	9	Jack & Sandra Kelly
Ch. Sham-O-Jets Luvamike	SB211403	5	John & Joan Kipping
Sherrydan Tag, WC	SA166523	8	Shelia Fowler
Sidram Buc of Rusticana, UD WC	SA207834	5	Edith E. Munneke
Ch. Sidram Simon	SA98663	10	George & Gretchen Abbott
Sir Charles of Mt. Whitney ***	S649332	2	John D. Feeback
Ch. Sir Duncan of Woodbury	SB023769	20	Lynne Lounsbury
Am.Can.Ch. Southern's Gold-Rush Traveler	SC074688	6	Clark & Colleen Williams
Ch. Spannen's Rainmaker	SB17209	10	Jack E. & Jacqueline A. Waggoner
Am. Can. Ch. Speedwell Pluto	839660	(Honorary)	Samuel S. Magoffin
Ch. Sprucewood's Ching	S665065	5	Mr. & Mrs. M.C. Zwang
Am.Can.Ch. Sprucewood's Chocki	S665061	14	Mr. & Mrs. M.C. Zwang
Ch. Star Route Stormy Hurri	SA537520	5	Glenn L. & Phyllis A. Butler
Am.Can.Ch. Star Spray Maria's Rayo Del Sol, WC	SA165405	11	Pauline Ring

303

OUTSTANDING SIRES

NAME OF DOG	AKC NO.	NO. OF CHAMPIONS	OWNER(S)
Stilrovin Bearcat	S857475	3	Elmer J. Sievers
Stilrovin Bullet ***	A367770	4	E. L. King, Sr.
Dual Ch. Stilrovin Rips Pride	A561185	5	Kingswere Kennels
Ch. Stilrovin Shur Shot	A947110	6	Ralph G. Boalt
Ch. Sun Dance's Alexander	SB969338	9	Shirley & Wm. Worley
Ch. Sun Dance's Bronze, CD	S854854	15	Opal Horton
Ch. Sun Dance's Dancer, UD	SA157509	5	Harry A. Lyle
Ch. Sun Dance's Esquire, CD	SA441192	18	Shirley & Wm. Worley
Ch. Sun Dance's Moonlight Gambler, CDX WC	SA194110	12	Howard & Marcia Henderson
Ch. Sun Dance's Rainmaker	SB721460	7	Anthony & Penelope D'Alessandro
Ch. Sun Dance's Rarue	SB043462	13	Shirley & Wm. Worley
Ch. Sun Dance's Sir Ivan, CDX	SA21127	5	Oscar F. Frenzel III
Am.Can.Ch. Sun Dance's Vagabond Lover, CDX	SA171198	6	Violet Topmiller & Laura Ellis Kling
Ch. Sunset's Happy Duke	SA241789	12	Charles Cronheim
Ch. Sutter Creek Goldrush Flyboy	SC142905	5	Susan G. Breakell
Tigathoe's Brass Blade	S743193	3	John & Helen Casky
Dual Ch.-AFC Tigathoe's Funky Farquar	SB170187	5	Dorothy Ramsey & Elinor L. Tribon
Toby Of Yelme	S131003?	3	Charles E. Snell
Tonkahof Admiral	A390569	3	Mrs. Gerald G. Carnes
Ch. Tonkahof Bang ***	A489313	10	Joseph Mac Gaheran & Henry W. Norton
Am.Can.Ch. Topbrass Durango Brave, CDX WC	SB112284	7	Betty Waters
Ch. Trigger's Royal Diamond, CDX ***	SA165992	7	William Beltzer
Am.Can.Ch. Tulachard Robinhood, CDX	S525126	5	H. Frances McKenzie
Am.Can.Ch. Vagabond's Cougar Bill, CD	SA534602	14	Wm. Zimmer & Laura E. Kling
Am.Can.Ch. Valhalla's Amber Waves	SB094735	8	Kathleen M. & Lawrence G. Liebler
Victorious Of Roedare	A940555	2	Charles E. Snell
Ch. Wochica's Okeechobee Jake	SA679062	62	Susan Taylor

"All bitches which have produced two Field Champions; one Field and one Show Champion; or three Champions of any kind (Show, Field, and/or Obedience) are included. A dog holding a Utility Dog or Utility Dog Tracking title is the same value as a Show Champion." (G.R.C.A. requirements.)

NAME OF BITCH	AKC NO.	NO. OF CHAMPIONS	OWNER(S)
Ch. Aldercrest Cinnabar Sand	SA495624	3	Joyce & Richard Arnold
Amberac's Sunburs+ Sun-Brave,WC	SB863726	4	Judith Ciganek & Ellen Manke
Amberac's Reeva Rustelle	SB150153	5	Ellen L. Manke
Antonia Iowana	A787117	3	Walter E. Flumerfelt
Auroras Sunshine Sadie	SB357577	4	Robin A. & Raymond M. McCarthy
Beaumaris Ainsel Meghan	SB003154	3	Reginald S. & Josephine Willson
Beckwith's Amiga Mia	SA864252	4	David W. & Delores M. Berby
Am.Can.Ch.Beckwith's Apricot Brandy, UDT	SB864253	6	Mr. & Mrs. R.E. Beckwith
Ch. Beckwith's Autumn Wind, CD	SA864251	4	Ronald F. & Darlene J. Smith
Beckwith's Chickasaw Jingle	SA457628	5	Kathleen M. & Lawrence Liebler
Beckwith Chrys-Haefen Belinda	SA399876	4	R.E. & L.L. Beckwith
Am.Can.Ch.Beckwith's Frolic of Yeo,CD	SA257350	12	Connie Gerstner & R.E. Beckwith
Beckwith's Gayhaven Fancy	SA319961	4	Mr. & Mrs. R.E. Beckwith
Am.Can.Ch.Beckwith's Highland Holly, CD WC	SA394517	5	Jane Libberton & Connie Gerstner
Ch. Beckwith's Ingot's Ember,CDX TD WC	SA635758	3	J.H. Newton, Jr. & Nancy D. Newton
Am.Can.Ch.Beckwith's Malagold Cherub, UDT	SA746856	8	Mr. & Mrs. R.E. Beckwith
Am.Can.Ch.Beckwith's Malagold Omega *	SA669063	4	Bonnie Sprude & John J. Sprude
Ch.Beckwith's Malagold Starfarm	SA616528	9	Carol T. Vogel
Am.Can.Ch.Beckwith's Nutmeg,CDX	SB149183	5	Ludell L. Beckwith
Am.Can.Ch.Beckwith's Terra Cotta,CD	SB362805	3	Mr. & Mrs. R.E. Beckwith
Ch. Bonnie Island Heather,*Am.Can.UDT	SA637968	3	John B. & Roberta Anderson
Ch.Bowman's Bonnie Breeze	SB130158	4	Shirley A. & C.M. Shipp

NAME OF BITCH	AKC NO.	NO. OF CHAMPIONS	OWNER(S)
Ch. Bowman's Kindelle of Krisha, CD WC	SB039788	4	Gloria Kerr
Ch. Brackenhollow Sherry, WC	SA229246	2	Sheila Fowler
Ch. Braevue's Vixen WC	SB17803	5	Edna & Harvey Gardenier
Ch. Brandywine's Tansu D'Oro	SA878791	6	Mr. & Mrs. Benjamin J. Gikis
Brynmar's Cinderella	SA952611	3	Frank J. & Rachel H. Pehr
AM.Can.Ch.Brynmar's Millicent, CD	SA567449	5	Rachael H. Pehr
Braun's Taffy	S290097	3	D. Lee Braun
Ch. Brittby's Golden Sunset	SA246042	5	Rita B. Simpson
Buff of Square Shadows	S950659	3	James M. Corrigan
Ch. Butch's Gypsy Maid, CD	S253697	3	Eleanor H. Burr
Ch. Callipan's Semper Fidelis	SA417485	5	Margaret O. & J. Wallace Scott,Jr.
Ch. Cal-Vo's Nickle Nehi	SB941283	5	Sharon C. Smith
Candle Glow of Arlington	SA189529	3	Richard E. Adams
Ch. Casseopia of Nerrissida	SA142599	3	Margaret C. Scott
Cayenne's Happy Thought **	SA571947	2	James D. & Marjorie R. Browning
Celloyd Bess of Nashoba	S542745	4	Celloyd Kennels
Celloyd Ginger of Inverness	SA185758	4	Katherine G. Weed
Celloyd Serenade	S766698	4	Frances S. Hargrave & Lloyd M. Case
Am.Can.Ch.Chafa Honeybun of Jungold, CDX,TD WC	SB484287	4	Cherie N. Berger & Sara Lynn Jung
Champaign Lady of Wochica	SA487790	4	Janet L. Bunce
Ch. Chebaco's Brandywine	SA969275	5	Joyce A. Fitzgerald & Jeffrey H. Gowing
Am.Can.Ch. Chee-Chee of Sprucewood	S448601	16	Mr. & Mrs. M.C. Zwang
Cherie of Brookshire,UD WC	SB822837	3	Ronald M. & Carolyn M. Ochylski
Ch. Cheyenne Golden's Sunshine	S542421	4	Cheyenne Golden Kennels
Ch. Cheyenne Goldens Queen Mary	SA324913	3	Cheyenne Golden Kennels
Ch. Christmas Cactus Flower, CDX WC	SA755084	3	Anthony & Sara Lynn Jung
Am.Can. Ch. Cimaron 'D Dazzle Dust, CDX TD WC	SB393523	3	Cherie N. Berger

NAME OF BITCH	AKC NO.	NO. OF CHAMPIONS	OWNER(S)
Ch. Cloverdale's Sweet Sadie	SB558192	5	Richard & Jane Zimmerman & Bob Stebbins
Ch. Copper Kettle Cinnamon Glory,CD*	SA420324	10	Louis & Suzanne Grasso
Copper Penny of Oak Hill, WC	SA645667	3	Peter & Ursula Lanino
Copper's Artistic Rhythm	S386329	3	G.L. & F.W. Bergloff
Cragmount's Annabelle	SA562968	3	Carol T. Vogel
Ch. Cragmount's Auster, CD	SA562965	5	Betty B. Hoggard
Cragmount's Easy Lady	SA79220	3	Arnold Veerkamp
Ch. Cragmount's Tiny Cloud	SA8424	4	Mrs. C.W. Engelhard
Ch. Cummings Dame Pepperhill	SB143731	5	Barbara & Jeffrey Pepper
Am.Can.Ch.Cummings Golden Princess	SA292329	8	Lynn H. Cummings
Ch. Czar's Lassie	S284364	3	Czargold Kennels
Dame Karlor of Cullen	SA598729	3	Shelly R. Berner
Darlington Del-Beth Rochelle	SA670187	3	William C. Prentiss
Ch. Dealer's Donation To Duckdown,CD	SA349252	6	Jack & Jacquelyn Waggoner
Can.Ch.Deegoljay's Amorous Aspasia,CD	SA931917	4	David A. Hilliard
Deerflite Selina	SB372450	3	P. Anne Bissette & Maralyn Y Ferrari
Ch. Deerflite Sunset,CDX	SA667777	4	J.F. Bissette
Am.Can.Ch.Deirdre's Bran Or	SA598577	5	David R. Reynolds
Des Lacs Golden Heart	S833898	5	Mrs. W.C. Zwang
Ch. Des Lacs Goldie,CD **	S137860	4	Mrs. R.S. Peterson
Am.Can.Ch.Des Lacs Lassie, CD WC	A994369	7	Des Lacs Kennels
Ch. Des Lacs Lassie II	S137859	3	Dr. & Mrs. D.D. Fischer
Ch. Des Lacs Shellie	S831944	4	Ira E. Denson
Double-J Jim	SA934940	5	Jack D. Godsil
Ch. Dub's Duchess, UD	S799236	3	W.T. Armitage
Ch. Duckdown's Tiffany Tomboy	SA456761	3	Jack & Jacquelyn Waggoner
Ch. Duckdown's Utterly Fantastic,CDX	SA511385	3	Eliesa H. Enloe
Ch. Duckdown's Voodoo Charm, UD	SA611626	3	Joan A. & Thomas M. Stoppleman

OUTSTANDING DAMS

NAME OF BITCH	NO. OF CHAMPIONS	AKC NO.	OWNER(S)
Ch.Duckdown's Veronica Laker,CD	6	SA620747	Laura E. Kling
Ch.Duckdown's Vesper Challenge	5	SA655277	Jack & Jacquelyn Waggoner
Ch. Early Autumn Sunshine	4	A654682	Mrs. Jeanne O. Parks
Eastgate's Golden Elizabeth,CD	3	SA972797	Marilee Gee
Eastgate's Golden Legend	3	SB248342	William E. Bedingfield
Ch. Eastgate's Golden Genie	7	SA351134	William E. Bedingfield & Jack Valerius
Ch. Etta Zoloto	5	A768800	Cheyenne Golden Kennels
Ch. Faera's Rusticana Megapup,CD	3	SB507375	Rhonda E. & Michael J. Hovan, MD
Farmingdale's Copper Wendy,CD	4	SA448469	James E. Brinton
Feather of Little Hill	4	A343113	Taramar Kennels
Featherquest Golden Quill **	2	S450803	Ingrid de Besche
Ch. Featherquest Golden Zoe	3	S983187	Oliver & Janet Wilhelm
Ch. Finderne Folly's Jubilee,CD	6	SA204032	Frances Hargrave
Ch. Finderne Gypsy of Nerrissida	5	SA114208	Frances Hargrave
Firegold Frisky Fawn,CD	3	SA903427	Michael & Margie Vogt
Ch. Fireside Auora Belle, CD	3	SA556323	Frances J. Ripley
Ch. Fireside's Princess MArgaret	6	SB211011	Emma L. & Raymond D. Hendricks
Ch. Gayhaven Harmony,CDX	6	S849142	Helen W. Gay & Marcia Schlehr
Gayhaven Slightly Cinnamon,UDT WC	3	SA516637	Pamela & Keith Ruddick
Ch. Gilier's Wingra Belle	4	S462965	N. Bruce Ashbey
Gilnockie Coquette	7	A241931	Ralph G. Boalt
Ch. Gilnokie Vixen of Goldenloe,CD	5	SB288552	Eliesa H. Enloe
Glen Willow's Happy Talk	4	SA86357	Charles A. Chronheim
Glittering Gold	2	A89912	Winnebago Kennels
Glorybee Dusty Ruffles,CD	3	SA494182	B. Jean & Ralph Madsen
Ch. Gold Button of Catawba **	4	S122040	Mrs. G.H. Flinn,Jr.
Ch.Goldendoor Cover Girl	3	S898497	Mrs. Patricia G. Corey

OUTSTANDING DAMS

NAME OF BITCH	AKC NO.	NO. OF CHAMPIONS	OWNER(S)
Ch. Golden Gal of High Farns,CDX	S537241	4	Ruth E. & Robert C. Worrest
Ch. Golden Girl Enid,WC	S641800	5	Pauline T. Ring
Ch. Golden Knoll's Ballerina,CD	S230866	3	Dr. Henry C. Shaw
Golden Knoll's Tonkabelle	S495339	5	Bryan D. Miller
Ch. Golden Lassie II	S129020	3	Mr. & Mrs. Malcolm Mac Naught
Goldenloe's Glory Be	SA182720	3	John F. Bissette
Ch. Goldenloe's Junior Miss	SA529382	6	James C. Enloe
Ch. Goldenloe's Taffy Apple	SA472235	3	B. Jean Kistle
Ch. Goldenloe's Tawny Tiger,UD WC	SA529377	6	Anne S. Couttet
Ch. Golden Pine's Bambi's Lady	S786274	4	Golden Pine Kennels
Ch. Golden Pines Down Payment	SA185488	4	Mary Luise Seamans
Ch. Golden Pine's Finale Miss	SA344763	4	Wallace K. Bishop
Ch. Golden Pine Glorybe	SA721919	12	Mary Luise Seamans
Ch.Golden Pine Glorybe's Angel	SB89529	12	R. Ann Johnson & M.L. Seamans
Ch. Golden Pine Just-A-Minute	SB247628	6	Leslie Dove & Mary Luise Seamans
Golden Pine Mrs. Cratchit	SA892890	6	Mrs. Josiah T. Seamans
Ch. Golden Pine's Punkin Pi,CD	SA423852	9	Mary Luise Seamans
Golden Pine Sandpiper,CD	SB29326	3	Virginia V. Rutter
Golden Pine's Twink	SA349236	3	Jane Engelhard
Ch. Golden Pine's Yuletide Glee	SA454073	4	David E. Crook, Jr.
Ch. Goldenquest's Thistledue	SB745150	3	Carter F. & Diana V. Foss
Ch. Golden Sherry of Liberator,UDT	SA940698	3	Dorothy A. Texeira
Golden Surprise For Xmas,CDX	SA88044	2	Dory Van Duzer & Morris W. Stroud
Golden Treasure	A511261	4	Leslie C. Brooks
Goldrush's Birch of Bearwood,CD WC	SA22910	14	D. Jean Baird
Ch. Goldrush's Caprice, CD	SB459364	6	D. Jean Baird
Ch. Goldwing Rhythm-N-Blue	SB816229	3	Leslie Dove
Greenfield Jollye	A432574	4	Reinhard M. Bischoff

OUTSTANDING DAMS

NAME OF BITCH	AKC NO.	NO. OF CHAMPIONS	OWNER(S)
Ch. Hayes' Golden Lady,CD	S745341	5	Mr. & Mrs. R.E. Hayes
Heatherington Jeane, CD	S595301	5	Barbara & Edward O'Laughlin
Ch.High Farm Band's Glockenspiel	S993912	3	Ruth E. Worrest
High Farms Beau Brittany	SA922158	3	Richard A. Zimmerman
Ch. High Farms Mary Poppins	SA334165	8	Violet Topmiller
Ch. High Seas Agatha Cristie, CD WC	SB733232	3	Lisbeth Short & Michael J. Short, MD
Ch. Hillcrest's·Marigold, CD	S933683	5	Mr. & Mrs. S.B. Bowles
Hilltop's Gold Dust	SA155105	3	Barbara Retzlaff & Ray E. Sherman
Honey Bear XIII	SB198316	4	Janie Bsharah
Honeysuckle of Yeo	SA525176	3	John A. & June Ryden
Ch. Honor's Chances Are, CD	SA347051	4	Avis Swanson Friberg
Ch. Honor's.Charade	SA707436	4	Avis Ekdahl & Mrs Elaine Parent
·Ch. Honor Coed	SA460797	8	Avis & Dick Ekdalh
Honor's High Stakes	SA832613	5	Patricia Klausman, Kitty Cathey & Avis Friberg
Honor's Pekay Kiss Me Kate, CDX TD *	SB225912	7	Patricia Klausman
Am.Can.Ch.Hunt's Annabelle of Vegas, CDX TD WC	SA458247	6	A. Roberts Dismukes, Jr.
Hunt's Early Bird, CDX	SB017467	3	Gillian M. Masemore
Ch. Indanda Thembalisha	SB181704	7	Dr. John B. Lounsbury & Tina Lewesky
Indian Knoll's Cricket's Love	SB234511	5	Joan A. & John A. Kipping
Ch. Indian Knoll's Zonta, CD	SA1499	3	Barbara Retzlaff & Ray E. Sherman, Jr.
Ironstreams Pavlova	SA256903	3	Mary E. Johns
Ch. Jana Roc Jessica	SA872740	3	Nancy H. Rockaway & Mrs. Robin Lewis
Ch. J's Kate	SA186222	8	Ronald W. Akers
Ch. Joe-Dee's Misty Day of High Farms	SA309937	3	Joseph Dainty
Ch. Jolly Peachy Pistönpacker	SB615146	4	Robert & Sheila Humphreys
Jolly Victoria of Misty Morn	SB682909	3	John Lounsbury & Peter Lewesky
Ch. Jubilee's Lady Love,CD	SA799081	4	Tryna Sutfin

NAME OF BITCH	AKC NO.	NO. OF CHAMPIONS	OWNER(S)
Judy of Stonegate	A904409	4	Mrs. Luther H. Blount
Ch. Jungold's Gold-Rush Hope	SB622211	5	R. Ann & L.C. Johnson
Jungold's L C's Lady Ambassador	SB474680	8	Gail Capaldi-Brown & R. Ann Johnson
Kami's Kama Shetani Malaika	SA732895	9	Margaret H. & Steven R. Scheele
Ch. Karlor's Gold Sunset	SB261029	3	Peter Trapp
Ch. Karmilock Morgan of Sundance	SB431805	3	Margaret H. & Stephen R. Scheele
Ch. Karmilock Silver Charm	SB247812	3	Peg Scheele
Katrinka	S38565	3	Grace E. Rowley
Kelley's Keir of Kieps	S735418	4	Ruth E. Kelley
Ch. Kelley's Round N' Round	S876607	3	Ruth E. Kelley
Ch. Kelley's Tribulation	SA48929	5	Mr. & Mrs. William V. Kelley
Khetha Thembalisha	SA807713	3	Edward A. French
Kingdale's Toast	S95456	3	Mrs. Russell S. Peterson
Am.Can.Ch.Krishna's EZ Livin'	SB724325	6	Buzz & Lyn Splittgerber
Am.Can.Ch.Kyrie Loch Ness of Terra-Hoh	SA773093	6	Diane M. Lavene
Ch. Lady Butterscotch, UDT ***	SA437695	3	Anna M.L. Van Rooy Currey, MD
Lady Du Beau	S937829	3	Richard A. Telvick
Lady Hance	A418642	2	Sid N. Marchildon
Lady of Roedare	A782899	2	S.F.D. Roe then Harold J. Kaufman
Ch. Lady Sonots	SB640959	4	James F. & Marilyn E. Schmiesing
Ch. Lark Mill Genevive,CD	SB245463	18	Gloria Kerr & Gail Sprock
Ch. Laurell's Amiable Caboose	SA551580	4	Laura Ellis Kling
Ch. Laurell's Flower Drum Song	SA975137	3	Patricia Hardy Haines
Laurell's Honor's Gibson Girl CDX	SB13912	4	Susan Fisher & Sylvia Donahey
Laurell's Itti Bitti	SB267106	4	W. Stuart & Christy Brown
Laurell's Jaunty Jinn-Jinn,CDX	SB348370	4	Cherie Berger
Ch. Laurell's Kilimanjaro	SB540296	8	Thomas C. & Laura E. Kling
Ch. Little Bit of Laurell	SA934491	5	Charles W. Kling

OUTSTANDING DAMS

NAME OF BITCH	AKC NO.	NO. OF CHAMPIONS	OWNER(S)
Little Dawn of Chickasaw	SA198728	4	Janet L. Bunce
Ch. Little Dipper of High Farms	S747822	3	Ruth E. Worrest
Ch. Lorelei's Fez-Ti Za-Za	SA215263	5	Reinhard M. Bischoff
Lorelei's Golden Tanya	S270651	9	R.M. Bischoff then C. Willard Gamble
Lorelei's Golden Poppy	S53795	3	Celloyd Kennels then Ironstream Kennels
Ch. Lorelei's Happy Ti-Ji-Gee	S915141	5	R.M. Bischoff
Lorelei's Lucky Penny	S339172	6	Dr. Irene Kraft
Lorelei's Marsh Jay	S580147	3	Rachael W. Elliott
Malagold Beckwith Bootes	SA616530	10	Gerald H. Hershberger
Ch. Malagold Svea	SB305263	4	James E. Anderson & Connie Gerstner
Ch. Maple Leaf's Princess Pat	SA175925	5	Clarence & Irene Gingerich
Marshgrass Coquette	S590116	5	Mr. & Mrs. Malcolm Mac Naught, Jr.
Meadow Creak Ko-Ko	S785373	3	James N. & Allan L. Ramsay
Am.Can.Ch.Meadowpond Dazzle's Sparkle, CD	SB974935	4	Cherie N. & Alan F. Berger
Ch. Milaur's Aphrodite	SA259419	4	Shirley & Wm. Worley
Ch. Milaur's Aurora	SA259412	5	Charles E. Barlow
Ch. Miss Liberty O'Lark Hill	SA567699	3	Cecilia S. & Jack W. Sarlls
Missy of Nottingham, CD	SA823210	5	Robert J. Polley
Morningsage Malagold Honey	SB261008	3	Joanne A. Lastoka
Ch. Morningsage Sandpebble,CD	SB801137	4	Joanne A. Lastoka
Mueller's Sparkle	S350326	3	Kurt W. Mudler
Nancy's Golden Dawn	SA175693	3	Richard Kerns
Ch. Nugget's Golden Candie,WC	SA368102	3	Ronald L. Berg
Oakcreek's Golden Wren	S226513	2	J.V. Owens
Oakcreek's Lady Amber	S48435	2	Charles E. Snell
Patsy of Woodend	A563469	2	George D. Alt
Ch. Penelope of Blue Hills	SA550196	3	Wm.E. Bedingfield,Jr. & Jack Valerius
Ch. Pepperhill's Return Ticket	SC380211	3	Barbara & Jeffrey Pepper

OUTSTANDING DAMS

NAME OF BITCH	AKC NO.	NO. OF CHAMPIONS	OWNER(S)
Pink Lady of Audon **	S571001	3	Stilrovin Kennels
Princess Lou	SA285117	3	Lewis Purdy
Princess Pat of Los Altos	S710032	4	John & Maryanna Railton
Ransue's Daffodil	SA982566	4	Dr. Stanley R. Grim
Ch. Reddigold's Peaches N'Cream	SB770189	7	Lynda Reddington & Judith Anderson
Ch. Rockgold's Wild Honey	SA307936	5	Eleanor H. Starkeson
Rockhaven Judy **	A87255	3	Woodend Kennels
Am.Can.Ch.Rockhaven Regina	S182255	6	Russell D. Law
Ch. Royal Flush of Yeo,UDT WC	SA477800	3	Horatio C. Hoggard III
Ch. Rozzy-Duchess	S791942	8	Mrs. C.W. Engelhard
CH. R. R. Echo V	S75685	3	Mrs. R.S. Peterson then Dr. George Tennison
Ruanne Yankee Pride	S619531	3	Barbara D. Miller
Ch. Rusina's Golden Whirlwind, CD	S682077	3	Russell D. Law
Am.Can.Ch.Russo's Pepperhill Poppy	SB666153	6	Barbara & Jeffrey Pepper
Rusticana Happi Talk, CDX	SA825950	3	Albert J. & Edith E. Munneke
Ch. Rusticana Kandi Kane, UD	SA304053	5	Albert & Edith Munneke
Rusticana's Sancy, UDT WC	SA667785	6	Jeannie Fox
Am.Can.Ch.Sar Barr's Niamh Cinn Or Ib	SB186265	3	Deirdre Reynolds
Sanchar's Sasha,CDX	S346314	3	Bryan D. Miller
Sandia's Flaxen Babe,CD	SA451148	3	David & Mary Merwin
Sassafras of Willow Acres,UDT	SA742279	3	Walter C. & Thelma E. Ross
Satinway Wildmist of Sidram	S950399	5	James R. Mardis
Shadowbrook Molly	S928306	3	Jane D. & Charles E. Cooney, Jr.
Shenandoah of Stilrovin, CD ***	SA237713	5	Philip F. Uehling
Sherrymount Sarah	S285311	3	Mrs. Patricia G. Corey
Ch. Shur Shot's Lassie	S439422	3	Dr. & Mrs. D.D. Fischer then Mrs. Wm.A. Vogt
Sidram Kapering Korky	S787303	7	James R. Mardis

OUTSTANDING DAMS

NAME OF BITCH	AKC NO.	NO. OF CHAMPIONS	OWNER(S)
Ch Sidram Shady Lady, CDX **	S649122	3	Lloyd S. Foltz
Ch. Sidram Shining Star, UD	S192367	4	James R. Mardis
Spannen's Carrie Nation	SB415013	3	Robert N. & Carole S. Jones
Ch. Spannen's Harmony	SA716177	6	Jack E. & Jacqueline A. Waggoner
Ch. Spannen's Sugarfoot	SA942395	4	Jack E. & Jacqueline Waggoner
Sparkle Plenty	SB816103	3	John F. & Elizabeth H. Deardorff
Ch. Speedwell Tango	873199	2	John K. Wallace
Ch. Sprite of Aldgrove **	A89523	2	Henry B. Christian
Ch. Sprucewood's Glamour Girl,CDX	S998543	9	V.F. Topmiller
Ch. Sprucewood's Harvest Sugar,CD	SA62237	19	Marcia Henderson & Jackie Overly
Ch. Starfarm's Carolina Ginger,CD	SA912202	5	Arthur D. Jr. & Shirley O. Cahoon
Starfarm Donnegal	SA983107	7	Marly L. Keffer & Betty B. Hoggard
Ch. Star Spray Enid's Glorieta	SA71769	7	James C. Enloe
Ch. Star Spray Enid's Maria	SA71764	3	Pauline T. Ring
Am.Can.Ch.Star Spray Maria's Gloria	SA165402	4	R.E. & L.L. Beckwith
Ch. Star Spray's Poly's Follygirl	SA25375	4	Frances Hargrave
Fld. Ch. Stilrovin Katherine	A396109	4	Mrs. James A. Austin
Sudden Sandy ***	S75176	2	John Romadka then Earl M. Donner
Ch. Sun Dance's April Fool	SB110206	11	Shirley & Wm. Worley
Ch. Sun Dance's Athena,CD	SA83078	7	Lisa Anne & Shirley Klein
Ch. Sun Dance's Contessa	SA799287	12	Lisa Klein
Sun Dance's Flare	SA31590	6	Harold & Sheila Fowler
Sun Dance's Gold Ingot,CD	SA86118	4	Howard & Marcia Henderson
Sun Dance's Heather,CD	SA157107	4	David Stewart then Jean Madsen
Sun Dance's Scheilah	SA146003	3	Stanley Brothers
Ch.Sun Dance's Sprig of Holly,CDX**	SA127719	3	Lisa & Shirley Klein
Ch. Sun Dance's Susie Q.	SB273094	6	Patrick Worley
Ch. Sun Dance's Taffeta Doll,CDX	SA546820	6	Shirley & Wm. Worley

NAME OF BITCH	AKC NO.	NO. OF CHAMPIONS	OWNER(S)
Sun Dance's Vintage Punch	SA171200	4	William Worley
Ch. Sun Dance's Vivacious Sock	SA171199	6	George & Gretchen Abbott
Sunkist Flirt of Whitebridge	A502192	4	Henry de Roulet
Ch. Sunset Royal's Near Miss,CD	SA616994	4	Dr. Alan & Kathleen McDowell
Ch. Sunshine Sundae,CD	SA163285	3	F.M. Broders
Ch. Sunstream·Gypsy of Topbrass	SB575915	3	Joseph & Jacquelyn Mertens
Sunstream's Little Echo	SA522961	3	Ralph & Emily Wallace
Ch. Sunswept's Shooting Star	SB730948	4	Lynne A. Hallee
Sweet Penny	SB026842	3	Brenda Wood
Synspur Beckwith's Stacey,CD	SA739429	4	Mrs. R.E. Beckwith & Jane Libberton
Ch. Tabby of Goldendoor	S553490	4	Martha & Warren Winterhalter
Ch. Tammy of Railroad Mills	SA228233	4	William N. Stahl
Ch. Tangelo's End of The Rainbow,CD*	SA900692	3	Lynn W. & P.L. Fletcher
Ch. Tansy of High Farms	S960165	3	Harry & Dawn Erickson
Ch. Tempo's Nassau Miss	SB520481	11	Shelia M. & Edward P. Huser
Tigathoe's Chickasaw ***	SA240341	4	Mrs. George H. Flinn, Jr. & Mrs. Robert Sadler
Ch. Tigathoe's Gold Digger,CD	SA285453	3	Alica A. Burhans
Ch. Tonka Belle of Woodend	A215130	2	Tonkahof Kennels
Ch. Topbrass Ad-Lib's Bangor,CD***	SB053708	2	Joseph & Jacquelyn Mertens
Ch. Topbrass San Francisco Flame	SB169520	3	Joseph & Jacquelyn Mertens
Tri-Stada Golden Dawn	S1522	4	Tri-State Hunting Dog Association
Ch. Truell Pond Lucy of Liberator, CD WC	SA636208	4	Nancy S. Garrison
Ch. Tulachard Clover,CDX	S359285	3	H.F. McKenzie then Phyllis R. Mayo
Ch. Uthingo Thembalisha	SA337354	4	Edward A. French
Valentine Torch of Topbrass,WC	SA655957	11	Joseph & Jacquline Mertens
Ch. Valhalla's Amber Kate,CD	SB202943	3	Kathleen M. & Lawrence Liebler
Valhalla's Autumn Mist	SB187851	3	K. & L. Liebler then Mercer Russo
Valhalla's Golden Valkyr	SA945424	3	Kathleen M. Liebler & Margaret J. Tajc

315

OUTSTANDING DAMS

NAME OF BITCH	AKC NO.	NO. OF CHAMPIONS	OWNER(S)
Valleyheart's Golden Sherry	S841969	4	Wade R. & Betty B. Drury
Vickersby Astra	S793597	4	Franklin J. Veno
Vickersby Beretta,CDX	S793596	3	Doris E. Deschene
Vickersby Vickers	S639365	3	Eleanor H.Burr
Virginia Dare of Boot Lake	A791814	2	Joseph S. Herring
Ch. Walkir Lafayette Burgundy,CD *	SA513229	7	Anne M. & Herman A. Plusch,Jr.
O.T. Ch. Wessala Naughty Nannette *	SA585507	3	Joel W. Prouty
Ch. Wessala Pride of Golden Pine	S634858	6	Golden Pine Kennels
Westmont's Diana,CD	SB496412	3	Vicki & Carol Falberg
Willow Lane's Golden Kimbyeya	SB273061	4	Frances D. Childrey
Winsome Winnie of Wildwood	A771997	3	Eric S. Johnson
Ch. Wochica's Gold-Rush Bonanza	SB187060	3	R. Ann & L.C. Johnson
Ch. Wochica's Sand Piper,WC	SA627318	7	Janet L. Bunce
Ch. Wochica's Windsong	SA698952	3	Karin L. Fisher
Ch. Yorkhill's Coin Collector	S533269	5	Mary Beth Helm

Index